THE LEDGE

THE LEDGE

AN ADVENTURE STORY
OF FRIENDSHIP AND SURVIVAL
ON MOUNT RAINIER

▲ ▲ ▲ ▲ ▲

JIM DAVIDSON
AND
KEVIN VAUGHAN

BALLANTINE BOOKS

NEW YORK

Published in the United States by Ballantine Books, an imprint
of The Random House Publishing Group, a division
of Random House, Inc., New York.

BALLANTINE and colophon are registered trademarks of Random House, Inc.

Portions of this work were originally published in different form in the
Rocky Mountain News.

Grateful acknowledgment is made to the following for permission
to print previously unpublished material:

Scott Anderson: excerpt from a card from Scott Anderson
to Jim Davidson from 1992. Used courtesy of Scott Anderson.

Joanne (Markowski) Donohue: excerpts from the journals of
Joanne (Markowski) Donohue. Used courtesy of Joanne Markowski Donohue.

John Madden: note from John Madden to Jim Davidson.
Used courtesy of John Madden.

Don and Donna Price: writings, including journal entries, by Mike Price.
Used courtesy of Don and Donna Price.

The Ruess family: quote by Everett Ruess. Used courtesy of the Ruess family.

Mark Udall: excerpt from a letter from Mark Udall to Jim Davidson
from July 1992. Used courtesy of Mark Udall.

LIBRARY OF CONGRESS CATALOGING-IN-PUBLICATION DATA
Davidson, Jim.
The ledge: an adventure story of friendship and survival on Mount Rainier /
Jim Davidson, Kevin Vaughan.
p. cm.
ISBN 978-0-345-52319-8
eBook ISBN 978-0-345-52321-1
1. Mountaineering accidents—Washington (State)—Rainier, Mount. 2. Mountaineering—
Washington (State)—Rainier, Mount. 3. Davidson, Jim. 4. Price, Mike. 5. Mountaineers—
United States—Biography. I. Vaughan, Kevin. II. Title.
GV199.42.W22D38 2011   796.52'209797782—dc22   2011010515

Printed in the United States of America on acid-free paper

www.ballantinebooks.com

2 4 6 8 9 7 5 3 1

First Edition

Book design by Victoria Wong

Dedicated to

Mike Price

June 23, 1992

Dear Mike,

Jesus, man, I'm sorry! I can't believe this happened to you and to us ... I swear to God, Mike, I didn't mean to fall into that crevasse and I certainly didn't want to pull you in behind me ...

Everyone tells me that it was all an accident and that it could have been the other way around just as easy. I suppose they're right.

I really enjoyed our climb ... God—weren't our bivouacs wild? We were like real alpine hard men—as you said, this climb should make some great stories ...

I apologize if my nervousness made you mad or frustrated. Perhaps it was a lack of courage. Perhaps it was foreboding. My crevasse fear did build and build right up to the last few hours and minutes—perhaps I knew.

I assure you that had you gone in first, I too would have dug in for all I was worth and then would have gone right in behind you. I think you know that, though. I truly felt we were friends and partners ...

I shall strive to take this second chance I've been given and unfurl my wings and fly with it, not turn inward into a dark ball. I shall strive to live a strong, forward-moving, vivacious life in your honor.

Take care, Mike.

Your friend,

Jim

PROLOGUE

I peer off the ledge into blackness. Pressing my gloved hand against the ice wall for balance, I tilt my head to the right and stare past my boots, half-buried in loose snow. Squeezing my left eye shut, I look straight down my right hip and leg, as if I'm sighting along a rifle barrel. I am desperate to see the bottom of this dim cavern.

Nothing. Empty space drops below us and vanishes. My stomach clamps tight, and I swallow hard.

Even through my thick climbing gloves, cold seeps out of the ice wall and stings my fingertips. I pull my hand back and exhale a ragged breath.

Fear forces me, for the moment, to block out the ominous space looming around and below, so instead I study the ledge we're on. It's been a few minutes since the collapse happened and we crash-landed here. My eyes have now adjusted to the muted blue light filtering down from far above. Our frozen shelf is about seven feet long and two feet wide. Mike lies on the snow ledge lengthwise, his feet dangling a few inches over the far end. I'm standing next to him, with the toe of my left mountaineering boot touching his climbing harness.

I step back to give him some room, but right away my shoulder bumps against the frozen wall behind me. When I reach forward, my hand hits the far ice wall before I can straighten my arm. A mild wave of claustrophobic tension ripples through my chest, but I push it away and shuffle about to find more space. But with Mike, his pack and gear all jumbled across our small ledge, there's nowhere else for me to stand. One long strand of yellow climbing rope loops off the ledge just beyond Mike's head, so I bend over to reel it back in before it snags on something.

With my head down low, I feel wetness drip off my nose. I run my forearm across my face and see dark smears on my jacket sleeve. Blood.

Retrieving the rope forces me to confront the dark space beneath our ledge. Fighting to stay calm, I focus on trying to figure out where we are inside the glacier, and how much deeper the crevasse stretches beneath us. The rope droops down at least twenty feet without touching anything; beyond that, I see nothing. Deep below me, the glacial sidewalls are nearly as black as the crevasse itself—I can distinguish them only by the glint of weak light reflecting off the ice. The walls pinch closer until the gap between them is less than a foot across.

I'm not going down there.

To my right, the crevasse stretches laterally away from me as it tunnels more than one hundred feet farther into the mountainside. It's like looking into a dark, narrow alley, just two feet across, squeezed between towering buildings. At the far end our fissure burrows even deeper beneath the glacier and the gloom fades to impenetrable black.

I turn and look in the opposite direction, along the crevasse's long axis as it stretches down the mountain. Peering out over Mike, I figure the crevasse extends about two hundred feet that way. I pull in a sharp breath and hear my hiss echo off the ice wall. This slot is enormous.

▲ X ▲

Slowly, I face the awful truth: We're stuck on a tiny ledge, trapped alone inside this miles-long glacier. God only knows how far down we are—I haven't dared to look up yet. But there's no question about it: We're deep, deep inside.

It happened so fast. One second we were descending the mountain, nearly finished with the most remarkable alpine climbing experience of our lives, just hours after summiting Mount Rainier. Then a step, a single treacherous step, in the wrong spot.

A snow bridge collapsed, and in a second, I was falling, falling—dragging Mike in behind me. Falling, falling.

And now, *this*. Trapped in a crevasse.

I drop my head and stare at my green plastic boots. I'm shocked by the massive space below us, on both sides of us, above us. It feels as if the weight of all the air in the huge cavern is squashing me.

By looking down and to the sides, I had hoped that I might find a simple exit. But now it's clear: The only way out is up.

I steel myself to face that reality, to determine how far the distance to the glacier's surface really is. Leaning my forehead against the ice wall, I close my eyes, blow out a long breath, and try to find some calm. I need a minute before I can look.

Rocking from one foot to the other, I hear the snow squeak beneath my boots. When I shift my arm, my Gore-Tex jacket crinkles against itself. Water drips on my sleeve, falling from somewhere high above me.

Stoically I straighten up tall and begin lifting my gaze. Twenty feet above me I see the side walls of ice flare away from each other as the crevasse gap expands to around four feet across. Then maybe six.

My eyes travel up...up...up. Forty feet above me, I see the walls, now separated by about eight feet, leaning back inward in an ever-steepening overhang. In the blue light closer to the surface I can make out lumpy blobs of ice frozen to the side walls.

My neck strains. About sixty feet above me, the left wall juts out, forming an overhanging ice roof that would be impossible to free climb. A sense of dread washes over me.

Resting my right hand on the wall for support, I curl my upper body backward so I can finally stare straight up. Far above, back at the glacier's surface, the entire crevasse is capped by a huge roof of snow. In some places up there, the snow bridge that spans this crevasse is thick enough to block all light, and from beneath, the bulbous ceiling appears black. In other places, the deceptive snow layer is so whisper-thin that soft light glows from its underbelly.

My eyes lock on the most vital feature: Directly over my head rests a small, irregular circle of bright white light. It's sunlight spilling through the jagged hole that opened beneath my feet and swallowed us. The sky above the glacier is presumably still blue, but I can't see it—the intense light pouring in blinds me. That sunlit hole is the only way out of here, the only way back to life.

And that hole is roughly eighty feet away, straight up.

I hear a quivering voice.

"Oh, we're in trouble," I say to Mike. "We're in big, big trouble."

THE LEDGE

CHAPTER 1

▲ ▲ ▲

THE AIRPLANE'S ENGINE droned rhythmically, the only sound in an empty sky. Mike Price peered out the window, taking in a snow-covered landscape that unfurled as far as he could see. He'd studied a map of this area for weeks, but even that hadn't prepared him for the reality of the Yukon.

Glaciers wider than mighty rivers; ice-streaked peaks reaching into the evening sky; a brilliant white blanket undulating across a barren landscape.

It was June 11, 1981, and Mike Price was on the cusp of one of the greatest adventures of his life. In the coming weeks, he and three friends would trek and ski ninety miles across this isolated stretch of uninhabitable expanse, lugging eighty-pound packs, aiming for the summit of a desolate peak called Mount Kennedy.

It was Mike's job to drop two plastic barrels of provisions along their route—and to know with certainty that they'd be able to find them days later, when they'd be out of food, isolated, alone. The plane swept in low over the snow, and Mike pushed one of the barrels out, watching as it crashed to the ground in a spray of powder. He marked the precise spot on the coffee-table-sized map.

A little later, deeper in the frozen wilderness, he dumped the second barrel, and again marked the map. The hired bush pilot banked the plane and headed back to base camp.

Later that night, in his tent, Mike cracked open a leather-bound journal, lifted a black ballpoint pen to page 46, and began writing.

"Tomorrow we're off! For real."

The magnificent desolation he'd seen out the plane's window riveted him.

"I find it difficult to write. The visual experience simply does not translate to paper well. Awesome."

To emphasize that entry, he took a blue pen and underlined the words.

In the coming weeks, Mike Price would learn things about himself that would help shape his destiny, that would one day lead him to a snowcapped mountain near Seattle.

During those long, muscle-numbing days in the Yukon, not only did he see things he'd never forget, but he was able to reaffirm in himself something he'd always known, something his parents had seen, too, when he'd boxed older, bigger boys as a kid, or when he'd loaded up his backpack and headed into the woods alone as a teenager: Mike Price was tough. He could survive hunger, weariness, and fear.

Mike was twenty-three years old in the summer of 1981. A native of Pauls Valley, Oklahoma, the son of an air traffic controller, he'd already led an exciting, nomadic life. Military school; college in Colorado and Montana; work in Wyoming. And lots of time in the mountains.

Now, the four friends—Mike, Andy Thamert, Bob Jamieson, and Bob's brother, Lee—were ready to reach for a dream that was as audacious as it was difficult. They planned to make their way across the ice and emptiness of the Saint Elias Mountains in the Canadian Yukon, then climb Mount Kennedy, a steep, snow-crusted peak. Named in memory of the late president after he was murdered in

Dallas, it had first been climbed in 1965 by Robert F. Kennedy and a team of experienced mountaineers on a trip sponsored by the National Geographic Society.

Mike and his buddies would spend thirty-seven days in unforgiving country, beginning in the mud along the Slims River and then, roped together in their climbing harnesses, trekking through endless fields of ice and snow. They would cross seven major glaciers, go thirty-four days without seeing another human being, run short of food, fight off overpowering boredom and tension, and skirt yawning crevasses that threatened to consume them.

"I will always remember the trip as being equally difficult, beautiful and desolate," Mike would write near the end of the journey.

NO ONE WHO'D known Mike Price as a kid would have been surprised to learn that he would one day possess the confidence to set out into the Yukon with three friends and that they would rely on their wits and little else to get home alive.

Small and skinny all his life, with a bowl cut of blond hair, he was self-assured beyond his size and years. After he advanced in a junior high spelling bee, he told a reporter for the local paper that he wasn't surprised.

"I've got momentum," he said. "The Price is right."

He was barely a teenager when he uttered those words, but they illustrated the combustible mix of mischievous joy and wit that would form the core of his personality.

He drove his mother crazy at times, his curious preteen mind fueling a motor mouth that seemingly wouldn't quit. They'd be out in the station wagon, Donna Price up front, Mike leaning over from the back seat, yammering on about the army, about soldiers, making it up as he went, like a junior Dick Vitale, one sentence crashing into another and then another, no hint that an ending was coming.

Sometimes he'd go on for so long that his mother would think silently about offering him a dollar to just be quiet.

Over the years, as he grew older, his parents and his younger brother, Daryl, saw a gentle transformation. Mike grew to be more introspective, and he would sit in a gathering and listen rather than yammer.

After his family moved to Colorado, an abiding love of the outdoors blossomed in Mike, and as it did he developed an inner confidence. He was the son who, as a teenager, ventured up Poudre Canyon, west of Fort Collins, Colorado, camping out in weather so cold that—family legend would have it—he used a frozen stick of summer sausage to drive his tent pegs into the icy soil. He was the traveler who blew into town the day before his first class at the University of Montana, found an apartment, and got a part-time job in a ski shop—no worries.

"He did what he wanted to do," Donna would say years later. "How many people can say that? How many people have the chance, and the courage?"

There were times, when Mike was out in the desert or up in the mountains, that concern, even alarm reverberated in the minds of his parents. But Don and Donna Price were determined that their boys would stand on their own, that they would make their own way in the world.

MIKE CARRIED HIS bravado with him to the Yukon, where the four young men—"unknowns and never-wases," as he described them beforehand—fought through at-times horrific weather in their quest to climb a peak few had ever visited.

Near the summit of Mount Kennedy, rocked by blasts of wind, blinded by sheets of snow, they found they could go no farther. Bitter cold froze their eyelashes together when they dared close their eyes for longer than a blink. In that no-man's-land, only a few hours from the summit, Lee Jamieson, then just seventeen years old, stopped, his hands numb. Bob, seven years his brother's senior, sidled up to Lee and slipped off his frozen mittens, replacing them with his own.

"Andy and I move behind," Mike would write of the moment. "At 12,500 feet the climb is over. Simultaneously all four of us know it, but stand dumbly in the blowing snow, waiting for Bob to speak... Less than 1,400 feet from the summit, no one wants to be the first to give in. We are so close. We have come so far."

It was July 4, 1981, their twenty-third day in the mountains.

As they started down and began the ninety-mile trek back, a sense of dread swept over Mike.

"Thinking about the descent I worry about falling on the steep slopes below," he would write. "I picture myself sliding sideways, head downward, into an open crevasse, with snow pushing up the sleeve and collar of my jacket, packing into my clothes."

As he skied, roped to one of his partners, it almost happened.

"Bracing into a tight turn above a particularly ominous crevasse, I push my skis and nothing happens. I try again and am still unable to drive the tails around and into the slope. Picking up speed I am shocked to hear the icy skitter continue. Already I can see into the depths of a dark hole vaguely ahead. I feel the blood pulse through my neck, grip my ski poles tightly, and give an all-out oompf! into the mountain, slamming to a stop."

Later, as he crawled across an eight-foot snow bridge spanning a giant glacial crack, one arm punched through. He scurried across, shaken, and then sweated it out as each of the others crossed. Everyone made it.

A day later, Mike lay in the tent, tired, hungry, homesick. A kind of melancholy gripped him. He'd filled his journal, even writing inside the back cover. Now he unfolded his map of the Yukon and began writing of the experiences, people, his parents in Kansas City, and even Patches, the dog he missed.

"I long for warm days in the woods, the aspen trees, the green pines, the blue lakes, dirt and rock under my feet. And very much for the hot sun deck in K.C., listening to the ballgame on the radio with Dad and Patches, Mom cooking supper, snacking on chips, having something 'real' to drink, in anticipation of a large, tasty, brim-filling meal of solid food. I think I am the most pronounced in the group in missing these, though I don't bitch about it—just say that I miss them and let it go at that."

Handwriting—some of it neatly printed, some of it wandering sloppily downhill—would eventually fill every inch of the map's milk-white back side.

"We are completely isolated. No contact whatsoever with the outside world. No radio. We have not seen another person in about three weeks...

"Psyched for the return only because each step is a step toward home. It cannot pass quickly enough. Like waiting for Christmas when I was a kid...

"I'm so moody and sensitive both. And I'm finding out that while I have a lot of stamina, I don't have endurance on the same plane. Day-in day-out heavy-duty ski-packing wears my body down badly...

"I look forward to this fall and even before then—I look forward with unprecedented eagerness to see Mom, Dad, Patches, Daryl and the relations at the family reunion. The cloud has passed from my sun...From this trip, I have restored my pride—fiercely—but even more so and unexpectedly so have gained a sense of humility—of niche—I've never had before."

CHAPTER 2

▲ ▲ ▲

HOLDING THE ICE ax in my right hand, I probe the glacier ahead. The ax shaft sinks in six inches and the snow feels solid, so I step forward. My boot settles into the soft, wet slop up to my ankle. Probing before each step is exhausting but necessary as I check for hollow snow bridges that could conceal yawning glacial crevasses.

I probe again, feel firm snow, and sink to my ankle as I take another step.

The air is calm, and the midday sun is strong on this first day of summer, June 21, 1992. We can't see or hear any other climbers. The snow before me lies smooth and flat and blindingly white as we descend from the summit of Mount Rainier. I flip aside the rope that leads back fifty feet to Mike. Looking at the glacier in front of me, I see no cracks, sags, or aberrations.

I stab my ice ax shaft into the snow, and it sinks in the usual six inches before resisting. Stepping forward, I press down my right boot. I sink to my ankle, and then my shin.

Snow seems deep here.

Momentum pushes me forward, and more weight rocks onto my front foot. Oddly, my boot is still settling into the soft snow.

It should feel firm by now.

I sink almost to my knee.

What the...?

The ground beneath my foot caves.

Snow's collapsing!

A burning electric shock of fear jolts my body. Before I can even say it or think it, my body knows what's happening: I'm on a snow bridge across a hidden crevasse, and it's giving way.

I'm falling...into...the mountain.

Instincts take over. As I scream a warning to Mike— "FALLING!"—my right leg locks to avoid stepping down any farther. But there's no stopping; inertia carries me forward, and I sink faster into the snow, up past my knee. My scream sounds like a scared shout from the other end of an empty house, and the confused terror in my own voice sends a second wave of adrenaline burning through my veins.

I dart my eyes sideways and think about scrambling to the solid ground behind me, but momentum and my backpack's weight drive me down face-first. There's no turning back. My left leg also crashes through the weak snow bridge, and in a heartbeat I'm in up to my thighs.

I vaguely hope the wide bottom of the backpack will spread my falling weight across the weak snow and somehow stop me; instead, with a muffled *whompf* the fragile bridge ruptures further, settling and sagging all around me.

I drop faster into the ever-widening hole, and I instinctively thrust my left arm to the side. Through an open crack, I see blackness underneath.

I'm going in!

I'm slithering downward, my chest above the snow, my belly encased in the disintegrating snow bridge. In the void below, my legs churn madly. There's nothing but air under me now. Only the side walls of the snow hole dragging against me hold me up.

Just a split second has passed, but my mind has slowed it all down. It's as if I'm watching a movie, and someone else is in it.

Gotta stop.

As I sink to my sternum, I slam my ax down hard. The pick bites deep into the snow surface in front of me.

My right arm snaps ramrod straight; I grip the ax shaft even tighter, preparing for the impact, expecting the 220 pounds of me and the pack to rip my shoulder joint. I don't care—anything's better than going into the crevasse.

But the pick tears through the wet, granular snow in a spray of slush. There's no resistance.

"FALL...!" I scream. My one last attempt to warn Mike ends abruptly as my face smashes into the crevasse lip, ramming ice crystals up my nose, into my mouth. Just one or two seconds after the collapse of the snow bridge started, my helmeted head vanishes below the surface.

Gravity yanks me from the warm world into the belly of the glacier, as though something evil has a deadly tentacle around my feet and is dragging me deeper. The monster has me.

As my head passes through the snow bridge, blackness and menace envelop me, and crunchy snow grinds against my ears. Sharp ice crystals scrape skin off my nose and forehead.

My shoulders feel pressed from the sides as they squeeze through the snow bridge. Then the battering and scraping and squeezing suddenly stop. For maybe half a second I'm relieved.

Then I get it: It's not that I've stopped falling; I've been spit out the bottom of the snow bridge. I frantically wave my arms and legs in the blackness, but feel nothing. I'm no longer touching anything. With no sensory input, for a split second I feel magically suspended in midair. In reality, though, I'm accelerating down.

In a vain attempt to stop, I swing my ice ax blindly in front of me as I fall. It swishes though the air. I can't reach either side of the crevasse. My gut warns that I am going for a big ride. I start guessing how far I'm falling.

Ten feet.

Mike's on his belly, digging in hard with his ax and boots—the fall should be short.

When he gets hold, the rope will jerk taut and stop me—any second now.

I feel no reassuring yank of the rope.

Twenty feet.

I try to swing my ice ax again, desperate to hook something, but my arm feels funny; the nylon leash has slipped off my wrist. My ax is gone.

I can't stop myself now.

Thirty feet.

I'm going too fast. Mike should have stopped me by now—something's wrong.

Barely controlled fear erupts into terror. I've been falling feet-first, but now the high-centered weight of my pack rotates me sideways as I plummet. Instinctively, I jab my arm out into the darkness, groping for a place to grab hold. I can't see it, but I feel an ice wall, hard as concrete, race past my gloved fingers, the nylon screaming as it skims along.

Forty feet.

We're almost out of rope.

Fifty feet.

If I'm really in fifty feet, that means Mike's been dragged almost to the crevasse lip. He's running out of space . . .

C'mon, Mike! . . . Dig in! . . . Dig in! . . . Stop us!

The rope tied to my waist harness jerks, and for a brief instant I think Mike's done it, that his ax and boots finally caught hold and he's arrested my fall.

We're going to be okay . . .

Then the rope goes slack and I accelerate even more madly than before.

Lost in my own fear, fifty feet below him, I can't hear or see Mike. But I suddenly feel his presence. I know he's here—I have dragged my friend into the crevasse with me.

Without Mike as a counterweight, digging in, we're both headed for the bottom. Roped together, we soar through the blackness.

We've had it.

CHAPTER 3

▲ ▲ ▲

DAD WRAPPED THE rope around his waist twice and briskly tied the knot without a word. I heard his voice in my mind anyway, repeating the mantra he'd taught me for tying a proper bowline: "The rabbit comes out of the hole, around the tree, and back in the hole."

I was twelve years old.

The tawny braided manila rope draped along the leg of his paint-splattered pants. He handed me his lifeline and our fingers touched. His wide calluses made my hands seem pathetically soft.

"Do ya understand what ya hafta do?" he asked as we stood on the building's roof.

"Yeah, I think I got it."

"Good. I outweigh ya, so back over the other side."

The big storage shed hunkered in a remote corner of the federal Natick Labs in Natick, Massachusetts. I slid my butt off the building's crest and moved downhill two feet. Struggling for purchase on the slick metal roof, I edged one boot against a panel seam and dug my other heel into a jagged rivethead. From below us, back down the ladder, I heard a steady mechanical hum. The spray gun idled, ready for Dad to squeeze the trigger and shoot a thick coat of protective tar onto the roof.

Having me on the opposite side from Dad let me see him but gave us some mechanical advantage in case he fell. The extra force required to drag me back up and over the roof's apex should slow us both enough so that I could probably stop him.

It was my first time pulling ropes for anyone, and I was terrified. Dad was going to spray, and I'd been recruited to hold his safety line. I knew that once he started, the big pneumatic pump would chug out viscous tar so fast that Dad would have to run back and forth to prevent a thick mess we would then have to clean up. With the tar flying and Dad scrambling, my job was to pull in rope when he ran toward me and feed out slack when he scampered away. Take in the rope too slowly, and the excess would pile up and trip him. Feed out slack too slowly, and the line could jerk him off his feet. If Dad stumbled for any reason, I had to make sure he didn't plunge off the roof to the pavement thirty feet below. If I blew it, my dad was going to hit the ground.

"Ya ready?"

"I guess so."

"There's no 'I guess so.' Ya have to keep me on the roof."

"I know. But what if I get tired or can't hang on?"

"Wrap the rope around your arm or your leg. Bite it with your teeth. I don't care; just hang on. Remember, there's no letting go."

Trying to look brave, I nodded my head at Dad, and he nodded back. He pulled the trigger, the spray gun screamed like a jet, and high-pressure tar blasted out. Dad dashed down the sloped roof, and my arms flailed as I let out slack. When he got one step from the edge he extended his reach and coated all the way to the drop-off. Then he scurried up the roof, spraying his way back toward the ridgeline. Loose rope piled around and on me as I yarded it in.

We maintained this frantic pace for a few minutes before Dad released the trigger. He stopped near the roof crest, a jumbled cocoon of slack rope coiling around me. We both panted for a minute, inadvertently pulling the heavy petroleum vapors deep into our lungs. Dad broke the silence.

"This baby pumps out some juice."

"Boy, I'll say."

"Ya doin' all right?"

"It's wild, but I got it."

"Keep it up."

He hit the trigger again and the mêlée resumed. We had started at six A.M. to beat the July heat. Now it was seven o'clock, and warmth boiled off the metal roof and mixed with the muggy New England air.

By midmorning we had the job almost half done. During a break, Dad checked the thermometer he had placed on the roof surface and blew out a low, long whistle.

"It's maxed out past a hundred and twenty," he said. "Gettin' awful warm up here."

"Maybe we can finish today, though," I interjected. "Should we just keep going?"

He looked at the sun, then the thermometer again, then at me, thinking.

"Nope," he said after a three-second pause. "Better quit before someone gets hurt."

We returned to the job site the next morning in the dark, and climbed onto the roof at first light. As the sun crept higher, the gun screamed, Dad scrambled, and my tired arms spooled the rope in and out once again. Coarse fibers protruding from the three twisted manila strands pricked at fresh blisters on my hands, but tacky tar blotches on the rope gave me a good grip. By ten A.M., we had finished.

That evening, when I took my regular seat at the dinner table, I was surprised to see my green paycheck centered, almost ceremonially, facedown on my empty white plate. Puzzled, I flipped it over.

Dad gave me a sideways glance while he sipped his scotch and water. The amount was double my normal pay.

"There's a mistake. You paid me too much."

"No mistake," he said. "Pulling my ropes, ya did the work of a full painter. So ya should get paid like a full painter from now on."

Thrilled but stunned, I looked across the table at Mom. She said softly, "Your father said you worked hard. Take it."

"I didn't go off the roof," Dad said, "so ya did your job right. Ya earned it."

I lifted my milk and clinked glasses with Dad.

"Atta boy, Jim."

AS FAR BACK as I can remember, I hung around my dad and uncle as they operated their painting business out of our barn. Two stories tall, with white clapboard siding, it sat beside our century-old house in Concord, Massachusetts. Behind its massive sliding doors, several rough-hewn horse stalls converted to shelving overflowed with ladders, brushes, and hundreds of half-empty paint cans. The aging building leaned a little to the west, and there were a few dinner-plate-sized holes in the wide-plank flooring of the rope-storage loft upstairs, but it served fine as a paint shop. I didn't appreciate at the time how hard their work was, and how vital; my dad had four kids, Uncle Bob had five, and as co-owners of the business they could lose their shirts or make a year's profit with a single job.

I loved the ever-changing crowd of men arriving each morning— beater station wagons and rusty vans backing up, their occupants grabbing job orders, loading paint buckets. After an energetic scrum of preparation, the convoy would pull out. As a preschooler I often asked to go to the job site, too, and since I usually couldn't, Dad sometimes appeased me by handing me brushes and a bucket of water and telling me to "paint" the wooden bulkhead that led to our fieldstone cellar. Brushing the water on the green boards made their dark surfaces glisten, just as if they had a fresh coat.

At age nine I worked several forty-hour weeks during the summer for Lincoln Painting Company, scraping off old paint and cleaning brushes. Dad paid me ten cents an hour. At age ten, I worked full-time for half the summer, as well as some weekends during the school year. Dad had taught me how to walk sloped roofs and how to spray paint by the time I was twelve. On hundreds of jobs, I observed my father interacting with his partner, his customers, his crews. I watched and listened and learned.

I can still hear his voice in my head.

"Think it through before ya commit...Make sure ya know what you're doing...Better hit it early...You're tired today? Well, hired, tired, fired...Stick with it until ya get the job done...Do it like ya mean it."

And more than that, I can feel in my bones the lessons I took away from all of it. That when you committed to "foot" a ladder, anchoring it while another man climbed high, you could never, ever leave your partner; even if the ladder slid away and fell, you rode it to the ground, protecting him as best you could all the way. That when you "pulled rope"—keeping hold of another painter's safety line to prevent him from falling to the ground—you dedicated yourself to hanging on for all you were worth. If your partner took a tumble, you never let go of the rope, even if it yanked you off the building, too.

Just before I pulled rope for Dad on an extra-slippery roof, he said to me, "If I go off and hit the ground, ya'd better be coming off the roof right behind me, still holding my rope."

Once, I was on a roof with our foreman, Rocco Ciraso, and a new hire. As a scrawny twelve-year-old, I was too light to anchor Rocco, whose beer belly and thick-limbed Harley-riding physique brought him in at about 230 pounds, so the untested new guy was going to pull Rocco's rope. Even after Rocco drilled into him the importance of never letting go, the guy seemed noncommittal. Rocco didn't trust him, so I didn't either.

"Stick out your arm," Rocco ordered.

When he did, Rocco tied the rope to the shocked man's wrist. When the newbie complained and reached for the knot, Rocco gave him the cold stare he had perfected back in his badass biker days and warned, "Leave it on."

"There," Rocco said after cinching the knot tighter. "Now I know you'll try hard."

He did try hard that day, and he did okay, but he never came back. When Rocco told my father the next day why the new guy quit, I heard Dad reply, "Fine. If he's not going to stick with it, then we're better off without him."

DAD AND UNCLE Bob did a lot of industrial painting for the federal government. In the summer of 1976, they won the bid to paint the Wyman Avenue bridge, a primary access point for traffic entering the Portsmouth naval base. About three hundred feet long and two lanes wide, the unassuming metal structure looked like most other highway spans. The job seemed straightforward: Sandblast the faded gray paint off the bridge's steel underpinnings, then spray two fresh coats back on.

Nothing on the job went right. The bridge stood on the border between New Hampshire and Maine where the Piscataqua River meets the sea, and saltwater mist filled the air. So we had to sandblast and paint in small, inefficient chunks, or risk the newly cleaned steel rusting and needing to be stripped all over again.

On summer break after eighth grade, I joined Dad on the job site. I scraped metal handrails, shoveled sand, and tried lugging one-hundred-pound sandbags. Because I outweighed the bulging brown paper bags by just twenty pounds, initially I could not move them very far. By the summer's end, I could carry them with ease.

Each workday started when Dad and I pulled out of the driveway at five-thirty A.M., so we'd be the first ones on-site by seven o'clock. We were the last to leave, at around six each evening, which got us home by seven-thirty for a reheated dinner.

Dad and Uncle Bob taught me about sandblasting so Dad and I could work alone some weekends. He blasted; I tended the sand pot.

Blasting at this scale required enough compressed air to pump a ton of sand every hour through one hundred feet of thick hose with enough force to instantly strip three layers of paint off steel. The racing air roared like a jet engine and the surging blast hose writhed like a giant anaconda. Dad could hear nothing, say nothing, and see very little because of the protective canvas hood he wore, so I was his eyes and ears. My job was to watch him intently and adjust the blasting pot according to his demands.

He taught me our company hand signals for more sand or less, for when he was all right, and for when he needed me to cut off the gushing machine immediately. Stopping the blaster on demand was the most important aspect of my pot-tending job, as it only had two speeds: off and full tilt. When Dad waved his forearm in a sharp arc, I sprinted to the pot and hit the pressure-relief valve. That cut the compressor flow and bled air pressure from the line. A safe shut-off was confirmed first by the hissing escape of air, and then by a reassuring clunk as the blasting pot's metal lid dropped loose from its seal, released by depressurization. One second later the air-driven sand would cease shooting from the nozzle, giving Dad a rest. Without a committed pot tender, the blaster could be compelled to wrestle and direct the thrashing blast hose until the compressor eventually ran out of fuel.

An insidious and dangerous part of the system was the connecting hose that routed pressurized air from the compressor over to the sand pot. This high-pressure hose was skinny and flexible, like a beefy garden hose. Its two ends had forced-fit metal couplings. Occasionally the huge pressures and mechanical vibrations caused the fitting to slip from the sand pot, which let loose an uncontrolled, whipping air hose. The air pressure was so great that the untethered hose end swung, flopped, and gyrated in large erratic circles anywhere from two to twenty feet in radius. As it danced wildly about, the metal coupling end whooshed through the air, arcing one way, then the other, in a blur.

Such a loose hose obviously had to be stopped, then fixed. But therein lay the danger. To stop the hose, you had to stop the compressor. But to reach the compressor, the pot tender first had to capture the lashing air line without getting clobbered by the flying metal coupling. In essence, work would be at a standstill until we seized control of the aggressive, whirling air line. As pot tender, I needed a lesson in subduing a wild hose.

Dad let the throttled-down compressor bring to life an intentionally disconnected air hose. Even at half pressure, the black rubber tubing stood up like a king cobra and skittered sideways. The gray metal coupling sliced and circled through the air like some giant bola. As the moving hose dragged on the ground or slipped across its own smooth coils, it would suddenly change its swing radius, speed, or direction—or all three at the same time.

Talking loudly over the compressor, Dad said, "Now, don't just charge in there like a dummy. Study it. It looks crazy, but there are some patterns and limits. Watch."

He was right. After two minutes of seemingly random thrashing, I saw a rhythm to the movement. The possessed hose made three or four clockwise rotations, then stalled out for five seconds. Then it slipped sideways a few feet and rotated back the other way, repeatedly coiling and uncoiling itself.

"Yeah, I see it now," I said.

"Good. So use that to make your move. Then race in there and grab that thing."

"Okay."

"Don't go in there half-committed, change your mind, and stop. That'll get you whacked in the head. When you go after it, do it like ya mean it."

Not wanting to be chicken in front of my father, I got ready to make my first practice charge at a loose hose. Dad tapped my shoulder and gestured me close to him. He leaned in.

"A few more things. When ya grab it, don't grab down the line from the coupling, because then those last few feet will really start swinging. All the pressure and motion will get pushed to the loose end ya don't have control over. That metal end will whip around twice as fast and get ya. So always snag it right behind the coupling, like you're grabbing a snake. If ya control the danger, it can't get ya."

That made sense, and the logic comforted me.

"Assess it, charge it, control it—okay," I said. "Anything else?"

"Don't be surprised if it changes all of a sudden and the hose starts whipping around a new way."

He turned his palms to the sky, shrugged, and half-smiled.

I scowled and said, "Great..."

The hose mostly danced the same steps, so it seemed doable. Hunched down as if I were going to steal second base, I watched for the start of the lull. The next time it cycled around, I charged. The scariest part was when I was about ten feet away, because I was close enough to get smacked by the coupling but not close enough yet to grasp the hose. Three more fast steps and I grabbed the hose about two feet from the end. I knew that was not best, so I snapped my other hand up and seized the serpent three inches behind its coupling head.

Got it!

The pressure kicked back, and the hose thrashed like a snake trying to turn on me. I stepped on a moving coil to keep it trapped. A bit surprised and fairly pleased, I turned to look at Dad. He crinkled his face tight and stacked his fists together like he was clutching a baseball bat. It was the signal for me to hang on tight. I nodded and held my prize up to show him I had it captured. Then Dad whistled loud and gave me a throat-slashing signal to cut off the compressor. I walked the captive hose end back to the compressor and hit the kill switch. The revving compressor died, and the snake hose went limp in my hands.

"Atta boy. Ya didn't hesitate."

"Yeah, that wasn't too bad."

"Remember, that was half pressure. At full pressure the hose will be faster, and if it gets ya, the coupling will hurt like hell."

"Are we going to do a full-pressure practice?" I asked hesitantly.

"It would be nice to try, but it's not worth losing a tooth."

"I've got a question: When I do it for real, should I wear my coat for protection or take it off so I can move faster?"

"It'll be up to you. I won't be standing there telling you exactly what to do. Remember what I taught ya, then do it like ya mean it."

DAD HAD A knack for landing unusual gigs. Over the years we had painted cranes and churches, fire hydrants and radar dishes, even the gondola towers at the Cannon Mountain ski area, in New Hampshire. But one job beat them all: We were to paint a high-voltage electrical switchyard located adjacent to an enormous power plant. I was eighteen the year my dad took on that job.

The inch-thick wires coming out of the generator building fifty yards away carried 230,000 volts and enough amperage to electrify a swath of eastern Massachusetts. All that power dumped right into the complex routing switchyard where we stood, the electrified air above buzzing as if swarmed by angry bees. Vertical steel beams supporting a welded lattice of smaller crossbars formed the switch-yard's frame. The intricate structure was designed to support the wires and heavy equipment needed to distribute the electricity into a network of power lines fanning out across the county.

To keep the voltage from electrifying the framework, a series of ceramic insulators shaped like oversized doughnuts isolated the siz-zling wires from the steel. It took a string of fifteen or twenty insu-lators to make the switchyard's steel safe to touch. Even then, when you grabbed the steel to climb, stray voltage sometimes crawled across your skin like stinging ants.

"All right, guys," Dad said. "Just a little more safety training, then we'll call it quits."

Dad turned us back over to the power company safety man, Frank, who had spent the day scowling and trying to scare us. It worked—we were terrified.

During our day-long safety lecture at the switchyard in Fall River, Massachusetts, Frank had intermingled tips and techniques with horror stories of people losing limbs, dying—even literally ex-ploding after mistakes made near the 230,000 volts. The steady hum of electricity above our heads underscored everything Frank told us. He said the juice was so high that we could never actually touch the lines, even if we tried. If one of us got within three feet of a live line, the massive voltage would leap out like lightning and destroy us.

After this brief class, it would be our job to go up there and paint the steel framework, with the hot power lines buzzing and snapping four feet away. The power company would deactivate one switch-yard square at a time for us, but the other sections around us had to remain fully charged. Every man was responsible for watching out for everyone else, Frank warned. Electricity always tries to run to the ground. If any one of us got zapped, the power racing down the steel frame we climbed would also electrocute every other man below him on the tower. Frank also demanded that we follow the orders of our ground crew. The ground crew would be Frank, another veteran lineman, Dad, and Dad's foreman, Rocco, who had been working with us for seventeen years. If any of us tower climbers strayed out of the safe zone or got too close to the wires, a ground man would blow a whistle.

"When you hear the whistle," Frank bellowed, "do not turn around. Do not move sideways. Do not lift your arm. Don't even get a hard-on. Just FREEZE! We'll talk you down. A few years ago, one guy was getting too close to the wires and I blew the whistle to warn him. Unfortunately, his buddy, who was actually in a safe spot to start with, didn't freeze. He thought I'd blown the whistle at him, so he turned around to go the other way. He walked right into a hot zone."

Frank paused.

"He's dead."

We were silent.

The sun was down, and daylight receded from the muggy air. Frank's voice boomed across the yard: "Okay, gather up."

Eight of us assembled near a corner of the switchyard.

"I have one more thing to show you," he hollered.

Frank pulled on cumbersome insulating gloves while his assistant unlocked a steel cage that secured a large switch. Frank pointed thirty feet above our heads and asked, "See that big copper switch rod up there?"

We all craned our necks. I spied a copper rod about four feet long and two inches in diameter.

Frank leaned toward us with a sneer on his face, his two mangy eyebrows merging into one bristling hedgerow of gray hair.

"If you don't listen to me, this is what will happen to you," he snarled, grabbing the control switch with two hands and yanking it down hard. The copper switch rod above our heads moved in an arc—a thirty-foot-tall power switch sweeping toward its cradle.

Before the switch could connect, a hot white bolt of jagged, crackling electricity shot out of the switch rod, lighting up the night air. When the rod settled into the receiving seat, a crisp click of metal preceded one last angry pop of electricity. The hum above us grew louder.

I thought about what my body would look like if that voltage tore through me. Frightened, but not wanting to look so, I glanced sideways at the older painters around me. Wide-eyed and blank-faced, they stared up, silent.

"Class dismissed," Frank said simply, then walked away.

We painted the switchyard through August, and no one got hurt. The dangerous work had helped me grow in immeasurable ways by fueling an inner confidence and by igniting a passion for challenges that made me stronger.

A YEAR AFTER we painted the switchyard, the same power company offered Dad another electrical-system painting job. Lincoln Painting Company was one of the few firms willing to take on such risky jobs.

So, for the summer of 1982 we climbed and painted high-voltage transmission-line towers. The open steel frameworks ranged from eighty to two hundred feet tall, and they ambled across the fields and woods of eastern Massachusetts. Every tower had six lateral arms extending over open space. At the end of each arm was a snapping, humming metal power line carrying about 230,000 volts.

Compared to the switchyard, the height of the towers greatly increased the consequences of a fall. Instead of getting badly hurt from a thirty-foot switchyard fall, if one of us plummeted eighty to two hundred feet from a tower, it would certainly be fatal. High on the steel towers, with the wind whistling around us and a void beneath us, we shooed away fear by bandying about dismissive phrases like "After a forty-foot fall, the outcome's the same, so don't worry about the height." We wore safety belts at first, but the risk of a loose leash dangling down into a live wire outweighed the benefits. So we mostly climbed free, untethered to the tower, and hung on tight as we walked the paint-splattered steel beams.

Although the voltage was about the same as it had been in the switchyard, the risk of electrocution was greater. Because we four tower painters were so high up, the ground men had a harder time judging how close the climbers were to the wires. The work was nerve-racking at times, and to find the four of us who painted the towers that summer, Dad tried out more than thirty men. Some lasted less than a day, some less than an hour. One guy showed up, walked under a tower for ten minutes, looking and listening to the voltage sizzle, and then just left.

One night, we brought home photos of us on the towers, and Mom and my sisters freaked out.

"You're going to get your son killed!" Mom blurted out.

"Oh, c'mon now, Jean—" Dad started to reply, but Mom pushed back from the dinner table and stormed out of the kitchen.

A moment of silence passed.

"She doesn't get it, does she?" I asked.

"No," Dad said wearily, "she doesn't."

Even then, I felt I was part of something special. And I thought the company, and Dad, needed me. I was one of the four-man crew that would scale each tower to the top, a disposable hospital hood tied over my head to cover my hair, a gallon bucket of olive drab paint clipped to my belt. Once we reached the highest point, we'd paint our way down, slathering the steel girders as we moved.

We called it "bringing down the tower," and the switchyard rules from the previous year still applied. Get within three feet of the power lines—or drop paint or dangle a rope near the wires—and you would die, and probably kill the other three men on the tower, too. Only now we were much higher off the ground, with the steel digging into our knees as we spread the paint, reaching out to coat bare spots we couldn't always see while Dad or someone else on the ground followed our progress through binoculars.

The diamond-shaped tips on the ends of the lateral arms were the worst. I would inch out, on my belly, as far as I dared, with electricity coursing above and below me, stretch one arm through an invisible, shrinking safety zone, and run the brush over those tips. I couldn't see what I was painting—I'd just blindly dab paint while Dad steered me from the ground with hollered instructions.

"To the right—more to the right," he'd yell. "Creep out a little farther."

He'd also yell out if I missed a spot.

"Ya left a skippa," he'd holler, and I'd reach out again, swabbing the brush over the tip until it was covered and dripping with paint. Once I finished painting, I would crawl backward along the arm, with the steel edging bruising my limbs and power lines snapping above my head.

All these years later, I can close my eyes and feel the tingly surge of that electricity pulsating through my body, as if ants were biting me everywhere. I can hear the incessant hum of power throbbing along those wires.

At times I felt apprehension, even raw fear, but I learned to contain it. You couldn't be afraid the whole time, but if you weren't at least nervous or scared some of the time, I figured, you had to be insane. Ignoring the risks was not an option; succumbing to fright, however, would have made me a danger to myself and everyone on the crew. Staying controlled, pushing the fear down, and keeping a clear mind in the face of danger and difficulty—that's what I learned on those jobs with Dad.

CHAPTER 4

▲ ▲ ▲

I PLUNGE INTO the mountain. Rocketing through the gloom, my arms and legs windmill desperately through the air. My eyes are open, I think, but I can't focus on the malicious ice walls rushing past me.

Partway down, I slam sideways into a thin snow platform that spans the crevasse—an old snow bridge, maybe. I feel the hit across my body and sense myself slowing a bit, and briefly I hope that the fall is over. But I tear right through, and sail deeper into the mountain.

Gravity pulls me in quicker as I career toward disaster.

Just three seconds ago, I was on the snowy surface of the glacier, anxious to get off Mount Rainier, eager to toast our summit climb with Mike later tonight, antsy to get home to my wife, Gloria. Now I'm plunging down into a crevasse, and my mind seizes a new, more horrifying fear.

Please, God, don't let us cork.

The threat of corking is real. If you fall into a crevasse and your partner can stop you, you'll wind up hanging from the rope, maybe hurt, maybe not. Fall far into a crevasse along with your partner, with nothing to catch either of you, and there's every chance you'll both slam to a stop wedged into the fissure's maw, like a cork in a bottle. Unable to move, unable to do anything but wait for death's slow, cold march. Corked.

This can't be real. But the terror burning a hole in my chest says it is. We're going all the way to the bottom.

Flopping like a rag doll, I sense I'm going to hit very hard, very soon. An image of myself as a loose-limbed falling man flashes in my brain. This takes my mind somewhere unexpected—to the old *Wide World of Sports* TV show's iconic footage of a ski jumper tumbling out of control on a takeoff ramp and crashing limply to the ground below as announcer Jim McKay intones something about "the agony of defeat." In spite of his brutal landing, that skier had not been seriously hurt, I had read somewhere, because he had not tensed up during his wild fall.

Voices erupt in my head—the same ones I'd heard in difficult situations for years, playing out my options.

Go limp.

You think that's going to make any difference?

That's all I can do.

Just then, the right side of my face grazes the icy wall—merely a kiss of a touch, but it's enough to deflect me the other way. I bash into the opposite wall hard, snapping my head sideways, and pain knifes through my left shoulder.

I pinball back to the first wall, smashing against it with my right side, jamming my helmet down over my forehead and into the bridge of my nose. The blow stuns me; then I ricochet into the far wall again, faster and harder this time.

Aaah—my leg!

I can't take much more.

The ice walls are pinching closer together. I'm getting near the bottom of the crevasse.

It'll all be over soon.

My heavy pack is underneath me, dragging me down. Trailing behind me, my arms and legs flop wildly, smashing against the ice walls. I'm starting to go head-first, a perfect setup to get corked.

And then . . . *WHAM!*

My back hits first, and it feels like someone has driven a two-by-four right between my shoulder blades. I hear the air forced from my lungs in one loud, grunting burst. My torso has stopped, but my limbs arrive a fraction of a second later. Both my legs smack to a stop, splayed out; then my arms bounce off hard walls and flop to rest across my chest.

My head snaps back violently, wrenching the tendons in the front of my neck, shooting hot pain through my chest muscles.

I blink and gasp and try to grab a staccato breath in that panicky moment that comes after the wind has been knocked from me. Gulping air, I touch a wall with my right hand, and my glove makes no noise. I reach out with my left hand and feel another wall right next to me. Again, silence. Since the side walls aren't moving, I'm not moving either. Slowly, my brain becomes convinced that I'm no longer falling.

Joy briefly flickers through me.

I'm alive.

I JUST FELL all that way, I'm alive, and I'm not too badly hurt.

I suck in a smoother breath, wiggle, and feel pain stab down my neck. I'm on my back, with my feet a little lower than my head, and I'm looking straight up through the near darkness toward a small point of light far above me. The crevasse walls are about two feet wide here—just inches from my shoulders.

Bewildered, for an instant I don't understand why I stopped. I can only assume I landed on a snow pile on the crevasse bottom.

I see moving darkness, a confusing image as the pinprick of light far above my head vanishes and reappears, almost as if some unseen being is waving a dark curtain in front of a distant spotlight.

Then something about the size of a grapefruit lands on my belly. *Whump*—a handful of wet, clumpy snow. The pinhole of light flickers again, and a double handful of sloppy snow hits me in the face. The light blinks once more, and another load of slush splashes down onto me. It's falling faster and harder, like someone up there is dumping slushy snow and ice down the crevasse onto me.

Whump, whump, whump.

Arriving faster now, the snow pours in like concrete rushing down a chute, filling over my shins, my thighs. I stare dully at the pile growing on me. Like a lone voice trying to rouse a stuporous crowd, some small corner of my brain urges me to respond. My sluggish mind finally realizes that the light above me sputters off when falling snow blocks my view. The light flickers rapidly. More snow's coming.

The momentary relief I felt when I realized I had survived the fall vanishes as fear rushes in. I try sitting up, but my shoulders are pinned. More desperate now, I attempt to force myself upright and feel my stomach muscles burn with the effort. The harder I try curling my body up, the deeper I feel the pack straps cut into my shoulders and hold me back. I can't get up. I'm trapped.

You're going to get buried. Dig.

I throw my hands up in front of me and dog-paddle as fast as I can, pawing at the falling snow, shoving it away in a race for survival. The slop splats onto me ever faster, and I feel its building weight press down my belly.

My thrashing arms feel weak, and a tinge of hopelessness rises within me.

You're losing. Dig faster! Keep that snow off you!

I flail my arms like some crazy cartoon character whose limbs spin perpetually but don't really accomplish anything. Snow covers my inclined body from my chest down to my toes. My legs feel heavy and compressed.

Keep your face clear.

Now it's really pouring in. Far above my head, the hole we punched through the sun-rotted snow bridge has made it even weaker. The bridge, I realize, is disintegrating and collapsing in on me. The cascading slop rumbles in my ears as it sprays in around me.

The light far above me goes dark, and doesn't switch back on.

Something big's coming. Cover up.

In that instant, I throw both my hands over my face and turn my head slightly to the right. Survival tips from old avalanche classes race through my mind, so I open my mouth to grab one last breath before I'm covered. I gulp in the air, but I'm too slow closing my lips, so the incoming snow packs grainy wet crystals into my mouth.

A huge load smothers me in a swirling crash, blowing my right arm away from my face. My head's buried now. I can't see. Rough ice crystals poke my cheeks. Still pouring in, the wet debris builds up above my ears and sounds become muffled. I hear more snow landing on the pile that grows thicker upon my head.

No deeper—just stop, please.

The sound of each impact is softer than the last, and I know the top surface of the snow is moving farther away as I get buried deeper.

No more—that's enough.

Stop!

CHAPTER 5

▲ ▲ ▲

BY THE MID-1980s Mike Price had found a kindred spirit in Everett Ruess, a young Californian who'd ventured into a still-wild West in the early 1930s, wandering and thinking, writing and painting. Setting out while just a teenager, Ruess explored the California coast, the mountains of the High Sierra, and the deserts and canyonlands of Arizona and Utah. He captured the stark beauty of the wilderness on his notepad and in his photographs and memories, and he carved those scenes onto linoleum blocks that were used to make prints.

Ruess's writings underscored his love for the outdoors, for the mystery waiting over the next hill, his words a poignant articulation of what drove him.

"I prefer the saddle to the streetcar and star-sprinkled sky to a roof, the obscure and difficult trail, leading into the unknown, to any paved highway, and the deep peace of the wild to the discontent bred by cities. . . . It is enough that I am surrounded by beauty."

Ruess scaled remote canyons, and he sometimes scrawled "Nemo" high on rocks—Latin for "no man" or "no one," or possibly a reference to Captain Nemo, who fled civilization in his submarine in *Twenty Thousand Leagues Under the Sea*. Then, in November 1934, near Escalante, Utah, he inexplicably vanished into the wilderness, never to be seen or heard from again. He was just twenty when he disappeared, and over the ensuing decades, theories abounded. Perhaps Ruess had been murdered. Plunged to his death while climbing a canyon wall. Set out on an adventure with no intention of returning to his old life.

A half century later, Mike Price became fascinated with Ruess, ultimately deciding to write his master's thesis in English literature on a young man who, like himself, represented a confluence of intellectual ability and love of the outdoors.

And as Mike set out to write that thesis, he didn't only research it; he lived it.

TRYING TO UNDERSTAND the meaning in Ruess's life—and maybe in his own—Mike struck out into the red rock desert canyonlands of southeast Utah, not only searching for answers to an enduring mystery but pursuing the romantic ideals that had inspired the young wanderer. Mike did not check into the Motel 6 in Moab and take a couple of day hikes. Instead, he slept alone in the sand, hiked under the blistering sun, hunkered down in torrential rains, and scaled canyon walls, all as he looked for clues about Ruess, for those hand-scratched "Nemo" marks.

Mike slept on the ground along a river turned silver in the moonlight, nothing covering him. He awakened at dawn, the call of canyon wrens the first sounds he heard. He sat in the rain reading, oblivious to his soaking clothes—or the protection of his nearby truck.

And he wandered the canyonlands, searching. He climbed into a cave, where he found strange drawings of human hands on the wall. Later he recounted the experience in his thesis.

"The hair on my arms stands on end; goosebumps march down my skin. But the markings lure me on; my fingers tremble; I burn from inside. The closer I get the more the burning increases; my hands are on fire when I reach the back wall of the cave. Ruess was here. I feel it. I feel it. When I lift my hands to the strange green hand prints my fingers match the fingers on the wall; my palms match its palms."

Overcome with weakness and nausea, Mike took a nasty spill—falling out of the cave and crashing to the sand in the canyon below, knocking himself out. As he awakened beneath the unrelenting desert sun, Mike soothed himself by writing of cooler places he had been: "Waterfall ice under the coldest cold a Colorado winter can offer... The outlet streams after a week of subzero nights... Time and motion both stopped, frozen into a moment lasting days, weeks, months until stirred into life again by the springtime sun."

BY 1990, MIKE was an established instructor at the Colorado Outward Bound School.

The program took young people out into the wilds for weeks or even a month. There, leaders like Mike taught them the outdoor skills needed to survive, and led spiritual journeys of self-discovery that encouraged the students to contemplate the meaning of their lives.

In late September 1990, Mike backed his battered pickup out of his brother Daryl's driveway in Colorado and headed west on Interstate 70, bound for Utah and a month-long canyonlands course in the windswept country that called to him as it had to Everett Ruess.

Near Grand Junction, just a few miles from the Utah border, Mike pulled alongside a car and glanced over. He recognized the woman at the wheel—Deb Caughron, a fellow Outward Bound instructor also on her way to teach—and he held his speed steady with hers. For the longest time, she didn't glance over; she was a woman, traveling alone, on a lonely highway. But Mike just held his truck right there, a giant cowboy hat on his head.

Eventually, she looked over, and when she did Mike tipped his hat and winked. The gesture earned him the nickname "Cowboy Bob."

A year later, Joanne Donohue, a slender New Jersey girl with tumbling locks of golden hair, came west for a thirty-day Outward Bound canyonlands course. For much of it, Mike was the only guide for Joanne and five other crew members (an assistant instructor joined them late, then exited soon after to walk out an injured student). As her crew worked its way through the desolation that is red rock country, Mike's gentle guidance, goofy songs, and quiet confidence settled on her.

Each night, she lay in her sleeping bag with a pen and her journal. Much of what she wrote was about her being twenty-three and living a great adventure. But day after day, at some point, her thoughts turned to Mike, and how he was able to make her believe in herself in a way that helped her get through one of the most challenging experiences of her life:

"I popped up and made this incredible climb up over this hump. The wind was actually shearing me off of it. Mike was running around, bounding back and forth on this moon-like landscape taking pictures! Then the most sweetest thing anybody has ever done— Mike starts singing that hickish cowboy song [with the line] 'You Don't Have to Call Me Darlin', Darlin'.' I'm groaning over this unbelievable climb with no handholds and I'm inching up with the wind screaming so hard that I can barely hold on and Mike is off to my right singing as proudly as can be, singing this cowboy song. I knew why he was singing it, so that maybe I wouldn't tense up and get frustrated on the rock. I just can't not laugh when he sings that song and he knew it. I was laughing so hard that I almost couldn't make it up. But I did... You're in these life/death situations and it is so reassuring to hear his voice because he guided you from the beginning. I'd trust Mike with my life. If there was anyone on Earth I'd trust it to—it would be Mike."

On the sixth day of the adventure, Mike and his charges ascended a three-hundred-foot sandstone face in Arch Canyon. Joanne struggled, slipping as she started up the rock, unsteady and unsure.

"Relax, relax," Mike told her.

She turned to him.

"Mike, I don't think I can do this," she said.

"You can," he told her, and grabbed the back of her pack and hoisted her and it up.

A little later, she complained again, unable to steel herself.

"You keep saying, 'I can't,' Joanne," he said.

They were the last words he uttered to her. She climbed to the top.

"He allowed you your own raw discoveries, and the rewards that come with it; they are the only ones you remember anyway," she would say later. "He knew that. We didn't. And in those terms, he was the ultimate guide."

MIKE PRICE'S ADVENTURES in the desert working on his thesis were another step in the journey he'd begun during those thirty-seven days he and three friends spent in the Yukon. In that frozen desolation, Mike had tested himself in extreme weather and examined his own being in an unforgiving landscape. Near the end of the trip, he opened a green spiral-bound notebook—his third journal of the trek—and looked out on his surroundings.

"Our 34th day almost over," he wrote. "Three more. And off the ice by tomorrow night! And then—'somewhere over the rainbow' in Kansas. Should be able to maintain a good psyche the rest of the way. Esp. as we get off this ice.

"Everything on the glacier is melting, shifting, cracking,

avalanching—we are just now watching a three-quarter-mile-long all-rock avalanche from a mile away!—and making all kinds of noises, reinforcing the air of instability. Incredible. I would enjoy the 'wonder' of it all a lot more if I did not have to camp on the ice again."

Mike's blue ballpoint pen moved across the paper, and in the words that flowed from him he found some answers. And maybe some insight into the biggest question of all: Why do people climb?

He opened one passage by noting a friend's admonition to heed another writer's description of a mountain's beauty as something more than the tableau of its colors and shapes and textures. And so he sat outside the team's crimson tent, in the late-afternoon light, and poured out his thoughts:

"Seeing the long-shadowed brown furrows cut into the low green-gentle slopes of Observation Mountain is a landmark symbol to me. Perhaps the most important-inspiring one of the trip—to me. Overlooking the Slims Valley, the Kaskawulsh and the South Arm's lower stretches, Observation Mountain is the last bend. Once around it, the homestretch 15 miles of dirt, grass, flowers and trees is all that's left. Soothing . . . Observation Mountain. 5,300. A low peak—a 'nothing' mountain—but very beautiful, even more so than Mount Kennedy, in its own right. Green and living, shadowed in the evening arctic sun of mid-July . . . Nothing awesome, nothing forbidding; a simple easy convergence of peace. The weary way-worn sailor has nearly made it home. The worries of Odysseus are not over . . . I think I am on the road to being satisfied and it is a road to peace."

Mike turned a page and kept writing.

"Pure quiet—except for the 'making camp' noises and the sound of water running on the ice . . . I am in the best spirits now of the entire trip . . . Tears in the corners of my eyes—of pure emotion—joy—happiness . . . I feel totally unburdened. The load has been lifted off my back, off my mind. I have to do nothing more to prove myself.

This is not for others but for me—and to me. Observation Mountain is a beautiful place. A beautiful rare mood. A few precious moments of ecstasy somehow not meant for—or translate-able into—words. Language fails where the tears begin."

As Mike sat and wrote, a crystalline blue sky stretched over his head. The red tent the four shared was at his back, and in every direction he looked snowcapped peaks reached for the sky.

Sitting on his backpack, he kept pouring his thoughts down onto the pages of the spiral notebook.

"I think it was Thoreau—or Krutch—who said you must see a place a hundred times before you've seen it. I've seen Observation Mountain a hundred times, probably twice two times that, under a varying guise of names and places. But only now I've 'seen' it. As far as peaks go, it is commonplace. Nothing special. Nothing that would attract a mountaineer. But it has touched me—the hopeless-helpless romantic—and I am filled with the energy of life—my spirit is restored—my wounds healed... From the most desolate ice desert I've ever been on. I don't have to 'prove myself' to anyone... If I never climb a peak higher than Longs or harder than McHenry's—it will be o.k.—I will have done well... And this pertains not only to mountains... but to everything I do... There are not ulterior motives. No lusts, no wild drives, to be 'satisfied' like a junkie's habit. Just 'the seeing' and 'the doing.' Mystical... The sublime beneath the dust...

"A chill wind picks up from behind, blowing through my clothes and urging me to get up. Things to tend to, things to do. Always. 34 days out for a few brief moments of ecstasy—no summit could ever possibly offer. The exchange rate is not equitable. Life isn't either. It isn't meant to be. But I have something here. I have something—I cannot accurately and easily express it—but I am onto something for sure...

"The view from Observation Mountain. Not from the summit, mind you. But from within. I 'saw' for the first time. I saw a mountain! I saw into a mountain!"

THAT COMBINATION OF introspection and wonder was well developed five years later as he ventured into those desolate canyonlands, looking for the secrets of Everett Ruess, and for insight into himself. On one of his many forays into a no-man's-land, he found himself in a precarious predicament, isolated in a maze of narrow canyons as a storm-churned sky swirled over his head. He headed into a meandering slot barely three feet wide, looking for a way to escape the powerful rains he sensed looming, realizing that this narrow canyon could be a death trap—a cloudburst could easily, and quickly, leave it teeming with rushing water. Finally, he reached a cavern with a slot ten feet up that looked promising, but as he struggled to climb to it, his feet clawed ineffectively on the water-slickened rock.

He yanked off his pack, fighting his nerves, looking for an answer. He found it within himself—deciding he could climb out of the cavern without his pack and drag it up after him with his rope. The ascent from the narrow slot pushed his mind back to the Yukon, back to a crevasse that nearly claimed him.

"A sharp crack like a gunshot rings in my ears, and suddenly I am falling, falling through a hole in the ice and snow that widens as I crash through it. My feet dangle and kick helplessly in the open air, but the top-heavy load on my pack forces me to fall forward, driving my face into the lip of the crevasse. Somehow I manage to plant my ax and arrest the downward momentum. For a moment I teeter on the brink of the abyss, my body a lever against the icy mouth of the crevasse, my chest the fulcrum. Gingerly, I am able to slither out of the hole without dislodging the ax."

CHAPTER 6

▲ ▲ ▲

WHEN I TOLD my parents that I was going camping in the dead of winter, Dad was skeptical and Mom was distraught.

It was just after Christmas in 1980, and I had five weeks off between semesters at the University of Massachusetts but hardly any money. So I cross-country skied through the woods near our Concord house and I read mountaineering books from the library, and in them I saw that most expedition chronicles contained horrific stories of surviving brutal snowstorms. Though I had backpacked in summertime, I wanted to find out if I was tough enough to sleep out in the snow. I did some research and gathered gear for my first winter campout. To minimize the risk, I decided to camp in an area I knew well—and one that offered a fast retreat in case things went awry—so I chose Boy Scout Island in Warner's Pond, just a quarter mile from home.

After having me explain the plan a second time, Mom leaned across the kitchen table toward me and said, "Honey, this doesn't make sense. Is there something wrong?"

Confused, I asked, "Do you mean, like, am I in trouble?"

"No, with you."

"You mean mentally? Why would you think that?"

"Jimmy, it's not normal to want to leave your nice warm home and go suffer in the cold."

I tried clarifying that this was a critical step on my path to adventure, but I failed to sway her. To prove that my plan was sound, I pointed out the built-in fail-safe: "Besides, it's so close that if my feet freeze, I can even crawl home from there."

I was surprised that instead of making me seem wise, this perspective somehow confirmed to her my apparent instability.

Despite Mom's concern, on the afternoon of January 27, 1981, I marched out of the yard wearing the only backpack our family owned: my sister's bright yellow pack with the Girl Scout logo emblazoned across the top flap. Though embarrassed by the feminine label, I doubted I would run into any buddies from the neighborhood. Following the old credo "Wet wool is warm," I'd stuffed my ill-fitting pack with itchy wool clothes, along with a summer sleeping bag and a hammock. To toughen myself faster, I'd eschewed a tent.

By firelight that night, I dutifully scribbled in my first journal: "I already suppered on franks, beans and canned potatoes with baked apple for desert." After storing the morning firewood in a waterproof stuff sack, I crawled into my hammock and thin sleeping bag. Within ten minutes, I made my first wilderness survival discovery: Hammocks are miserable in winter. The strings underneath compressed and nullified the sleeping bag's meager insulation. Chilled air from the frozen pond blew all around me. Shivers kept me awake.

An hour later I heard a measured crunching in the woods. My imagination ran wild; then I reeled it back in, confident that nothing scarier than a raccoon lived on the island. But the footsteps grew louder and were coming right at me. Just as I became certain they were large, human, and probably from an escaped murderer, I heard "Jim!" It was Dad.

His showing up at my campsite in the dark was surprising enough. But his appearance that frigid night was truly stunning as Dad hated the cold. A lot.

With his old black Bakelite flashlight in hand, he zeroed in on my return shouts and walked up to my camp. Waving his work thermos, he asked, "You want some hot cocoa?"

"Sure. You came over here just for that?"

"Your mother was worried, so I'm here to check on you."

He arched his eyebrows and scrunched his closed mouth in mock disdain.

"How about some more wood on this fire?" he asked.

I slid out of the sleeping bag, tugged on stiff boots, and stoked the blaze. As the heat and light built, Dad flipped back the fake fur hood of his snorkel jacket. He held his hands over the snapping flames while I sipped hot chocolate.

"Well, thanks for checking on me," I said.

He reached deep into a parka pocket and pulled out a fist-sized object.

"Here, Joanne sent these," he said, handing me a baggie.

Ah! My sister had baked her gooey chocolate chip cookies. As I wolfed one down, he reached into another pocket and pulled out two cans of Budweiser. He popped the top on one, handed it to me, then opened his. We clinked cans. He knew I drank beer in college, but since I was still eight months under the legal limit, I was surprised.

"So, how's it going?"

"Okay, I guess. My boots are frozen and the hammock's cold."

"Ya gonna stay?"

I paused before answering.

"If I'm going to learn this stuff, guess I'd better stick it out. Besides, I said I was going to, so I think I should."

"Uh-huh."

"What do you think, Dad?"

"I think you're right."

With orange light dancing on our faces, we stood near the heat and sipped our beers. We discussed the nighttime temperatures and the thickness of the pond's ice. Then we found the North Star and pointed out the constellation Orion, just as we always did when we stargazed together. He shoved the empty cans into his pocket.

"I'll tell your mother you're doing fine."

"Okay. See you in the morning. And thanks for coming out."

He nodded once in response, then smiled and said loudly, "Have fun, baby!"

After listening to his steps grow distant, I crawled back into the pathetic sleeping bag and hunkered down. I pondered why he hadn't tried to talk me into leaving. I guess he thought that me staying warm was less important than me staying.

I KICKED MY climbing boot into the snow and stepped upslope. Stabbing the rented ice ax into the snow gave me something to lean on, so I bent over, panting, watching my breath form mini clouds of ice fog.

The climbing guide waited patiently ten feet higher. He was the first guide I had ever met, and he seemed just as I'd imagined one would be: fit, rugged, confident.

My college buddy Randy Hopping was twenty feet below me, struggling, like me, to find the elusive smooth rhythm that the guide had coached us to use. While our skills were lacking, for nineteen-year-olds we had at least shown pretty good judgment in recognizing that we needed a guide for our first snow climb. Randy had earned his Eagle Scout rank back in high school, but he was no mountaineer. I knew how to take care of myself outdoors, but steep winter climbing was a big step up for both of us.

Randy's suggestion, in 1982, that we attempt a winter ascent of Mount Washington had both thrilled and scared me. Anyone who read the weather section of the *Boston Globe* got a daily update on Washington's deadly potential. The fortress-like weather station atop the 6,288-foot summit regularly reported winds in excess of one hundred miles per hour, and for three-quarters of a century, Mount Washington had held the world record for wind speed: 231 miles per hour, measured back in 1934.

As we ascended the Lion's Head route, Mount Washington barely flexed its weather muscles. The temperature was fifteen degrees, with breezes fluttering at a paltry twenty-five miles per hour—as good as it gets in March on this infamous New Hampshire peak.

The guide had warned us several times that if the weather deteriorated he would pull the plug. Tired, but overflowing with enthusiasm, I hoped we would make the top. Higher on the slope, the effects of the arctic environment and savage jet stream winds left the short, gnarled trees so beaten down that they sprawled across the ground like knee-high creeping vines—krummholtz, the guide called it.

Another two hundred yards of snow hiking and I found myself above the tree line for the first time. Gazing a mile across the rolling flanks of the mountain's upper shoulder, I saw nothing but boulders, snow, and wind-blasted bare spots. A strong gust came out of the northwest, shoving us back. Instinctively, I leaned forward, dropped my head, and drove my shoulder into the wind.

The gust left as fast as it came. When I lifted my head, my tense cheeks ached. It wasn't from cold wind, though; I was smiling. What a wild, spartan, invigorating world I'd found myself in. Stark wilderness surrounded me, and the opportunity to experience a rare place, the frozen summit of Mount Washington, was tantalizingly close.

Another wall of wind slammed us, and I kept my head up to face it straight on. I thrust my arms straight out to the sides, the metal ice ax clutched in my right hand. When the wind pushed this time, I leaned into it, not pushing back but embracing the gust, cackling with laughter, whooping joyfully.

The mighty weather gods were kind that winter day, and we reached the highest point in New England.

One day I would look back on this moment and realize that it encapsulated all that it means to climb, to push yourself in a way you might not normally imagine is possible. That if your stamina, skill, and luck were sound, you would get to stand on top. That if you weakened, or your resolve faltered, or conditions worsened, the summit would elude you. I came to understand that respecting the landscape around me and knowing the landscape within me were both key. If I was to wisely balance desire, risk, and self-preservation, I would have to expand my external skills and deepen my internal knowledge. I would have to learn who I was, who my companions were, and what we were capable of achieving. The challenge was harsh, the outcome uncertain, and the growth potential unlimited. I realized that with climbing, I'd found something that nourished my soul and could forge me into a better version of myself.

FOUR MONTHS LATER, I was back in New Hampshire, taking the next small step on my journey to becoming a climber. Though still a poor college student, I had saved enough through tower painting to take a rock-climbing course in the White Mountains.

Two of us stood there—untested beginners waiting for our instructor, Kurt Winkler, to decide which of us would belay him as he ascended a granite wall. Probably because I had told him earlier about my tower painting work, he chose me.

Kurt had already set a bottom anchor at the base of the cliff, wrapping nylon webbing around a stout tree. So with a locking snap-link carabiner, I clipped my harness into the anchor to secure myself. With our guide tied to one end of the rope and me to the other, we were connected, but I still had to put him on belay. I grabbed the rope close to Kurt's end, wrapped it around my waist for friction, then positioned my stronger right arm and hand as the brake. Then I held the rope in my brake hand to anchor him fast. As he climbed, I would feed out slack slowly, ready to tighten my grip and catch him if he slipped.

"I'm not going to fall on this—I've done it a hundred times—but if I do, I'll yell, 'Falling.' Then what do you do, Jim?"

"I squeeze the brake hand hard and wrap the rope even tighter around my waist," I said, pantomiming the actions. "And I never let go."

He smiled and gave me a thumbs-up. Then he got serious and started the commands we had practiced.

"On belay?"

"Belay is on," I answered.

"Climbing?"

"Climb on."

With that, Kurt left the ground and began ascending the steep granite slab. His movements were smooth and graceful—not the rushed, jerky twitches of us students. He seemed to naturally grasp the best handholds on the first try, though he would sometimes re-fine his grip. When Kurt moved his feet up, he looked down and placed them deliberately on small rock nubbins.

Kurt glided up about fifteen feet, then found a comfortable stance. I wanted to do well when it was my turn to follow, so I tried memorizing the rest spot and his movement patterns. He selected a metal wedge from the sling of climbing gear he wore over his shoul-der like a bandolier. Then he slid the piece of protection into a crack, moved it down into a narrower section of the crevice, gave it a sharp tug to set it, and snapped a carabiner through the thin perlon cord dangling from the piece. He added another nylon sling to extend the leash coming off the piece, and finally clipped the sling's end to his rope with a second carabiner. Knowing he was safer now, I exhaled.

With that gear clipped, if Kurt slipped, I would be able to tighten my grip on the belay rope and catch his fall—assuming, of course, that the protection piece did not pull out or I did not stupidly let go of the rope. I was so determined to uphold my end of the safety bargain that the knuckles of my death-gripped belay hand turned white.

As Kurt led out the 150-foot rope length (also known as a "pitch") he placed more protection pieces (or "pro") in the crack. Watching the mechanics of how the rope ran, with a little foresight, I could see how the danger increased the farther he climbed above his last piece. Because he was leading, if Kurt were positioned ten feet above his last piece of pro and slipped, he would fall twice that distance before the rope began to catch him. Even then, the rope would stretch out another foot or two before he stopped.

While placing protection frequently might seem to decrease the chances of getting hurt, there is a counterpoint. Stopping to hang from one hand while setting gear with the other is strenuous. A balance has to be struck between placing gear often enough to be safe but not so frequently that the leader wears himself out. Watching our guide switch between moving and protecting himself, I tried imagining the calculations, estimations, and gut feelings he had to blend to determine when to go and when to pro. I had a lot to learn.

We were on Cathedral Ledge, a classic granite cliff just a few miles from downtown North Conway. Other climbers and tourists milled about on this sunny summer day, but I ignored them; giving the belay my undivided attention was paramount. My brake hand grew tired, but I heard Dad in my head: "There's no letting go."

Kurt finished the easy pitch quickly. He stopped on a ledge and set a solid anchor so he could belay me up, and then the other student. Once secured to his anchor, he shouted down, "Off belay,

Jim." I replied, "Belay off, Kurt," then dropped the rope and held both hands palms-up toward him to be clear. He waved and yelled back, "Thank you."

Since I had belayed him, I got to go first. I unclipped from the anchor tree and waited to exchange commands with Kurt. Once I heard "Climb on," I was ready to ascend. Before I even touched the rock, I relaxed by inhaling and exhaling three slow breaths. To psych myself up, I muttered aloud, "I can do this."

I stepped one stride across the forest floor and laid my palm atop an obvious round knob high and right. My left hand skimmed the face, finding a second hold. Remembering Kurt's example, I looked down at my feet. I raised one foot onto a small, flat lip, then the other, and I was ascending the white-and-black granite.

Haltingly, I moved up the rock face from one good set of holds to another. At each spot where Kurt had placed a piece of climbing protection, I worked to fiddle the metal hexes and wedges out of the cracks. I was following the pitch well, and was feeling pretty good about it.

Then, just below Kurt's belay ledge, I stalled at a section with no obvious holds. After two minutes of visual scanning, and running my hands across the warm slab, as if reading Braille, I realized that the first edges I had touched were probably the best.

Clutching the two marginal seams, I smeared the bottoms of my tennis shoes on steep, crystalline rock. I was on the holds but couldn't move up on them, so I stayed plastered in place, wasting energy and puffing like a steam locomotive. Kurt, aware of my predicament, leaned off his belay stance above me and in a firm voice advised, "Trust your feet. Stand on them."

I pushed down off my feet, willing them to stay put. As I straightened my knees, I rose higher, but my balance grew precarious. I was committed to the upward movement, so I kept going, but I sensed that something good had better happen soon or I might fall.

As I reached full height, a deep-cut pocket the size of a soap dish appeared above my left shoulder.

Grabbing that surprise "Thank God" hold made it easy to keep my weight directly over my feet—there was no way I would fall. The rock had provided what I needed. I blurted out, "Yeah!"

I scrambled the short distance to Kurt and pulled onto a flat belay ledge. Kurt clipped me into the anchor pieces set in the crack and then took me off belay while I soaked in the view. Partway down the pitch I saw the tops of green leafy trees. The kernmantle rope I had trailed stretched farther down to the other student, waiting nervously at the cliff bottom. Above us rose several more pitches of salt-and-pepper speckled rock—the way to the top.

Standing on a ledge halfway up a cliff face, I felt almost as if I were hovering on a flying carpet. The magic that had powered us up here came from the skill, the will, and the effort we'd put in. Although my journey up the lower face had lasted but twenty minutes, along the way I had experienced doubt and confidence, fear and elation. Climbing's intensity seemed to compress the full range of human experience into brief stretches of time.

The demands and rewards of ascending were so forceful that I was fully engaged. The focused attention it required of body, mind, and spirit was clarifying—and, afterward, calming. My love for climbing was moving beyond just an appreciation for the pretty places it took me. Life seemed more intense and gratifying when I was engaged in the challenges of climbing higher. Persevering through doubt and overcoming scary problems nurtured my sense of determination.

IN SEPTEMBER 1982, I went west. I stepped onto the train in downtown Boston wearing my backpack and stepped off a world away at Glacier National Park, Montana. Officially, I was on my way to

Montana State University to spend my junior year there, on the National Student Exchange program. In essence, though, I was off to seek adventure in the Rocky Mountains.

After two weeks of hiking in Glacier and Yellowstone National Parks, I arrived in Bozeman, ready to start at MSU. Having already changed my major from engineering to geology, I signed up for environmental geology classes. I chose a light academic load so that I could also fit in courses with an outdoor bent, like snow avalanche dynamics, wilderness first aid, and cross-country skiing. The climbing classes and the eighty-mile backpacking trip I had taken back in New England had served their purposes, preparing me for bigger adventures in the Rockies. I took an advanced rock-climbing class that went to several different cliffs near Bozeman. It was there that I learned the fundamental aspects of aid climbing, in which you rely heavily on the gear to ascend very difficult terrain. After the snow fell, I took an ice-climbing class, scaling frozen waterfalls with spiky metal crampons on my boots and ice axes in my hands. I was spending all my spare time and money climbing. Along the way I met three experienced mountaineers, Joe Berlin, Tom Engleson, and Jim Seines, and the four of us climbed as a team through the winter. The adventures provided me with exercise, recreation, and a revitalizing energy—the exhilaration I felt confirmed that I had been right to move west and become a climber.

And something happened that I had not planned on. I fell in love.

At the welcome meeting for newly arrived exchange students, we went around a circle rattling off our names and home states. I realized that I was in a room of like-minded people—all of us had chosen to temporarily move to a very different state where we knew almost no one, with the intention of expanding ourselves. During the introductions, I was captivated by a brown-haired girl named Gloria Neesham.

During several more icebreaker events for exchange students, I kept gravitating to Gloria, who was from Bowling Green State University, in Ohio. On a white-water rafting trip, we chatted. Under the guise of getting exposed to Montana culture, I talked her into taking western swing dancing classes with me. That first date led to another, then another. Soon, we were in love.

By the spring of 1983, we had been together for half a year, but with the second quarter completed at MSU, we needed to return to our homes in Ohio and Massachusetts. We made plans for me to visit her in two months. Seeing her off at the airport, I handed Gloria a single rose, and she walked onto the plane.

I WASN'T EAGER to end my partnership with my three ice-climbing buddies, either. So we planned our own reunion. Before leaving Montana, we committed to an ascent of Mount Rainier, in Washington, in June 1983, just three months away.

My seven months in Montana had formed new and permanent foundations for my life. I had fallen in love with Gloria, found my vocation in environmental geology, and embraced my avocation of climbing. But for the time being, I needed to return home to save money by living at my parents' house and painting for Dad. We sandblasted and painted four-story buildings at Hanscom Air Force Base, just ten miles from home. Moving hundred-pound sandbags kept me in shape, and hanging the swing staging off the buildings honed my rope and rigging skills. Every time we moved the staging, Dad drilled into me the same rules I'd heard from him a thousand times: Double-check the system. Make sure you always have a backup.

Some weekends I went to UMass to visit college friends, but mostly I climbed. Since I had not been a mountaineer before my Montana trip, I did not know any climbers in Massachusetts. Thus I followed the time-honored tradition of buying some gear and dragging along innocent friends. A buddy of mine from sixth grade, Mark Piantedosi, was athletic and strong from years of working for his father's landscaping company. Even though our jobs were physically demanding, Mark and I would climb one night a week right after work—skipping dinner and staying on the rock until dark.

I had followed veteran climbers up routes in New Hampshire and Montana, but by default, I was now the more "experienced" team member. That meant I had to learn to lead. Leading demands more strength, judgment, and bravery than following. With about a year of climbing under my belt, and no one to teach me, I learned to lead the old-fashioned, risky way: I read up on it, then taught myself.

I devoured climbing books and magazines. The reading helped, but I learned protection placement mostly through trial and error. I finally got the courage to lead my first route—a short, simple climb at Crow Hill, in central Massachusetts. I sweated and groveled my way up the crack, but I made it through without any blunders.

The scheduled snow-and-ice climb of Mount Rainier was just two months off, so I began serious physical conditioning for the first time in my life, running laps up and down the creaky stairs of my parents' hundred-year-old farmhouse. I sprinted up, creating a racket, and the pounding descents were even noisier. As I got stronger, I carried my backpack with weights in it and wore my plastic ice-climbing boots. This magnified the racket twofold, and Mom struggled to tolerate the clomping, asking if all this was really necessary. Shouting downstairs over my noisy steps, I assured her that this was how the famous climbers trained.

With a month to go before Rainier, I spent a precious $200 on airfare to visit Gloria in Ohio. Over lunch she questioned me about the upcoming climb of Mount Rainier. She knew that at 14,410 feet tall, Rainier was about 4,000 feet higher than I had ever been before, and that the crevassed glaciers were also new to me. I assured her that I was fit, that my three Montana climbing partners had experience, and that one of them had been on Rainier before, so I was in good hands.

On our last day together before I flew home to Boston, Gloria surprised me. She pulled out a medallion on a tarnished silver chain and said, "This medal was blessed by the pope. I used to hang it from the rearview mirror of my Volkswagen Bug for protection. I want you to wear it on Rainier."

"I can't take this, Gloria," I said. "It's too special. What if I lose it?"

"I want you to take it. It'll protect you."

She put the chain over my neck, kissed the medal for luck, then kissed me.

"During the climb, don't take this off. Wear it the whole time, until you're off the mountain safe and you call me."

Feeling the dime-sized circular medal bumping against my skin, I pressed it against my chest.

"Thank you, Glo. I'll be careful with it. And I will be careful on Rainier."

"Promise?" she asked.

"Promise," I said firmly. She stared at me for two seconds, and then we embraced.

On the plane the next day, I absentmindedly fiddled with the medal hanging beneath my shirt. Worried about losing it, I decided that once I got home I'd take it off, and save wearing it just for the mountain. Rainier was going to be a big climb, and I could use all the good luck and watching over I could get.

"I DON'T THINK this is the right way," Tom shouted over the wind.

"I don't know, either," I yelled. "We can't stay here, though."

Thick clouds enveloped Tom, Jim, and me, dispersing the light from our headlamps. The rope coil at my feet grew smaller as our teammate in the lead, Joe, scrambled farther down into a gully of crumbly volcanic rock. When the slack disappeared, I followed him down the debris chute. Each step I took moved shovelfuls of loose rock around. With him straight below me, I knew that any stones I kicked off would get funneled right at Joe, so I treaded as gently as possible.

After I slithered down about twenty feet, I spied his headlamp beam below me. I shouted down.

"Joe! Are we on route?"

"Can't tell. But I don't think so."

"We don't think so either. You better come back."

There was a pause while Joe accepted that his efforts had been a waste and that he had to struggle back up the manky gully. Then he yelled, "Coming up."

We were at about 9,500 feet, somewhere above the Inter Glacier on Mount Rainier's northeast slope. It couldn't be far to the safety of Camp Schurman, but we didn't know which way to go. Although this would have been straightforward in daylight, our late start and the extra few miles of approach hiking along a closed road had left us short of camp three hours after sunset.

Near the top of the rock chute, we huddled to make a quick decision. We'd been on the move for nearly eight hours and were tired. We were not really lost, but in the darkness and gathering clouds, we might stumble around for hours before we found the rangers' hut at Camp Schurman. This could readily turn into a mess, or even a major debacle if someone got injured. Dad's words echoed in my mind: "Better quit before someone gets hurt."

We made the call to stop for the night, retreating to a flat spot we had seen earlier. After struggling to pitch the tent in rising winds, we crammed ourselves inside to eat candy bars and drink hot chocolate.

Disappointment showed on everyone's faces. The day had been filled with compromises already, and now we found ourselves unable to reach Camp Schurman.

Our original plan had been to try the steep and technical Liberty Ridge, a classic arête that cleaves Rainier's avalanche-swept north face. But after arriving at the park earlier that morning, we had learned that the weather was predicted to sour in a day or two. Even with good weather the Liberty Ridge was a severe challenge. Although only moderately experienced—me least of all—we were smart enough to know that heading onto serious terrain like the Liberty was a bad idea when the weather was expected to deteriorate. So we had switched to the more modest goal of trying the Emmons Glacier, a crevassed but technically easier way to Rainier's summit. Scaling back to the Emmons-Winthrop route had been the right move, but even that left our chances of summiting in doubt. If the weather cleared in the morning, we would be in a reasonable position to make a strenuous one-day push to the top. If it didn't, we might not even see the summit, let alone reach it.

That night I fell asleep at around twelve-thirty, hoping for some decent rest. Just an hour later, I awakened to a flapping tent wall beating my face. The boys fumbled with lights, and someone was trying to get dressed. In a tired stupor, I asked, "What's up?"

Tom, our most experienced climber, said, "Big winds from the south. A pole has snapped. We have to lash it down before it shreds the tent."

The wind screamed around our domed shelter—if the tent came apart while we were half-dressed and surrounded by unsecured gear, we would instantly be in epic disarray. We stowed loose items and hurried to pull on our climbing clothes.

Dawn was several hours away, so we hunkered in the tent, fully geared, and waited. With each big gust, I'd grab the nearest pole and hang on to support it. During lulls, we sat in the dark, waiting for time to pass. I kept pressing my fingertips against my jacket to check for Gloria's blessed medal. Feeling the round shape sink into my flesh calmed me. Around four A.M., we emerged from the tent and broke camp. As I wrote to Gloria in a letter after the trip:

"It was weird to be out and moving so early in the morning. The clouds were going crazy in the wind, doing things I've never seen them do before. The red sun gave the whole mountain a strange glow."

We shuffled down the Inter Glacier, across scree slopes, and back to the snow-covered trail. Far above us, the winds continued roaring at about ninety miles per hour. Battered, blistered, and exhausted from hiking twenty miles round-trip, we were back at the car less than twenty-four hours after we'd left the White River entrance. Mount Rainier had merely swiped at us and we had turned tail and retreated. I was chagrined at such sudden defeat, but knew we had made the right call.

We licked our wounds in Seattle for two days, then rallied for a consolation mountain. We chose the more modest Mount Baker, a 10,778-foot glaciated peak in the North Cascades. Though Jim's aching knee prevented him from joining us on summit day, Joe, Tom, and I roped up and climbed the glacier to the summit, under great weather. As I wrote to Gloria:

"YEAH—My first big mountain! We made the top at 10:25 A.M. on June 16th, 1983. The view was incredible."

I flew to Ohio on the Fourth of July to see Gloria. We spent the holiday hanging out with her friends and watching the fireworks over Tanglewood Lake. The next day, I tried giving her back the borrowed medal.

"This kept me safe, even when things got rough," I said. "Thank you so much."

I held out the medal, etched with the profile of Pope Paul VI, but she didn't reach for it.

"Are you going to climb more big mountains?" she asked.

"Probably. Well, yeah, definitely."

She gave me a slightly aggrieved look, but then the tension dropped from her face.

"Then you should keep it. It will always protect you and always remind you of me."

CHAPTER 7

▲ ▲ ▲

IN A HALLWAY at the Lory Student Center, I stood motionless, staring at a bright flyer tacked to a bulletin board, oblivious to the harried students racing to class around me. The photocopied announcement read:

EXPERIENTIAL LEARNING PROGRAM

1986 ACONCAGUA EXPEDITION (22,834 FT.)

Aconcagua, in Argentina, is the highest peak in the Southern Hemisphere. And the Colorado State University outdoor program needed climbers to join the team. This could be my first expedition.

I'd just arrived in Fort Collins to pursue a master's degree in environmental geology. Things had fallen into place quickly for me at CSU, a sprawling campus with a commanding view of the Colorado Rockies. I'd been selected for a research assistant position under a National Science Foundation grant, which meant not only a $683 monthly salary but a tuition waiver. This changed my fortunes from nearly broke graduate student who wasn't sure his paltry savings would last through a second semester to eager climber with a spare $2,000 who could contemplate a thirty-two-day expedition to South America.

I felt ready to grab this challenge. The last five years had been a time of intense mountaineering for me, from several seasons of winter mountaineering in New England to alpine rock and ice climbs in Wyoming and Colorado.

Briefly, I wondered if this expedition was a reasonable expenditure, given that I still had two long years of grad school in front of me. But those thoughts faded as logic, instinct, and desire all led to the inescapable conclusion that going on this climb aligned with how I wanted to live. The chance to experience high altitude, join a committed team, and travel to the remote Andes was too much to pass up.

The expedition's coleaders, Daryl Miller and Pat Rastall, interviewed me, and two days later I was on the team. After a busy fall spent studying and getting into shape, Christmas Day found us sweltering on the roof of the Hotel Crillón in Mendoza, Argentina, as we sampled possible foods for our expedition. Canned squid packed in its own ink made a melancholy substitute for the holiday feast I imagined my extended family enjoying back home in Massachusetts.

After several days of preparation and bus rides, we started the two-day hike toward base camp. I had been above 14,000 feet only twice before, and altitude sickness racked me as the six of us worked our way up the mountain. On my first trip to Camp 1, a subtle headache flared into pounding skull pressure by the time we'd dumped our equipment at the 17,750-foot campsite. Day by day, headache by headache, we plodded our way up and around the west and north sides of Aconcagua, with me usually slogging behind my better-acclimated teammates. Though we had intended to scale the more difficult Polish Glacier, a reconnaissance climb to 20,500 feet led us to abandon that plan for the nontechnical Ruta Normal, or normal route.

The route change and storm delays lengthened our sufferfest. Biting cold and fifty-mile-an-hour winds ended our first summit attempt at 21,300 feet.

"The mountain is winning," I wrote in my journal.

A slog back down to our food depot for more supplies let us extend our oxygen-deprived stay to a tenth night in a row above 17,700 feet. When weak sunlight hit us on the eighteenth morning on the mountain, we rallied for a final summit attempt.

Though wearisome, our multiple laps up and down Aconcagua's slopes had left us fit and acclimated. We moved well to 21,800 feet, passing several slower groups as clouds chugged toward the mountain from the direction of Chile. The last thousand feet to the roof of South America ascends La Caneleta, a steep gully of loose rock. Starting this section, I needed a five-breath rest every twenty-five steps. An hour later, I slowed to one-fifth that rate, gasping a one-breath rest after every halting step. I buried my sickness and exhaustion by focusing instead on drawing strength from spiritual connections with friends and family. Two hundred feet from the top, I sought positive energy by mentally naming a loved one with each desperate breath I sucked from the thin air.

"I felt like they were all practically screaming in my ears and pleading with me to continue," I wrote in my journal.

With one hundred feet to go, I saw my partners on the summit. Pat let out an encouraging whoop. I breathlessly yelled back, "Damnit...I'm...gonna...make it!" and we both cheered. The last painful steps somehow seemed fun.

Hugs from my elated teammates greeted me on top. Our last team member joined us ten minutes later, and after a summit photo by the sticker-covered metal cross, we descended with light snow swirling about. I had broken my personal altitude record by over 8,000 feet.

But the trip was notable for another reason, for it was through one of my teammates that I met a wiry young outdoorsman with a mop of unkempt sandy hair and a quiet demeanor.

His name was Mike Price.

Mike had wanted to join the Aconcagua trip, but he simply couldn't afford it. Still, when we'd departed for Argentina, he had gamely volunteered to drive us to the Denver airport. Amid a pile of gear-filled duffel bags, Mike and I had shaken hands good-bye. Grinning, he had wished us well, then driven off, madly beeping the van's horn as he went.

THAT I'D EVENTUALLY ended up at CSU was not a surprise, for it was the natural extension of the life I had built over the previous three years. When I'd returned to the University of Massachusetts Amherst in the fall of 1983, I had turned all my energies to geology and climbing. At twenty-one, I had already identified the focus points of my life.

I climbed with college friends whenever I could, learning the skills I would need for bigger, more challenging peaks. I found out I could endure subzero temperatures during a twenty-two-hour summit traverse across Maine's remote Mount Katahdin. I learned the value of diligent map work after a navigational mix-up forced us to march eighteen miles toward Oregon's Middle Sister with little drinking water. That mistake left us so dehydrated that we drank skanky pond water laced with swimming insects. Still, we summited the snowy volcanic peak the next day.

I explored the White Mountains of New Hampshire, taking in the adage that if you can deal with the harsh conditions of Mount Washington in winter, you can handle the weather on any peak in the world. Though my young ego hoped it was true, I had my doubts. I sensed that greater peaks must hold greater challenges, and so they must be the best places to learn more about the mountains and myself. And I wanted to find out. I longed for higher, harder peaks and began scheming ways to include such mountains in my life.

At an Appalachian Mountain Club course on winter outdoor leadership, I met a quiet and capable climber my age named Patrick Heaney. Together we went on an ice-climbing binge across New Hampshire. We started climbing short, frozen slabs that allowed us to discover each other's skills, strengths, and weaknesses in low-risk situations. Later we moved onto multipitch ice routes, where we took turns swapping leads. Soon we were chasing classic alpine climbs across the White Mountains, and I gradually became a competent lead climber on both rock and ice.

But I longed to return to a place where the mountains started at 10,000 feet and went up. After I graduated, in the spring of 1985, Patrick and I went climbing in Colorado. We hitchhiked and climbed our way through the Indian Peaks Wilderness and Rocky Mountain National Park, huddling under a green nylon tarp propped up by our ice axes at night, awakening at sunrise to the perfume of spring wildflowers and the gurgling of melting snowbanks. We scaled a half dozen high summits, including Longs Peak (14,255 feet), by the icy Notch Couloir. As we hobbled down the trail on our last day, Patrick said, "I hate to leave."

"Yeah," I answered, "it would be great to live here and climb these peaks all the time."

That Rockies trip strengthened my resolve to make a life in the mountains. The physical exertions and mental fortitude that the mountains demanded forced me to face fear, manage doubt, and take action, even in the face of uncertainty. In short, the self-imposed challenge of climbing made me more resilient. People find self-reflection and self-improvement in a variety of ways—through running or music, therapy or bonsai. For me, the moving meditation of mountain climbing yielded these benefits, along with the bonuses of visiting remote places and experiencing wild beauty.

AFTER A YEAR in Massachusetts working as an environmental geologist, climbing, and spending time with Gloria, I was accepted into graduate school at Colorado State University in Fort Collins.

Gloria and I excitedly made plans to move to the Rockies together, and in August 1986 we settled into a simple apartment about a mile from campus. Within weeks, I'd secured the grant-funded job, the tuition waiver, and a spot on the Aconcagua team. And I had a new friend, Mike Price.

One Friday afternoon, my Aconcagua teammate Scott Anderson, Mike, and I met up at a geology department beer party. Scott and I discovered that we hailed from adjacent towns in Massachusetts—he from Lexington, me from Concord. When Mike heard that, he asked me what I thought of the classic Concord-based book *Walden* by Henry David Thoreau. Though I had only superficial comments about the book, Mike got a kick out of the fact that as a kid I had taken swimming lessons at Walden Pond. A second-year grad student in English, Mike loved literature about wilderness, nature, and philosophy.

Mike stood two inches taller than me, at five foot nine, but was about thirty pounds lighter. Though he was not the most outspoken guy, his unassuming exterior hid an energetic fireball of a young man. I was impressed that Mike worked as an outdoor instructor and had been on a wild expedition deep into the glaciated wilderness of Canada.

While graduate school kept us both too busy to climb much, Mike and I socialized together and became good friends over the next eighteen months. We knew that we wanted to climb together, so as soon as I wrapped up my master's degree, Mike and I hit the crags. The spring air chilled our skin, but the rock was warm enough to climb. We set out on a moderate route in Eldorado Canyon, a popular climbing area near Boulder. The route included the Bastille Crack, a five-pitch ascent up a steep buttress of red conglomerate sandstone that sits right along a dirt road.

Mike was the better climber, so he led the first pitch, with its short, tricky section that required shifting from one crack over to the next. I followed him, and then I took the next pitch. We switched leads until we reached the top, about 300 feet above the canyon floor. This fine day of climbing confirmed that we moved well together. Our climbing partnership had begun.

TWO MONTHS LATER, Mike was busy, so I went to California to climb in Yosemite National Park with my old Appalachian Mountain Club buddy Patrick. Early one morning we watched the rising sun paint Yosemite Valley's soaring rock walls deep orange, then gentle gold. By the time they settled into a granite-white hue, we were huffing up the approach trail to Middle Cathedral Rock for our climb up the East Buttress. The fifth pitch of this 1,000-foot wall is the "crux" section—the hardest part of the route. This route's crux can be free climbed with difficulty, or it can be aid climbed using an existing series of eight drilled-in bolts. Aid climbing involves hanging from gear to assist with the ascent; free climbing means advancing by one's hands and feet with gear present only as protection in case of a fall. Almost all the climbing we had done over the years had been free climbing. The only aid climbing I'd ever done was fifty feet of practice six years earlier in Montana.

Aid climbing requires complex gear, rope, and knot systems that collectively allow a climber to move up. Many pieces of specialty equipment are needed for proper aid climbing, including aiders, which are flexible webbing steps, and ascenders, sliding, mechanical rope clamps that allow a climber to raise himself up a dangling rope.

We didn't have any special aid gear, so Patrick aid climbed the short bolt ladder in a quick and dirty style by clipping gear into the next highest bolt and then pulling down on the dangling sling.

I followed in a jury-rigged fashion, yanking on gear Patrick had left clipped to the bolts for me and standing in nylon webbing loops that served as barely functional substitutes for real aiders. This allowed me to swarm my way up the nearly blank section while Patrick belayed me from above. With a mess of gear dangling from my neck, I soon flopped onto his belay ledge like a netted tuna hauled onto a boat deck.

"Graceless, but effective," Patrick said.

I smiled, nodded, and panted.

Since aid climbing relied so heavily on gear, I had thought it wouldn't be hard. In fact, hoisting myself up the 30-foot section with no ascenders or aiders wore me out in just minutes. I now understood how tiring aid climbing could really be.

ENVIRONMENTAL GEOLOGY JOBS were plentiful in 1988, and though I already had a good offer in Fort Collins, I applied for a position as a corporate hydrogeologist with Shell Oil. The work would entail studying and remediating fuel leaks from underground storage tanks. It was a high-profile position overseeing subsurface cleanup projects across eighteen states. I was thrilled when Shell offered me this dream position.

There was only one problem: The job was in Houston, Texas.

I did not want to live in flat, humid Texas, and I didn't want to move away from Gloria, but in the end the Shell opportunity was too great to reject. I accepted the position with an unsettling mixture of professional glee and personal dread.

Our loose plan was for me to go there at the summer's end and start work. I would fly often to see Gloria in Colorado, where she was a sales manager, and in few months we would decide if she should join me in Texas.

Before I left for Houston, Gloria and I embarked on a big tour of western national parks. In the Northwest, we stayed for several days at Mount Rainier. The snow-covered volcano loomed above our campsite.

One morning, we hiked a trail on the mountain's southern flank to the Paradise Glacier ice cave. The ice tunnel burrowed under the glacier, and the oval entrance was thirty feet wide and twenty feet tall, squashed by the massive weight of ice overlying the cave's mouth. Having studied glacial geology, I knew this was a melt channel formed by a subglacial river. Although I tried convincing Gloria to join me, on the premise that no ice collapse was likely to happen during the few minutes that we would be in the cave, she refused to enter. Nervous but excited to actually experience such a rare geologic cavern, I scampered thirty feet inside the tunnel.

My eyes took a minute to adjust to the dark, but soon I could see the smooth, scalloped ice walls, dripping with meltwater. I stuck my hand out and caught a few frigid drops. Squatting, I poked a finger at the contact line where the underside of the glacier met the bedrock beneath. This basal interface is precisely where glaciers grind solid rock into a fine grit called glacial flour. Imagining the weight of all that ice above me and the titanic power required to pulverize bedrock, I suddenly felt small before such unstoppable forces of nature.

Crack! A stone clattered onto the floor, somewhere deeper in the cave. My head snapped up and I stared into the darkness, surrounded by the steady gurgle of water flowing among the broken cobbles littering the ice cave's floor. All this water had once been snow farther up the mountain. Growing unease urged me from the cavern.

I tilted my head back and stared up at the dark ceiling. The ice surface undulated in water-smoothed waves, and a few glacier-entrained rocks remained frozen in the cave's ceiling. Four feet to my right, a pumpkin-sized boulder hung down.

I should have a helmet on in here.

"Jim, come out of there," Gloria called from outside the cave. When I turned toward her voice, light pouring through the rough-hewn entrance nearly blinded me, yet I could make out her silhouette. Direct sunlight angling in illuminated a patch of the rock floor, marking the way out. I blinked while my eyes adjusted, then emerged from the gloomy ice room, back to Gloria.

"How was it?" she asked.

"Very cool, but scary. It's dark and damp. It's pretty creepy being underneath a glacier."

A FEW WEEKS later I was in Houston, miserable. The environmental job at Shell was great—everything I'd hoped for. But my personal life was nonexistent. When I tried to hike in a state park, the sun and the bugs drove me back. When I ran, I grew so nauseated from the heat that I sagged against a chain-link fence like a puking drunk. Gloria, my friends, and the mountains were all back in Colorado. I would have to make do with frequent Rocky Mountain visits attached to my many business trips. I settled into a pattern of flying to Denver every other Friday, and returning to Houston after forty-eight hours.

A month later, Gloria and I officially got engaged.

We agreed to a long-distance engagement so that I could finish out at least a year with Shell. We trudged through the next thirteen months, me flying to Denver about twenty times, and both of us traveling to Ohio twice to plan our wedding. I didn't see Mike or my other Fort Collins friends much.

Finally, in October 1989, I drove my overloaded pickup out of the

Houston sprawl, heading northwest, back to Gloria and the mountains. We got married two weeks later in front of eighty friends and family members near Gloria's Ohio hometown, and then settled into a new apartment in Fort Collins.

NOW THAT I was back in Colorado working as an environmental consultant, I could climb once again with Mike. He would be away for weeks or months with Outward Bound; then I'd come home to hear some variation of the same message on my answering machine.

"Hello, Jim and Glo, this is Mike Price. I'm in town and over at my brother's. Just wanted to say howdy and see if you wanted to drink a beer."

Hunched over frosted mugs a few hours later, we'd get caught up, then make plans for a climb.

Over time, we journeyed together on rock, snow, and ice. Mike and I developed faith in each other's abilities to climb well, to move safely, and, just as important, to extricate ourselves from trouble when it appeared. Each of us understood our own capabilities—and those of the other—and we gently spurred each other to strive harder. By urging me beyond my comfort range, and supporting me when I was out there, Mike helped me slowly push back the boundaries I used to define myself. This made me grow more capable, both on the rock and off.

With his higher skill level, I am not sure that I helped him improve much as a climber. But I was capable enough that he did not have to instruct me or watch me for mistakes. Spending eight months a year herding and fretting over his novice students wore on Mike. He once told me that he enjoyed climbing with me because he did not have to worry.

"Even when I can't see you or hear you," he told me, "I know you'll do the right thing and make it through."

His extensive wilderness time also meant Mike was always in better climbing shape than I was. My career as a hydrogeologist kept me office-bound, and that left me with slightly lesser skills and conditioning than Mike. That didn't seem to bother him, though, so I tried not to let it bother me. Because I could not be as good a climber as Mike, I worked hard to be a good partner. I carried my share of the weight, arrived prepared, and moved fast when my turn came. When things got scary or uncertain, I lightened the mood with silly comments or wisecracks.

One day, a rattlesnake surprised Mike on a trail west of Fort Collins, and he instinctively leapt off the path and bounded through scrub oaks to safety.

"What do you call that move—the Oklahoma Two-Step?" I asked playfully.

Later, though, he got even. When I jammed my fist into a three-inch-wide crack while I was leading on another climb, I sensed movement in the fissure, then peered in to see two onyx eyes and folded black wings near my hand—a bat. I let loose a startled yelp and scurried across the rock to get away. Mike laughed so hard he had to sit on a boulder to compose himself.

On the drives and trail approaches we talked and joked. We always aimed for a full day of climbing, but delays and rainouts didn't really matter because we had a good time regardless.

We climbed extensively on Lumpy Ridge's granite spires in Rocky Mountain National Park. We scaled frozen waterfalls. And we skied in the pristine backcountry, whooping and hollering as we dropped down through lustrous powder fields in the shadow of the Continental Divide.

ONE WARM JULY morning we headed to Lumpy Ridge for the third day that week, set on rock climbing in an area called the Bookend.

As Mike steered his midnight-blue pickup the last mile up the dirt approach road, I read aloud from the guidebook and pointed out landmarks to help us find the right cliff.

We pulled into the gravel parking lot, Mike glancing up at the crags while I intently studied the guidebook. Suddenly, the book slapped my forehead, the floorboard bucking and grinding beneath my feet as we slammed to a stop. Looking up at the cliff instead of out the windshield, Mike had driven right onto a basketball-sized boulder at the parking lot's edge. Startled, I looked up, wide-eyed. Mike seized the moment.

"Well," he drawled nonchalantly, "that oughta be close enough."

We moved well together that day, swinging leads, gracefully flowing up the rock. A day later, determined to keep our momentum, we hit Eldorado Canyon, outside Boulder.

The drive south to Boulder always provides a great view west over the mountains, and we noted a few puffy clouds looming on the horizon—the usual. After parking in Eldo, we hiked the short approach to Anthill Direct, a fine climb with steep rock and exhilarating exposure. The route goes up the biggest face in the canyon and requires a fairly complex descent.

Mike led the first two strenuous pitches. As I followed the second pitch, a hard wind picked up from the west, and the temperature plunged about fifteen degrees in minutes. Trying to hustle, Mike handed me the gear rack and I started leading the third pitch. As I traversed left, the wind screamed down the canyon and my confidence sputtered. While traversing, a good leader places rock gear in a crack to protect both climbers from a dangerous, swinging fall. While I struggled to set protection, the wind roared so loud that when I looked at Mike, just twenty feet to my right, I saw his mouth moving but heard no words over the din.

We were halfway up, with the hardest climbing behind us. The wandering nature of the rock face we'd already climbed made rappelling off from there an uncertain prospect. We might wind up in the middle of the face, away from the crack system, stuck with no rappel anchor options.

Mike and I each looked up and down the cliff, quickly considering whether to push on or bail off. I pointed down to indicate the rappel option, and waggled an open hand to indicate the iffiness of bailing from there. With pulled-down eyebrows, Mike shook his head, telling me he concurred that rappelling was a bad choice. I pointed my right forefinger up and lifted my eyebrows. With a firm nod, Mike agreed: The way down was up.

The situation was deteriorating, so I wanted more rock protection before starting the next steep section; we couldn't afford any mistakes.

I looked down at my right hip to select another piece. Just then the wind shifted, and a huge gust blew straight up the cliff. The webbing slings around my neck floated as if lifted by invisible puppet strings, and the updraft flipped the full chalk bag on my right hip upside down. As gravity dumped out my climber's chalk, the wind racing up the cliff threw that white cloud into my face.

Powder clogged my mouth, nose, and eyes. Clutching the handholds tighter, I spit and snorted and wiped my face on the shoulder of my T-shirt. I blinked but couldn't see much, and my confidence vanished. Groping blindly below me, I down-climbed, leaving the gear in place. Mike fed me slack through the protection I had placed, and I worked my way back to him.

I leaned in close and said, "If I keep leading, I might fall. You'd better take it."

Mike looked annoyed. He understood that I'd been shaken, but he didn't like it that I'd turned back. The rope work necessary to swap the lead around wasted more precious time.

In the minutes it took us to get reorganized, the sky darkened. With rock walls blocking our view westward, we had not been able to see the storm approaching—a fairly common situation on Front Range climbs. Now it was right on us. With my top piece protecting him, Mike flew across to my high point, then continued leading where I'd left off. I fed rope out, wiped chalk from my face, and watched the storm build overhead.

In awe, I saw the sky get so dark that the streetlights in the lower canyon blinked on. Big, heavy raindrops splattered onto my arms—not good. We were about to get clobbered. About half the rope had paid out, and Mike's pace slowed as rain slickened the rock. The rope twitched out more slowly, then stopped.

Come on Mike. Find a belay.

Squinting up into the driving rain, trying vainly to spot Mike, I saw rivulets of water rushing down the rock face.

Crap—how am I going to climb?

The rope pulled, then began racing out. I hustled to maintain a belay until I was sure Mike was no longer climbing but just yarding in rope. I fed Mike slack as fast as I could. As we neared the end, I worked the rope loop clear of my belay device. Then the rope yanked hard at my waist and I held my breath, feeling the cord for more tugs. *Yank, yank. That makes three—he's got me on belay.*

I removed the anchor pieces, confident that though we could not speak to each other, Mike's pace and signals meant he was ready for me to climb. Though sure he could not hear me over the pounding rain, out of habit I yelled, "Climbing!"

Already chagrined that I had relinquished the lead to Mike, I was determined not to come up short again. I had to climb fast and well, even though the route was growing more difficult with every raindrop.

Slightly crazed with fear, I pulled hard on whatever I slapped my hand on. Mike knew that it was desperate on the face, so he kept the rope tight. This was no longer about clean or stylish climbing; this was a rushed race for safety, and maybe even survival.

Taking out Mike's protection, I didn't waste the few seconds needed to clip it to my gear rack. I just let it pile up on the rope in a dangling jumble. When I cleared a steep section, the rock angle eased. But horror gripped me—water was pouring down the rock slab in a broad sheet. It was as if someone fifty feet above were soaking the stone face with a full-force garden hose. To touch the rock I had to put my hand into the moving veneer of runoff. My forearm presented a new pathway for the rushing water. Some of it rooster-tailed off my elbow, and the rest gushed into my armpit.

I pawed at the biggest holds and pulled. My smooth-soled rock shoes sometimes skated off the shimmering face as I struggled for a foothold. Finally, I saw Mike twenty feet higher.

Almost there. Don't blow it.

I slowed a bit to reduce the chance of a mistake. By making it safely up the slippery pitch in the lashing rainstorm, I had redeemed myself. Stepping onto our sloping belay ledge, I longed to clip into a nice strong anchor, but there wasn't one. Mike had been forced to belay from a sling draped over a mushroom-shaped rock protrusion the size of a saucepan. There were no good cracks, so he'd had to make do.

When I realized how marginal an anchor we had, and how close I had been to slipping off the wet face, a small wave of nausea hit me. A minor error by either of us could have been disastrous. We squatted on our haunches, trying to make ourselves a smaller target for lightning. Thunder echoed back and forth across the canyon. We hunkered together, holding our one daypack over our heads as meager protection from the heavy rainfall.

"Mike, that was an unbelievable lead with this weather," I said. "Awesome, man."

"I don't know how you followed in the gushing water. I was scared that you might whip off. Way to go."

"Thanks. Now if it'll just slow enough to let us off here."

We were about 150 feet below the top. The rock ahead looked easier, but we had to wait out the rain. Flat-bottomed thunderclouds scampered past the canyon and onto the eastern plains beyond, taking the rainfall with them. The wind settled into shifting gusts, which dried the rock face but chilled us. One of us swiped the rock every ten minutes, checking to see how it was drying. Two hours passed before we thought it was dry enough to climb. Mike shivered and seemed a bit withdrawn. For once, my extra body fat served me well—I was not hypothermic like my skinny partner. Seeking the easiest way off, I led us up and to the left. The angled direction of our escape route forced us to climb three pitches before we reached ground flat enough so that we could unrope and begin the tedious descent. Rappelling short cliffs and fighting thick brush, we finally reached the truck in the dark, utterly spent.

Though the day had been more scary and less fun than we'd planned, we had held it together. Climbing—whether on rock, ice, or snow—is a carefully orchestrated dance between partners. It requires teammates with skill, patience, determination, and strength, both mental and physical. It requires partners who can work together even when the mountain blocks their view of each other, or when howling wind and driving rain sweep away shouted instructions. That day in Eldo, we both had to be fully worthy of each other's trust.

Each of us knew that the other was, in the highest praise one mountaineer can give another, "solid."

Our partnership was cemented.

CHAPTER 8

▲ ▲ ▲

IN THE LATE fall of 1991, Mike Price hits town after leading another Outward Bound course in the canyonlands of Utah—just him and six young men and women, out climbing and backpacking in the solitude of the red rock country. Mike spends about two hundred days a year in the desert or the mountains, and he blows into Fort Collins between trips for three or four days, crashing at his brother's place, just a few blocks from my house.

We settle in at the end of the C.B. & Potts bar with stories to tell and plans to make. By now, we've been buddies for five years. I pay for two pints of 90 Shilling draft. Mike lifts the icy mug, stares at the amber liquid, and says, "Ah, my favorite type of beer: free."

Whenever we get together, Mike recounts his latest trip. I relish his tales—it's a chance to vicariously taste the life of an unencumbered wilderness teacher.

Tonight he's in his usual city clothes: checkered western shirt with shiny snap buttons, battered jeans, scuffed cowboy boots. His shoulders curve forward, a reminder of the scoliosis he endured as a kid. He's as even-keeled as ever—for him, life is an adventure that should be taken with equal parts seriousness and laughter, reflection and relish.

Mike describes his comical instructions to his field crew—his advice to them if they encountered another group on the desert trail, which might represent competition for a coveted camping spot near water. "Tell them," he had said, "that we are a prisoner-outreach program from the hospital of the criminally insane. People leave in a big hurry."

Most of these sessions are one-sided—Mike recounting his latest wilderness escapade, me with nothing similar to share. I hike and climb and ski with passion, but my work as a self-employed environmental geologist keeps me otherwise all too busy. And while Mike is single, I am married to Gloria. All that means that I struggle to rack up one-fifth the mountain time Mike does. But I'd recently logged some trail miles, and this time I have a story to share.

A few weeks earlier, Gloria and I set out to hike Longs Peak. Five hours after leaving the trailhead, at about 9,400 feet, we'd ascended 4,000 feet along rocky trails and rugged boulder fields. We were close to the summit when a horrifying scene unfolded in a place called the Narrows, a hundred-foot-long ledge only a few feet wide. Just ahead of us, another hiker stumbled off that ledge, cartwheeling 70 feet down the mountain and landing, seriously injured, among a pile of rocks. We were among a dozen volunteers who kept the patient alive in the first critical hours. In the end, I spent eighteen hours with him, staying to help some National Park Service rangers and a few other die-hard volunteer rescuers carry him on a metal stretcher through the night, buffeted by subfreezing temperatures and eighty-mile-per-hour winds. When loose rocks clattered toward us in the dark, the rangers shouted for us to lean over the patient to protect him. At dawn the next day, we handed him off to a second rescue team, and six hours later they got the young man onto a helicopter and to the hospital. I was thrilled that he survived, but the rescue strained my body to its limits—I lost ten pounds in twenty-four hours—and tested my technical-climbing and rope skills during our night-long effort to lower the man over 1,000 feet of craggy mountainside.

"Nice job, Jim," Mike says. "You guys put yourselves on the line, and got him down. You earned some stripes on that one."

Mike raises his beer in toast, and we tap mugs, but soon our focus shifts. We'd talked for years about climbing something "big." All serious climbers think, at least fleetingly, about Nepal, but at this point the Himalayas seem out of our league and beyond our budget. We've talked about the Grand Tetons, and other places too, but one mountain—Rainier, in Washington State—keeps creeping into our conversations. This night, in the cacophony of a college-town bar, we decide what I think we both have known deep inside for a while: that we will go there. The postcard-perfect mountain, its volcanic slopes covered with glaciers, attracts thousands of climbers a year, the bulk of them headed for the top via the Disappointment Cleaver route or the Emmons-Winthrop route. It is as unforgiving as it is beautiful—an average of two or three people lose their lives on the mountain each year, and in 1981 it was the scene of the country's worst climbing disaster, when an avalanche swept eleven people into a crevasse.

We recognize that there are dangers, but we accept them. For us, earning rewards in adventure and personal growth means challenging ourselves with bigger mountains and, sometimes, bigger risks. As we talk, our determination solidifies. Rainier it will be. And we aren't going to climb a standard route; we are going to push ourselves on an elegant but challenging ascent up the north side of the mountain. Up the Liberty Ridge.

SIX MONTHS LATER, during our final preparations, I call the National Park Service ranger stations on Rainier three or four times, checking snow conditions, ice coverage, and avalanche danger. I learn that it has been a low-snow year, that the crevasses on the Emmons and Carbon Glaciers are not too bad, and that it has been unseasonably warm. In one call, I speak with Mike Gauthier, one of Rainier's climbing rangers, who tells me the avalanche danger is nil and that upper parts of the Liberty Ridge are covered in hard water ice. If you're ready, he says, for technical ice—and we are—it may not be too bad. But he also says that snow bridges are melting rapidly, exposing crevasses.

"It looks like July around here," he says, as I scribble down the information.

Crevasses.

Clinging to Mount Rainier's flanks are twenty-six glaciers—giant rivers of ice slowly creeping downhill, replenished by the snow that pummels the summit all winter long. In a twelve-month span in the early 1970s, 1,122 inches of snow fell on Rainier. At the time, this set a U.S. record.

Rainier's glaciers are complex geological formations, hundreds of feet thick, layer upon layer of ice of varying consistencies and thicknesses that can stretch for miles. The Emmons Glacier alone is comprised of an estimated 23.8 billion cubic feet of ice. Glaciers pack an unrelenting force, carving valleys and pulverizing boulders the size of houses. Thousands of years after they have receded, they will have left unmistakable imprints on the land.

The movement of glaciers is a simple matter of gravity. Once enough snow accumulates and hardens to ice, the combination of mountain slope and the gravitational force exerted on the ice layer begins pulling the mass downhill. Free water beneath the ice accelerates some parts of the glacier, while a rough bedrock base slows movement in other areas. The glacier's different flow rates and directions open up tension cracks in the ice, called crevasses.

The top 150 feet or so of a glacier is under less pressure than the deepest layers, and so the shallow ice is more rigid—and more prone to fracturing under the enormous tension that builds up as the frozen mass unsteadily works its way downhill. Those ever-changing cracks can open slowly and later be concealed by snow and ice that freezes over the top of the slit. The process repeats itself innumerable times and is so insidious that a snow bridge a few feet thick can conceal a giant, yawning crevasse 10 feet across and 120 feet deep.

We have to prepare for the worst, so a couple of days before our flight, Mike shows up at the home Gloria and I share. On the lawn we uncoil a 165-foot length of Mike's 8.8-millimeter climbing rope—the perfect kind for tackling glaciers. We are going to practice a crevasse rescue system that one of us on top of the glacier could use to extricate the other from a slot.

Though we have both done it before, we want to practice setting up a Z-pulley system. The arrangement rests on a simple principle: Dividing one long rope into three smaller sections, all threaded through pulleys, greatly increases one man's leverage and lifting power. When rigged properly, the three sections of the rope form a giant Z. We practice for a simple reason: No matter what Hollywood movies suggest, no climber in the world can haul his partner back up a cliff, or out of a crevasse, without mechanical help.

We each know that if one of us plunges into a crevasse, the other must flop onto the ground and dig in with an ice ax to stop the fall. Then the climber atop the glacier will have a real chance to pull the other out with a Z-pulley lifting system.

So out there on the shaggy grass, we practice our backup system, just like Dad always taught me. On the mountain, our anchors will have to be ice screws and metal-bladed snow flukes buried securely in the glacier, but here in my yard we use a black walnut tree and the deck railing. Seventeen months ago, Mike spent a season in Antarctica, where he was on the McMurdo Sound search-and-rescue team that pulled two men and their load of dynamite from an enormous crevasse after their bulldozer crashed through a snow bridge.

Since he knows the details better, he leads me as we put together a Z-pulley. Then we take it all apart, and I do it on my own. Mike observes quietly as I feed the rope through carabiners and pulleys. Gloria stands behind him on the deck, grilling steaks for all of us. She watches and listens as we work with the rope, talking about different self-rescue scenarios.

"You guys seem to be putting a lot of effort into this," she says, scowling. "How likely is a crevasse fall?"

I'm quiet for a second. She is mountain-savvy and knows there must be some risk; otherwise we wouldn't be doing all this. But I don't want her to worry, so I say casually, "Well, not very likely. We're just being careful."

"Besides," Mike adds, "if anyone busts through a snow bridge, they usually go in only ten feet at most. Then the other guy can just haul on the rope to help them scramble back out."

Gloria looks at me, then Mike, seemingly unconvinced; then she turns back to the grill. I glance at Mike, eyebrows raised, feeling a bit guilty that we've minimized the danger. Still, her worrying the whole time we're on the mountain won't help anyone.

In the past, she has expressed her concerns about me getting hurt or killed in the mountains. But Gloria's climbed some rock and ice with me over the last decade, and she's seen how safety-conscious I am. She also knows how highly skilled a climber Mike is, and how well he and I climb together. So, although she's a bit nervous about Rainier, she doesn't press the issue.

I finish packing on June 16, 1992; then Gloria and I meet Mike at a local bookstore for a lecture by Royal Robbins, a Yosemite Valley rock-climbing legend. In his talk, he urges the audience to follow less-known paths in life. Dreaming of our departure the next day, I feel we are following Royal's advice.

At six in the morning, Gloria sleepily drags herself downstairs to see me off. As is our custom before all my big climbs, she kisses my protective medal, slips it over my head, and gives me a good-bye kiss to send me on my way. When I drive up to the home of Mike's brother, Daryl, Mike's bags are stacked in the driveway. Three hours later, our Continental jet is in the air. The adventure has begun.

ON A PHOTOGRAPH of Rainier's north face, the line up Liberty Ridge is, in the language of climbers, "elegant"—a distinct route up and up, toward the snow-shrouded summit. The cleaver-like ridge juts out between two great walls. On one side is the Willis Wall—4,000 feet of steep volcanic rock, interbedded with crumbling ledges of ash, mud, snow, and ice, much of it poised to fall away. On the other side of Liberty Ridge stands Liberty Wall, imposing at 3,000 feet and with a terrifying reputation for even more frequent ice-cliff collapses and rock falls.

Above both walls and the ridge sits Liberty Cap, an ice field hundreds of feet thick wrapping a subsummit of the volcanic mountain. The edge of that ice cap is in constant change, cleaving off building-sized slabs that rumble down the walls in explosions of rock and ice. These collapses sometimes trigger cascading avalanches that can sweep out a mile across the Carbon Glacier.

We know climbing Liberty Ridge will not be easy; we will ascend 5,000 feet during a five-mile approach through a forest and across two glaciers just to reach the foot of the ridge. Then there's Liberty Ridge itself. It will demand another vertical mile of muscle-numbing work, roped together, each of us hauling a pack loaded with fifty pounds of gear and supplies. There will be slow-motion glacial flows clogged with ice blocks the size of trucks, a knife-edge ascent up a ridge averaging about forty-five degrees, and a couple hours of melting ice for drinking water each day. It will mean probably four days of hard work and lots of simul-climbing, where to move faster we'll be roped together and climb simultaneously, neither of us belaying the other. When we simul-climb, we'll be fully committed to each other and will have to be completely confident that neither of us will fall, as a mistake could yank both of us off the mountain.

But we're experienced, and we're ready. I am twenty-nine; Mike's thirty-four. My climbing journey stretches a decade, and Mike's nearly fifteen years. And after the last of our gear tumbles from the baggage conveyor, we drive away from the Seattle-Tacoma International Airport in a red rental sedan and head for Mount Rainier National Park.

Even from ninety miles away, in Seattle, Rainier's hulking mass dominates the skyline. The classic volcanic cone is gouged by huge glaciers that chop the mountain into alternating swaths of ice and crumbling rock. Though scores of big and beautiful peaks populate the Pacific Northwest, locals refer to Rainier simply as The Mountain.

WE PULL INTO the White River Ranger Station, just about eight miles northeast of Rainier's summit. It's Wednesday afternoon, June 17. Seeing the rustic building among the giant conifers triggers my memories of having been here nine Junes before. Mike and I check with the rangers about the conditions on the mountain, the weather forecast, and recent climbs. We fill out little index cards, listing our names and addresses, the route we plan to take, and emergency contact information for our families. I jot down Gloria's name and our home number. My unmarried wanderlust friend lists his parents in Oklahoma.

An hour later, in the White River Campground, we dump out all our gear, talking about what to take and what to leave—a blending of risk assessment and climbing confidence and gut instinct. Some of it is easy. We figure to be out four days, maybe five, so we set out enough food for that period: oatmeal and bagels, granola, nuts and raisins, macaroni and cheese, quick-cooking noodles. We grab Gatorade powder and iodine tablets to purify our water, a lightweight backpacking stove, fuel, helmets, headlamps, sleeping bags and pads. We decide to leave the tent behind—it looks as though the weather is going to cooperate. Tossing the tent into the rental car's trunk instead of into our packs means seven fewer pounds we'll lug up the mountain.

But figuring out which climbing hardware to take is more difficult. Too much, and the packs will be too heavy for us to move fast—and the potential danger will rise. Too little gear, and we won't be able to protect ourselves sufficiently, so the risk will increase. We settle on two camming units—spring-loaded contraptions about the size of a baby's fist—for rock cracks; about twenty carabiners; two snow flukes, which look like shovel blades; and seven ice screws—each one a hollow tube about eight inches long with a sharp tip and a thread up the outside of the shaft.

As the sun slowly descends in the western sky, we take in the grandeur of Rainier. We see Liberty Ridge and, at its apex, nearly 10,000 feet higher than we are now, a huge frozen slope gleaming in the fading light.

WHENEVER I CLIMB, I experience moments when fear tries to grab me, and each time I fight to remain relaxed and move fluidly, not jerking my hands and feet from perch to perch. I tell myself to stay calm, to ignore my heart pounding harder, and to fight the compulsion to draw short, fast breaths.

Sometimes, my head becomes a battleground as two personas—a frightened self-doubter who is all emotion and a confident cheerleader who is all logic—bicker for control. Although I hear other voices when things get hairy—those of my dad, of old climbing buddies—it is most often this battle that grips me.

It seems different for Mike. No matter how difficult or risky the situation gets, he stays calm, a reassuring presence when things are toughest. Mike will sense me struggling and will say, "C'mon, Jim, you can do it," and I'll know then that I can't let him down.

WE RISE EARLY—it's time to go climbing. After shoveling down instant oatmeal, we set out from the campground wearing shorts and T-shirts and carrying packs brimming with gear. Sunlight filters through the woods in splotches as we follow a broad hiking trail for three miles, gaining 1,600 feet of altitude. The dirt path eventually wanders out of the forest and then, at an elevation of around 5,500 feet, the trees thin and we enter a grassy meadow. Ice hundreds of feet thick once covered this area in Glacier Basin, but now it is a rugged open valley of rocks, sand, and dust, birthed by a volcano and transformed by moving ice. The main trail angles south a short distance, to the smooth, milky surface of the tiny Inter Glacier—the toe of the Emmons-Winthrop route. We'll be coming down that way in about four days, depending upon how the climb goes. The pleasant sunshine makes the upper edge of the Inter Glacier look far less scary and dangerous than it felt during that driving nighttime windstorm almost a decade earlier. It's a lesson on how dramatically things can change on Rainier.

We cut west on a faint climber's trail that ascends a snow-covered scree field of broken rocks and continue on to an open saddle called St. Elmo's Pass, named for the electrical discharge known as St. Elmo's fire observed here in 1887. Weighted down by my heavy pack, I pant and sweat my way up the slope. When we reach the pass, we gaze to the southwest, awestruck.

A massive heaving sea of ice stretches for miles. Building-sized frozen blocks with ragged edges are thrust up in some areas, while other sections drop in a jumbled series of collapsing ice ledges. Mixed in are smooth ice fields the size of mountain lakes, neatly patterned with regularly spaced crevasses. Farther up the glacier sit swollen ice domes, irregular and unpredictable crevasses slashing around their edges.

Even more stunning is the looming hulk of the mountain, rising 7,000 feet above us now in a sweeping slope of unstable rock buttresses and shifting ice cliffs. Continuous erosion of the weak volcanic rock leaves long drools of dark debris on the glacier that look like mascara running down white cheeks.

We drop our packs, snap a few photographs, and bathe in the morning sun's warmth. About 200 feet below us rests the massive Winthrop Glacier, the beginning of serious climbing.

It's time to gear up. We wiggle into more clothing, then pull on our helmets and harnesses, one around the waist, one across the chest. We force our way into snug plastic climbing boots and put on our crampons—metal brackets ringed with twelve sharp steel spikes, two of them angled forward for climbing steep ice.

We pull out our ice tools. Mike and I each carry two, an ice ax and an ice hammer, and they are nearly identical. Each looks sort of like a small miner's pick—a long, straight handle with a steel blade sticking out of one side of the head. We use the sharp-toothed picks to dig into ice and pull ourselves up as we climb. On the back side of one tool's head is a hammer, which we'll use to drive in ice screws. On the back side of the other tool is an adze, sort of a curving sideways ax designed for chopping out ice to make a flat spot, or to cut through slop on the surface to reach hard ice underneath. At the base of each ice tool's handle is a spike, a spearlike metal tip with a carabiner hole in it.

We pull out 165 feet of rope, divide it roughly in thirds, and both tie into opposite ends of the middle third. About fifty feet of rope separates us, and each of us carries a fifty-foot coil across his shoulders. This coiled spare rope is reserved for hauling one or the other of us out of a crevasse.

Finally, we step off dirt and onto ice, walking across a relatively flat section of Winthrop Glacier slit again and again by crevasses. After zigging and zagging around obvious slots, an hour later we reach rocky ground on the far side of the glacier. We climb onto a rock outcropping called Curtis Ridge, a high point where we can survey the massive Carbon Glacier. Nearly six miles long and 700 feet thick, it is a stunning sight—tilted ice blocks crammed against one another up and down the valley.

From the high spot, we try to pick a route across the mottled whitish-blue surface of the glacier, one that will keep us away from obvious crevasses and avoid the dead ends we'll never see once we're down among the towering ice blocks. It is about three in the afternoon; roughly six hours of light remain. We are tired but not exhausted, and we want to get as far as we can before dark. Slithering down unstable slopes of rock debris, we leave Curtis Ridge and try accessing the Carbon Glacier. I try forging a way first, but get cut off by an uncrossable gap in the ice. Mike then takes the lead in a new direction, picking his way across teetering ice boulders before retreating after concluding that they're too unstable. Then he moves over thirty feet to a new set of glacial blocks, and I feed out rope, watching him forge a way across the tumbled mess.

Sensing a weak section ahead, Mike sinks an ice screw and clips his rope into it with a carabiner; then I put him on belay. After he makes it across, I let my breath out. He pulls in the rope as I follow his footprints across, treading lightly.

Now we move up the low-angled glacier simultaneously, without placing ice screws as anchors. The fifty feet of rope between us stretches taut as we keep our distance from one another, each of us trying to match the other's pace, mindful that when crossing a glacier a tight rope will minimize the length of a crevasse fall. Mike leads the way until fatigue, eyestrain, and tension wear him down; then I move out front. Over the next few hours, we swap the lead back and forth. A couple times, we find ourselves in a dead-end alley between house-sized chunks of ice, and we must retreat to find a new route. It is like picking our way through a frozen three-dimensional maze. As we move toward Liberty Ridge, we consciously veer away from the dangerous Willis Wall.

The sun sinks low in the sky, and although we are almost across the glacier we know we need to shut it down for the day. On a relatively flat spot between two crevasses—one slot ten feet away on the right, one slot thirty feet on the left—we probe the glacier's surface with our tools, decide it's safe to bivouac here, spread out our foam pads and sleeping bags, and light the stove.

After dinner, we lie in our bags in the twilight, looking north past our toes as the glacier stretches downvalley below us for five miles, satisfied with our progress. Darkness comes, stars explode across the sky, and every so often distant rocks and ice rumble down the Willis Wall.

Our muscles ache and our shoulders throb where the pack straps dug in, but we feel pretty good even as the cold seeps up from the glacier and through our sleeping pads, chilling us. Before sleep overtakes me, I tap my fingertips against my chest, making sure my lucky medal is there.

I FIDGET THROUGH the night—I never sleep well on rough ground—and at first light we are up. Melting snow for water consumes an hour as our stove, no bigger than a beer mug, hums beneath a battered two-quart pan. We sip tea and eat oatmeal and cram our sleeping bags back into their nylon stuff sacks, invigorated by the crisp morning air, by thoughts of what's ahead.

Around seven A.M., we pull our packs onto our sore shoulders and head off, crossing the last section of the Carbon Glacier.

Then we reach the flank of Liberty Ridge, and we start climbing up onto the ridge crest from the eastern side. A hillside covered with dirty ice—volcanic dust and pebbles embedded in frozen muck— rises above us. Mike leads, raising his ice ax as he sets out, stopping a little way up and forcing an ice screw into the hillside. He moves a few more feet and then stops, lifting his second ice tool off his belt. Watching Mike alternately swing both tools, I know it's getting tougher now.

Mike climbs a little higher, rams another screw into junk that's more frozen mud than ice. He turns back to look at me.

"Don't fall," Mike yells.

"Understood," I holler back.

His words unsettle me. It must be pretty shaky up there.

The rope tightens at my waist, urging me up, and I kick my crampons in and swing my ice tools and follow Mike's trail. We are simul-climbing, and it is scary—this ridge is really a mudsicle, not the dense water ice where we feel most safe, where the sharpened tips of our crampons and axes bite firmly. Twenty feet higher, Mike stops again.

"Do...not...fall," he shouts, and the anxiety coursing through me ticks up a couple notches.

"Understood," I answer. We make it another fifty feet before Mike stops again. By now, I have angled over to the right and jammed my body into a little cave where the ice meets the rock. Simul-climbing is too risky here. I toss a long nylon sling over a boulder for a quick anchor and put Mike on belay.

"You're on belay now," I shout.

"Thanks."

"You wanna keep going or you wanna come down?" I yell.

"I better come down," Mike hollers back.

A few minutes later, we decide to back off this section of the ridge. We've lost an hour, and we'll have to retreat and work our way around the ridge and approach it from the distant western side. Losing some more time, though, is better than risking a big fall. It is probably somewhere in that frozen, muddy hillside that we break a tooth off the tip of one of the ice screws. We still have seven screws, but now only six are fully functional.

IT IS ALREADY late morning, and we feel a twinge of disappointment about the wasted time as we cut downhill, around the toe of the ridge, and ascend the western side of Liberty Ridge, heading for a spot called Thumb Rock.

The snow is better on this shady side of the ridge, and we simul-climb again, sinking screws into the occasional ice patch for protection, moving in tandem as we zigzag our way up, swapping the lead.

The afternoon sun bakes the mountain, and the heat sometimes causes rocks to break free from the ice and tumble. I am out front when I hear a clatter above me. Climbers normally keep their helmets pointed uphill rather than risk a rock in the face, but I sense that it is still far away, so I raise my forehead and see a basketball-sized rock hurtling down the mountainside.

"Rock," I shout. And then, as it bounds crazily toward Mike: "Scramble right, scramble right."

Mike scampers sideways and the rock bounces over the rope between us, then crashes out of sight. We start climbing again. A little later, Mike, out front, stops suddenly.

"My foot's in a small crevasse," he says.

I take two steps downhill to stretch the slack out of the rope, drop onto my belly, dig my ice ax into the glacier surface to anchor us, and yell, "Go ahead." Mike pulls his foot free. The crevasse isn't big—maybe two feet across and thirty feet deep, hidden beneath a snow bridge. Mike steps across it easily, and I follow.

But it's a reminder that we are crossing ice sheets pocked with thousands of cracks—some obvious and open, some covered by snow bridges that conceal the danger. As we climb, we constantly scan the glacier's surface, looking for a swale, or a telltale sprinkling of dust settled in a low spot—clues to a sinking snow bridge.

Early in the afternoon, we reach Thumb Rock, where a lot of climbers attempting the Liberty Ridge route camp on their second night. Mike and I survey the clear sky and decide to push on. We still have seven hours of daylight.

I lead us up a short, steep gully during the hottest part of the day. The sun-softened snow sucks at our feet with each step. It's like walking in shin-deep oatmeal, and the risk of an avalanche is growing. We need the temperature to drop and the snow to freeze up again, so we stop and wait.

The stove thrums like a miniature jet engine, reducing chunks of ice to water, and we share soup and tea, resting for a couple of hours. At this point, high on the protective shoulder of Liberty Ridge, we are safe, but close enough to the Willis Wall to watch an incredible series of debris falls. We stare, mesmerized, at the explosions of falling ice, some so powerful that they trigger secondary avalanches, which rumble and roar as they rain down the lower wall. Balancing a half-full soup bowl on my knee, I watch a black boulder—who knows at this distance if it is the size of a refrigerator, a van, or a house—bounce off a ledge and plummet 500 feet before crashing onto the Carbon Glacier far below us.

As the sun swings around to the western side of Rainier, the mountaintop puts us into shadow and the temperature drops.

The snow firms up, and by around five o'clock we are moving again, starting a sort of second shift to the day.

We cross a rock buttress, and I place the spring-loaded, retractable cams into a rotten crack as I lead. Peering around a corner, I'm surprised by a sheet of ice more than 500 feet wide, stretched as far up as I can see. That ice sheet lies at about forty-five degrees, with a few steeper sections. It is the shimmering slope we'd seen from the campground the first night.

"Holy smokes," I say, staring up.

"What?" Mike asks from below me.

"You'll see when you get here," I say.

A few minutes later Mike reaches me, and his eyebrows arch up above his big round sunglasses.

"Whoa," he says, surveying the ice field. "Maybe three pitches."

"Four to five," I guess as we consider the number of rope lengths it will take us to get to the top.

"You're crazy," Mike says. "It isn't that long."

It's about seven o'clock, and there's not a flat spot anywhere to camp on, so we keep going, fighting the heavy packs, which shift back and forth. There'll be no simul-climbing here—a fall could mean a sickening slide before a deadly 2,500-foot plunge over the shoulder of the Willis Wall, like those boulders we watched earlier. I shake the unsettling image from my mind and double-check my belay station—two ice screws on an equalized sling, backed up by a deeply driven ice ax. We have no choice but to belay every pitch, a time-consuming endeavor. I feed the rope as Mike heads up the ice slab, a tool in each hand, placing the occasional ice screw for protection. After he reaches the end of the rope, he sets an anchor and slowly pulls the lifeline back in as I climb to him.

I lead the next pitch. It is hard glaze ice, and my crampons and picks bite into it solidly. About every thirty feet, I look for a low-angled ramp to stand on while I crank in an ice screw, hooking the pick of my hammer through the screw's eyehole and using the ice tool as a lever. It is awkward and tiring work. After clipping our rope to the screw with two carabiners and a nylon sling, I feel my tight shoulders relax and my heart rate slow a bit. I'm safer now, the potential fall shorter. I catch my breath, then resume leading.

Around eight-thirty, I look up and, for an instant, don't believe what I'm seeing: a single climber with no rope making his way down toward us. He moves slowly, backing down the steep, frozen mountainside, kicking in his crampons and swinging his axes, one at a time.

As he draws closer, I move about three feet to one side. I am afraid that if the guy falls, he might slide down and knock me over like a bowling pin.

"Hi, how's it going?" he asks after reaching me.

"Good," I answer. "How about you?"

"Tired."

"Where you coming from?" I ask.

"The top."

"The top of the mountain?"

"No, just the top of Liberty Cap."

"Where's your partner?" I ask.

"Well, I don't have one," he says in a scratchy voice. "He was gonna come with me but he got sick and he couldn't, so I'm soloing."

"How much more of this water ice?" I ask, pointing at the slope above us.

"A thousand feet," he replies. I don't believe him.

"I soloed up from Thumb Rock this morning, and I'm going back tonight. If you fall on this, you go all the way to the bottom of the ice slab, and you'd go right over the Willis Wall," he says, giggling.

"Yeah," I answer, "I guess you would." This guy seems wacko.

"You'll never reach the top before dark," he says.

He must be wrong, I think. But what if he's right and we're still on this ice slope when night catches us? I feel a surge of anxiety. He heads down, and I continue the pitch.

That's the thing about meeting someone going in the other direction. It can be invigorating: You're almost there. Or depressing: You've got a long way to go.

As he passes Mike below me, they exchange a few words, but there's no time for chitchat. Darkness is coming fast, and we are in a race. As I climb, I continually scout the terrain, trying to memorize it before we lose the light, searching for a place to sleep. Over to my right, I see the tops of some big rocks, suggesting the edge of the ice and maybe a flat area—our best chance to find a spot for the night. Otherwise, we'll have to lead more ice in the dark—a bad option. I set a quick anchor and belay Mike up.

"Why'd you stop?" Mike asks as he reaches me, seemingly perturbed. "We still had slack."

"I think there's a flat spot over there," I tell him.

It is so dark by now that we dig into our packs for our headlamps.

"Well, where is it?" Mike asks.

"It's off to the right," I say. "About seventy-five feet out."

I settle in to belay, using ice screws and my tools as anchors.

"Let's hope you're right," Mike says, flicking on his headlamp and heading into the darkness. As I feed out the rope, the light bounces off the ice. He moves in the middle of the glow, a ghostly image in a world of ice, cold, and blackness. I turn off my headlamp to save the batteries, and when the darkness closes in on me, fear rises in my gut.

As Mike angles farther away, it gets harder to see his light. Then it disappears behind an ice bulge. Two minutes go by. Then five. Then ten. The rope twitches a few inches, then stops. I mutter aloud, "Come on, Michael, find us something."

Now I know I'm anxious—I call him Michael only when the situation gets really serious.

"I got it," Mike finally shouts from somewhere off in the dark, and I breathe easier. We're going to be all right. After Mike pulls the rope tight, I traverse across the ice toward him, pulling out the screws as I move. Finally there, I see that the spot isn't great; the ice-and-rock shelf, about the size of a picnic table, tilts downhill. There's no flat place to set up the stove, and we'll have to sleep in our harnesses, roped to ice screws. But it will do.

It is eleven P.M., and exhaustion overwhelms us as we crawl uncomfortably into our sleeping bags, our rope ends leading out of the bags, back to the anchor screws. Through the night, we fight a constant battle, creeping down the sloped ice ledge to the ends of our anchor slings, awakening, then worming back up the hill in our sleeping bags and resting, fitfully, a little more.

I OPEN MY eyes in the early morning light. Below me, to my right, is the ice field we'd come up. Sunrise colors reflect off the slick surface for 500 feet below me, until the ice slab plunges off over the shoulder of the Willis Wall. It is a precarious place to awaken.

"Whoa," Mike says just then, and for a moment I assume we're both looking at the same stunning thing.

Then I turn and see that Mike is actually staring in the opposite direction. I wiggle over to him, the nylon of my sleeping bag scratching on the rocks, and suck in a sharp breath. We are looking right down the Liberty Wall, with 2,500 vertical feet between us and the glacier we stood on yesterday afternoon.

"Holy smokes," I say.

In the dark of last night, we'd stumbled onto this almost-flat spot just a few feet from the sheer drop-off down the wall. We are just below the Black Pyramid rock formation.

"Man," I say, "I've bivouacked out a little bit, but I've never bivied anywhere like this."

"I've bivied out a hundred nights," Mike answers, "and I've never bivied like this—I don't even know anyone who has."

Our nerves jingle and our muscles ache. Even in the daylight, there is still no good place to put the stove, so we carefully pack up and resume the climb, headachy and dehydrated, our water bottles nearly empty.

Mike leads first, then me. We swap the lead a couple more times, moving like molasses, hunger racking us. By ten A.M., we are out of water. We battle altitude and thirst, feeling as if we have hangovers, as if our legs and packs have doubled in weight.

Late in the morning, after crossing a badly crevassed area, we reach easier ground, light the stove, and melt ice. We eat, replenishing our bodies, and fill our water bottles. We're at about 13,300 feet, roughly 800 feet below the Liberty Cap.

We rest awhile, and then start up again. Mike takes the lead, kicking steps in the knee-deep snow. I lead for a short while, but I am so weakened by the altitude that I am painfully slow. Mike volunteers to take the front again. Out of guilt, I protest, but Mike correctly points out that we'll be faster if he just keeps leading. Chagrined, I bring up the rear, promising myself that whatever it takes, I will not make Mike wait on me. I force myself to match his pace.

Finally, we approach the last steep section, topped by a dead-vertical ice wall that is 40 feet high in places. Mike finds a section where the wall is maybe 20 feet high, swings his tools and kicks his crampons, and starts up, moving smoothly. He reaches the top, pulls himself up and over, onto solid ground. Still belaying him from below, I see handfuls of ice chips fly over the edge as Mike chops out the next belay spot.

The rope snaps tight, and I climb, my nose pressed against the steep ice as I struggle up. I reach the top, sink one of my picks, then the other, pull myself up, get a leg on top, and muscle my way over the lip.

"Welcome to the Liberty Cap," Mike says, a big grin breaking across his tanned face.

Too tired to respond, I bend over my ax and pant like a dog on a one-hundred-degree day. All the tough terrain is behind us—ahead is easy snow climbing to the summit.

I am finally feeling better, and at the same time Mike starts deteriorating, the toll of leading for so long wearing on him.

"Sorry, man," Mike says as we're getting ready to head across the next section. "I just can't kick steps anymore."

"No problem, amigo," I say. "You carried the ball for a while. Now it's my turn."

I'm glad that I am able to rally and lead again. We grind our way to the highest point on the Liberty Cap, at 14,112 feet. We snap a few pictures, eat a little, then start moving down the east side of the cap. Mike says he really feels cruddy—light-headed, ready to puke—so we move slowly. He grows quieter than usual, and when I don't hear a witty comment out of him for over an hour, I know he is hurting. Finally, we reach the flat saddle between Liberty Cap and the summit and knock off for the day.

We briefly consider going to summit and sleeping on top—the weather is so beautiful. But Mike just doesn't have it in him right now.

He sits on his pack while I jab the handle of my ice ax into the snow around us, feeling, making sure we aren't over a hidden crevasse. I pound two shovel-shaped snow flukes into the glacier, tie us to them, and settle in even as the sun still lingers in the western sky.

Mike crawls into his sleeping bag and immediately crashes, wiped out. I feel pretty good, so I stay awake. It is the kind of partnership we enjoy: When I struggle, Mike picks me up, takes the lead. Now Mike needs a little help, and I go to work with the stove, melting snow. An hour later, Mike wakes up, starts eating and drinking, and begins to feel better.

By the time we shimmy into our sleeping bags for the night, Mike is joking again. We are back in business.

AS THE LAST rays of the sun slip away, the lights of Seattle shimmer in the distance, 13,600 feet below us. Hours pass as I drift in and out of sleep, feeling the glacier's cold through my foam pad, through my bag, through my clothes.

Around four A.M., I open my eyes. Stars twinkle above us, the first wisps of pink brush the eastern horizon, and a trickle of relief courses through my achy muscles. The sky is still clear.

It is Sunday morning, June 21, Father's Day. The summer solstice, the day the tilt of Earth's axis will mean the sun is as far north as it will get. The longest, sunniest day of the year. I doze for another two hours, my rest broken by one overriding thought: *Man, twelve more hours of good weather, that's all we need. Then we'll be off the mountain.*

CHAPTER 9

▲ ▲ ▲

PINK-ORANGE ALPENGLOW from the rising sun marches across the summit snowfield of Mount Rainier, illuminating Mike's smiling face.

"Mornin'—feeling better?" I ask.

"Yeah, lots," Mike says. "Guess I just needed some sleep and water."

"Good, because the day looks awesome."

Mike coaxes the stove to life. At 13,600 feet, it grudgingly sputters but soon throws out heat. As the stove slowly melts ice to water, we busy ourselves getting ready for the summit, and our last day on the mountain.

While we sip weak tea and force down the last of the granola, we watch two rope teams trudge up the last few hundred feet to Rainier's 14,410-foot summit. They are on the standard northeastern route. We are a quarter mile west of them in the glacial saddle between the true summit and the Liberty Cap.

Stuffing my blue sleeping bag into my pack compresses the air out, and I catch a whiff of rank body odor: mine. We have been climbing, sweating, and sleeping in the same clothes for three full days. A hot shower is going to feel awful good.

Mike says, "Hey, let's make this easier and summit without the packs."

"Uh, I'd rather just bring them with us," I reply uneasily.

"Why lug 'em?" Mike asks. "Just leave 'em here, then get 'em on our way down."

I look again at the climbers on the Emmons-Winthrop route. After three long days of blazing our own path across glaciers slit by countless crevasses, I envy those climbers following the relative safety of the well-trodden snow trail. What Mike's proposing means cutting across additional unknown ground later this morning to reach the trail. Exhausted and wary, I'm apprehensive of traversing more untested glacier.

Studying the most direct route between us and the summit, the northwest snowfield, I see rocks around the edges and dirt sticking through the thin snow. No crevasses. I point at the snowfield.

"Let's go up this way and bring our packs with us," I suggest. "We'll summit and then just follow the main track down with every-one else."

"Why waste all that energy?" Mike responds. "After we summit, we can pick up our gear here, and then contour across to the trail."

I roll it over in my mind. Mike had been ill last night, probably from exhaustion and moderate altitude sickness, so we don't want to push too hard. I don't want to make an issue of a minor strategic difference, especially when we're almost done. The summit sits just 800 vertical feet above us, so reaching the top should not take very long. The packs can stay.

AFTER WE FINISH stowing our gear, we each shove an ice hammer into the snow, handle first, and clip our pack to it. Spaced our usual fifty feet apart, we tie back into the thin glacier rope that tethers us together. Grabbing the map, cameras, and one water bottle, we start up the final snowfield to the summit. Mike heads out, wearing his crampons, holding an ice ax in his right hand.

As he climbs, Mike probes the ground in front of him to check for possible crevasses hidden beneath the snow. Before each step, he plunges his ax handle in, feeling for resistance. When he pushes and the ax won't go any farther, he figures the ground ahead is strong enough to hold him.

Our fifty-centimeter, technical ice axes were perfect for the steep terrain we ascended the last few days. But here on the low-angled snow slope, an ice ax that measures less than twenty inches is way too short. Touching the spike to the ground requires bending over and reaching out. It's annoying, but we have no choice. It won't last long, so we hunch over and keep probing the snow as we go.

We climb this last simple section without helmets, switching the lead, taking turns out front as we share the joy of topping out on a clear, bluebird day.

We should be moving more quickly—we're not carrying any weight, and we both slept okay. But the air is thin, the strenuous alpine climbing wore us down, and the fire of exhaustion burns in our legs, so it's still a trudge. I pause briefly between steps to let my thigh muscles rest a bit.

Between panting breaths, I look west toward the Liberty Cap, which we climbed across yesterday. By comparing it to our current position, I estimate our elevation to be about 14,200 feet. We're getting real close.

Mike's out front. Atop a small, rocky ridge, he stops, turns to face me, and casually takes in the rope as I approach. He's not belaying me, so I know the climbing is easy and that he's waiting for me to reach him so we can summit together.

I crest the small rise and see that we are on the highest portion of the summit crater rim. Below us in the giant circular bowl are a dozen climbers, some resting and some creeping across the inner crater floor toward us and Rainier's true summit, the Columbia Crest. Savoring our sweet moment of success, we walk together one hundred feet westward, to the summit. Mike drops the coiled rope, throws both hands into the air, and says, "Hey!"

I step toward Mike and we execute a manly handshake–hug–back slap. We have the top to ourselves. Totally safe here on the dirt, we untie from the rope. After three long days and nights being tied to each other, it feels strange not to be tethered to Mike. But we relish strolling independently about the flat summit.

Looking south, I see the lesser Cascade volcanoes. Mount Adams is closest, and the exploded shell of Mount Saint Helens sits farther away. In the distance rests the white, blurry triangle of Mount Hood, in Oregon. Mike opens our water bottle and passes it to me without taking a sip. Only forty minutes out of camp, we aren't dehydrated and there is plenty of water, but I still appreciate Mike letting me drink first. I slug down two gulps of melted glacier and feel residual volcanic grit settle on my gums.

"We did it, man," I say as I hand the bottle to Mike.

"We sure did. You know, there're very few people I could have done that route with, even other instructors."

I'm stunned to be compared favorably to Mike's Outward Bound colleagues, and I'm pleased by his compliment and his confidence. I reply, "Well, there's no one else I could have done a route that serious with."

We grin at each other from behind our dark glasses.

Breaking out the cameras, we take summit photos of each other with the southern Cascades in the background. Soon another climber arrives, alone. I wonder if he ascended the whole mountain solo; or maybe his partners are resting down on the crater floor, unable to muster the energy for the last leg to the summit. He bubbles with energy and spits out that this is his one hundredth summit of Mount Rainier. Impressed, I offer my congratulations, then turn to

Mike and drop my jaw silently. Mike nods his head in approval and says, "His hundredth summit, our first. Only ninety-nine more to go and we tie him."

The climber then talks into a radio, describing the summit view to someone. Confused at first, we soon understand that he is talking to people in a small plane circling overhead. His friends in the airplane are there to celebrate with him and probably take photos. It dawns on me that our presence may be detracting from his big moment, so we shuffle off the summit a dozen yards. Gripping his ax in his right hand and the radio in his left, he throws his arms wide above his head and holds them there while the plane makes a low pass.

About then, a party of four climbers arrives at the summit. After they celebrate, I ask one of them to take our picture. The easterly wind puffs up my hood and whips around the drawstrings of Mike's wool hat. We toss an arm over each other's shoulders and the climber snaps a photo of Mike and me on the summit of Mount Rainier.

IT'S NOW AFTER nine A.M., and more climbers are arriving. I am surprised to see so many mountaineers, then remember that it's Sunday, June 21. I think of my dad, twenty-five hundred miles away, and silently wish him a happy Father's Day. About a dozen people tag the top, take photos, and leave, with most of them retreating south to the standard Disappointment Cleaver route. A few head back down the northeast side of Rainier to descend the Winthrop and Emmons Glaciers. Time for us to get going, too.

We rope up again and head back down the northwest slope of the summit cone, alone. Following our solid tracks in the snow, we reach our packs in less than thirty minutes and prepare to traverse eastward so we can join the standard route on the Winthrop and

Emmons. The Emmons itself is nearly five miles long, and together these two glaciers form the biggest mass of ice in the United States outside of Alaska.

With the solstice sun now high in the sky, we are sweaty, so we strip off our pile jackets, put our shell jackets back on, and then squirm into our chest harnesses. Staring eastward across the upper Winthrop Glacier, I see curved crevasses and ice blocks the size of vans thrust up out of the snow. I say, "Let's play heads-up here, okay?"

"You seem nervous as a cat. What's up?" Mike asks.

"I'm okay. I just don't like the looks of this."

Mike studies the untracked terrain lying between us and the established snow trail off in the distance.

"We've been through a lot worse in the last few days," he says. "We'll be fine."

By ten A.M. we are moving, with Mike leading the way. Cool breezes roll across the glacier as we navigate around some obvious crevasses. Seeing the cracks so close, I constantly scan right and left, looking for trouble, and I feel my confidence ebbing.

The warming snow balls up beneath our metal crampons. Quickly, the snow trapped beneath my boots grows several inches thick, and it's like walking with a tennis ball stuck to the bottom of each foot. I pause, lift one boot, and bang the side of my crampon sharply with the shaft of my ax, knocking the snow off. I switch legs and clean the other boot. Mike and I soon synchronize our crampon-cleaning breaks to reduce the number of stops.

We cut above some linear crevasses. I find myself nervously measuring our progress to the established trail ahead: We're halfway across; two-thirds; almost there.

A short rest would be nice, but with tilting ice chunks poised just above us, we push on.

Another one hundred feet and we finally reach the snow trail stomped out by all the passing climbers. I exhale deeply and let my chest loosen up. Now we are on the main descent route, and we are no longer alone. There are probably twenty people on the route, most above us, a few below.

We drop our packs onto the snow, taking a break. Mike picks through our food bag—there's very little left, but that's okay because we should be off the mountain in another four or five hours.

"You want the greasy cheese or the granola crumbs?" he asks.

"Uh, sounds great. I'll take the cheese."

I gnaw indifferently on the slimy yellow cheddar and grin as I watch Mike chase granola bits around a clear plastic bag. He licks a finger, stuffs it into a corner of the crumpled sack, and, like an anteater feeding, pulls out a few morsels. After he sees that I'm amused, he makes a big show of licking each crumb off his dirty finger. I shake my head and we both laugh. Steady wind from the east chills us, so we don't linger long. Mike heads right down the trail at a good clip, and when the rope between us tightens, I follow. The morning sun casts sparkles and shadows across the glacier.

Going straight down means that to stay centered over my feet, I have to bend at the knees and lower my butt. We're descending fast; after twenty minutes, my thighs are on fire.

When the snow softens a bit, I start plunging my heels into the glacier's surface. Driving my heels down dents a firm, flat platform for my foot. Mike is heel-plunging now, too. This takes more effort, but our pace doesn't slacken much. I feel a bit rushed and nauseous; maybe I'm altitude sick from sleeping so high last night. I shout ahead to Mike, "Hold up!"

Mike halts, then turns to face me.

"I don't think I've got the oomph right now to heel-plunge. Let's sidestep."

"That'll be slow."

"Yeah, but I don't want to trip."

Mike's right that we should keep moving downhill as best we can. But I can see he knows I'm fried, so he relents without making me feel bad.

"Okay, we'll try it for a while."

Turning sideways, I stretch my downhill leg below me and press the uphill edge of that boot into the snow. Next, I shuffle my higher foot down to join the lower boot, and then reset my ice ax down-slope. This jerky motion is slower, but the pauses give me the half-second rests I need. I settle into a rhythm, as does Mike, and we steadily descend the glacier.

We drop another few hundred feet, and three climbers with day-packs pass us. We watch them descend ahead of us and curve to the right. The trail down the glacier is an impromptu path of footprints stomped solid by scores of climbers. It has been over a week since the last snowstorm, so all the repetitive footsteps have consolidated a track in the snow at least ten feet wide. In some sections, mean-dering climbers have packed it out almost twenty feet across.

The path is reassuring: Dozens of others have trod here without trouble.

When the trail cuts abruptly in a new direction, sometimes the cause is obvious—like an open crevasse, a sagging snow bridge, or a teetering ice buttress. Other times, the reason for the sudden direc-tion change is not clear. Whatever the case, we follow the proven footprints before us. The next hundred yards of climber's trail is eas-ily seen, but farther ahead it intermittently disappears as it drops be-hind snow hills, swings below small ice cliffs, and meanders laterally across the glacier.

We stomp along for a while, passing ascending climbing teams. Some climbers notice our short ice axes and helmets and ask where we've been; one guy even correctly surmises that we climbed the Liberty. We are still wearing our helmets, which puts us in the mi-nority on the Emmons-Winthrop route. An hour earlier we had talked about taking the helmets off and strapping them on our packs. But since we'd have to lug the weight anyway, we figured we might as well keep them on our heads.

This downhill trudge gets monotonous. Mike must be feeling it too, because he suddenly turns around to talk. With a mischievous lilt in his voice, he drawls out, "Hey...Jim?"

"Yeah," I answer.

"Whatever you do, don't think about a hot fudge sundae."

"Aaah, crap! Why did you bring that up?" I say in mock disgust and anger.

"Don't think about the chocolate," Mike goes on. "Don't think about the nuts. I don't want you thinking about that."

"Thanks. Thanks a lot, Mike," I say.

We walk in silence for a minute while I scheme. Then I shout, "I promise not to do that, as long as you don't think about a cold, frosty beer with foam on it about two inches tall running down the side."

Mike groans in happy longing. Ha! We're even.

Motoring downhill, I give some serious thought to dinner. We should easily make it to the campground tonight. I know Mike's self-discipline and meager budget means he'll vote for generic pasta in the campground. But maybe I'll insist on treating us to steaks and beers.

THE SUMMIT CRATER far above us now blocks the wind, so it feels warmer, and the surface of the glacier is like wet oatmeal, three inches deep. As we descend, we pass a few climbers moving downhill more slowly than us. We zig and zag our way downhill, traversing onto the Emmons Glacier proper, and reach an elevation of about 12,000 feet.

Mike asks, "Feeling better now that the air is thicker?"

"Yep. I feel pretty good."

"Well, let's try and glissade."

Glissading is basically sliding downhill on the snow; you sit down on your butt or, more rarely, stand up and ski on your boots. When the slope's angle and the snow's consistency are just right, glissading can be a fast way to descend, and pretty fun, too. We know that if we glissade, we must pay strict attention to avoid losing control, going over cliffs, smashing into rocks, or plunging into crevasses.

Glissading would give our weary legs a break, so it sounds tempting. But we are still on the glacier. We should probably just walk the Emmons and then glissade later, on the Inter Glacier, where there are almost no crevasses. But I don't want to sound weak or be the naysayer by bringing this up. I'm afraid Mike will think less of me if I keep presenting risks. So I don't say anything direct. Instead, I waffle.

"Well," I say, "do you think we should?"

"Yeah, we'll make better time."

So we sit down and get ready. We remove our crampons— leaving them on would be asking for them to snag and break an ankle—and tuck them inside our packs, where they can't grab the snow.

We strap our ice hammers to our packs, move about forty feet away from each other, and sit down in the snow. I stay on the known climber's path while Mike places himself off the trail to my right, so we can glissade almost parallel to each other. We each hold an ice ax like a canoe paddle to steer ourselves and to use as a brake. With a mutual nod, we scoot our butts forward and begin sliding downhill on the wet snow. My nylon climbing pants hiss as they glide across the glacier's surface.

After a few minutes, Mike halts. Since we're roped together, I skid to a stop, too. I stand and scan the next section of glacier below us.

"Looks safe ahead, Mike. No drop-offs or anything."

"You're moving slower. Take your pack off and drag it behind, like me."

So I slip off my pack and clip it with a carabiner and sling to my waist harness. We push off at the same time and resume the glissade. Mike was right: Having my pack off makes me faster. But my tethered pack keeps flipping, flopping, and crashing into me from behind—a pain.

The descent path has been mostly straight so far, but now it angles left, so we stop, stand up, and brush off the clingy snow. We pull our packs on and walk laterally on the snow trail until we are above the next linear section. Then we plop down and glissade again.

Soon the snow path has so many meandering portions that we have to walk more and our overall progress is about the same as two other climbers who are hiking downhill. We pass them glissading, and they pass us each time we stop. Because we have our crampons off, when we walk laterally we're less secure and less speedy than the other climbers, so the two of them keep catching up with us, then waiting behind us. Mike is leading now, and as the follower I grow sick of feeling pressed by the other team's front climber, who walks right on my heels.

"Mike," I yell, "hold up."

I let them go by me, which means Mike must also. I trade friendly nods with the rear climber as he passes me.

At about 11,500 feet, Mike and I see the trail below us head into a long, linear section of the glacier. This semipermanent feature is called the Corridor, and its smooth, gentle slopes are known to have few crevasses. The Corridor is in the middle of the glacier, and the unrelenting ice pressure from the two sides probably closes many of the tension cracks. I can see that the trail runs fairly straight down the slope's fall line to about 10,000 feet. This should give us fast, easy access to the glacier's end at Camp Schurman, located at 9,460 feet, where a little humpbacked hut of a ranger station is tucked in against jutting volcanic rocks.

The two climbers who just passed us stop to eat and fiddle with their gear. We walk past them yet again, and line ourselves up at the upper entrance to the Corridor. Jumbled garage-sized blocks of glacial ice, separated by cracks and sagging holes, line both sides of this alley. Danger hovers on either side, but the clear path down the middle seems inviting. Across the whole landscape lies a deep blanket of snow.

It doesn't look like we can quite make a single straight run all the way down, but we will be able to slide downhill for quite a ways before having to move eastward so we can resume our descent.

I take the lead spot on the rope and step off the trail to the left. This allows Mike to stay on the wide communal trail to my right, and slightly above me. With a push of our ice axes, we are once again sliding downhill on our butts. I sit up as tall as I can and lift my head to look out for any danger.

About every hundred feet, we stop by digging the bluntly pointed spikes of our ice ax shafts into the snow. Then one of us stands to scout the trail ahead, make sure it is safe, and adjust our route if necessary. During one stop, I stand, then turn back and look over my left shoulder. We're several hundred feet below where we left those two other climbers. A snow-covered ice hummock lies between us and them now, so we can no longer see each other. Mike and I resume sliding downhill.

The smooth snow slope in front of me looks fine, but as we descend I sense the terrain changing off to my left. I can't see a section of the ground over there, which suggests that a drop-off lies ahead. I snap my left arm high above my shoulder with an open hand—the signal for Mike to stop. I grab my ax with both hands and brake hard.

I stand up and peer to my left. I still can't see the actual problem, but it doesn't feel right. When I look up at Mike, he is rolled onto his left side, ice ax held in both hands, poised to drive it into the snow for an anchor. Not knowing why I signaled for a stop, he is ready to belay me if necessary. He lifts his head a bit, glances the fifty feet downslope at me, and yells, "What is it?"

"Not sure. I think there are crevasses in front of us."

"Go take a look," Mike says.

I pull on my pack, shimmying into the shoulder straps, and make sure the rope isn't snagged on any ice protrusions. Looking upslope, I watch Mike stab the sharp pick of his ax firmly, and kick his boot toes deep into the snow as an anchor. Satisfied with his secured position, he gives me a nod. I return the nod and turn downslope.

Probing ahead of myself with my ice ax, I walk cautiously forward two steps, tightening slack from the rope. My internal danger meter kicks up a notch. I instinctively pump my left hand into a fist—the signal for Mike to watch me and hold on tight. I raise my voice: "Tension."

My attention is focused ahead, but I feel the rope tug reassuringly at my waist. Mike has me. Holding my ax at the ready, I creep forward another half step and see the ground drop off below me. I stare into a dark hole. My stomach clenches, and I suck in a short burst of air.

It's not a singular cliff but, rather, a series of descending vertical steps, each one formed by loose, leaning ice blocks the size of tractor-trailers. Each step drops off about ten feet more than the last, and between each tilted ice block is a gaping crevasse, mostly camouflaged by snow. It looks like an ice serac has collapsed from below and sucked the broken glacier pieces seventy feet deeper into the Earth. Beyond the collapsed hole I see transverse crevasses, all stretching east-west, contouring across the slope.

I look over my right shoulder and see the rope stretch tightly back to Mike. Still pinning himself to the ground, he is on his stomach, ice ax muscled diagonally across his chest in a classic self-arrest position. He stares at the snow an inch from his face, focused on being our team's anchor.

I ease back a step and the piano wire of a rope relaxes. Mike feels our lifeline slacken and looks over his right shoulder at me, but keeps us anchored. I exhale hard to force myself to calm down.

"Whoa, big crevasse down here, Mike. We're not going this way."

I back off a few feet to a safe spot. The slack rope flops to the ground, so Mike sits up.

"Okay," he hollers back, pointing. "Why don't you cross beneath me, to the right, to get away from it."

I walk a few steps back east and stand on the broad trail of footprints. The late morning sun beats down on us. Even though we are only wearing Gore-Tex shells over a single layer of polypro long underwear, sweat soaks my skin.

I look directly uphill at Mike resting on the snow trail above me and say, "Water up."

I drop my pack, and Mike slides out of his. As we drink, I survey our surroundings. We're at about 11,000 feet. Another hour and we'll be off the glacier. A few more hours of hiking over glacial scree, then through old-growth forest, and we should make it to the rental car tonight—and maybe those steaks and beers.

Time to get going. I pull my pack back on and study the communal trail ahead. By contouring to the right across the slope, I can traverse over five yards and align myself directly above the next straight downhill section of the climber's path.

I turn upslope to Mike, fifty feet away. He is on the stomped-out snow trail, watching me.

"Ready?"

"Ready," Mike says, nodding.

"I'm going to cut right."

"Sounds good," Mike answers.

I'm facing directly east, perpendicular to the slope's fall line. I'll go about fifteen feet or so, which will tighten the rope between us. This will leave Mike still on the snow path and put me on the right-hand side of the trail, where we can again glissade straight down.

I scan the snow-covered glacier surface before me, but I don't see any signs of trouble. No accumulated dust in a low spot. No cracks. No sags.

CHAPTER 10

▲ ▲ ▲

THE SNOW FEELS dense and firm as I shove the handle of my ice ax into the glacier's surface. Satisfied, I take a step and sink ankle-deep into wet snow before settling onto solid ice beneath.

I probe the snow again, and it feels strong, so I step forward; but in an instant my boot pushes deeper into the glacier than before. My mind tries to comprehend what's going on.

The next few seconds unfold in what feels like an eternity. As I tip forward and start sinking into the snow, I realize what is happening: I've walked onto a snow bridge spanning a hidden crevasse, a plank of snow crystals terribly weakened by the sun-baked days, and it's crumbling beneath my feet.

"FALLING!" I scream as loud as I can, trying to warn Mike. I can't see him behind me. But I know he's flopping onto his belly and ramming the pick of his ax into the ice, digging in, fighting to save me and, maybe, himself.

In the next fraction of a second, the snow consumes my legs as if it is quicksand. By now, I've sunk into the snow bridge to my abdomen. A hope shoots through my mind: Maybe my pack will jam and stop me. It doesn't, and I slam through the ever-widening hole.

I react instinctively, swinging the ax in my right hand, hoping to catch solid ice with the sharpened tip and stop my plunge.

The pick of the ax cuts into the mush in a spray of ice and snow. While shouting to Mike again, I feel my face crash against the crevasse lip.

A finger of pain shoots up between my eyes, and my feet flap in nothingness.

The fall is sudden, shocking. I slip through the snow bridge, and the icy, black crevasse swallows me. The most terrifying nightmare of glacier climbers has arrived.

For a moment, I hope that it's just a small crevasse. Ten feet deep. A hard landing, then a quick climb out. I feel fear but not terror. I know Mike heard me and saw me. I know he's solid. I know any moment the rope will jerk me to a stop.

But I don't slow down—I pick up speed.

My body explodes with adrenaline, and my mind furiously calculates as I plunge ever deeper.

Ten feet. Twenty feet. Thirty feet. I'm going too fast. Something's wrong.

I rocket through the gloom, crashing back and forth between the ice walls, squeezed ever more tightly in the grip of an enormous slot. The rope jerks hard, and for the briefest moment I hope Mike has stopped the disaster. But just as quickly the tension is gone, and I accelerate wildly. I know now I have dragged Mike in behind me.

I careen off the walls, get knocked sideways, and smash to a stop on my back. I hit so hard the air bursts from my lungs.

Blinking and gasping, I fight to get a breath. I touch the wall with my gloved hand, and there is no noise.

I just fell all that way, and I'm not too badly hurt.

I wiggle, and pain stabs my neck. Then something lands on my belly. *Whump.* It is a handful of wet, sloppy snow. A pinhole of light high above me flickers, and more wet snow hits me in the face. The light blinks again, and more slushy snow pours onto me. The snow falls faster and harder and bigger. *Whump. Whump. Whump, whump, whump.* The slurry pours in like a wet avalanche racing down a mountain, burying my shins, my thighs, my belly.

Oh my God. I'm being buried.

I toss my arms above myself; then the wet slop buries my head.

AFTER A FEW more distant impacts, there is silence and darkness beneath this cocoon of snow. I wonder whether it's quiet now because the snow has ceased falling or because I am buried so deep that I can no longer hear what's happening on top of the thick snowpack. The silence terrifies me.

I open my eyes—at least I think I do—but blackness envelops me. To make sure they're actually open, I blink a few times and feel sharp snow grains scratch my eyelids.

I see nothing. I'm buried alive.

Terror surges from my gut. I exhale heavily through my mouth and nose and feel the air flow out, then bounce right back onto my face. My left forearm remains draped across my face; it has preserved a small open space.

I need air.

I bash my forehead against the snow, trying to enlarge the small pocket around my face. The void around my head is half the size of a basketball.

I suck in hard, trying to grab a breath, but my mouth is half-filled with crunchy snow, so I pull in only a small gulp of air. I try chewing the snow to clear it away, but it is too much, as if someone has stuffed a Popsicle into my mouth. I work my jaw and tongue, struggling to push out the rapidly hardening snow clump. But it turns into a dense lump the size of a plum. When I rest for a second, the snowball settles back in my throat and gags me. Afraid that the obstruction will choke me, I push it forward and off to one side with my tongue. I can breathe a bit more easily, so I pant in a few strained gasps from my air pocket.

I know from avalanche classes that I must get out of the snow fast or I will die here. But I can't sit up—the wet slop sucks heavily at my arms and legs and chest. A great weight pins down my legs and torso. My pack, corked fast between the walls of the crevasse, anchors my shoulders, pinning me.

Full-blown panic sets in. I push with all my might, but I can't move. It feels as though I'm being held down by a thousand cold, wet hands.

Try again.

When I attempt to curl my torso up, my pelvic muscles feel like they're ripping. Sensing that the effort is futile, I stop, and my heart hammers in my chest.

Avalanches tumble their victims wildly, and buried survivors sometimes don't even know which way is up. I worry that maybe I'm not even facing upward, and that I am trying to go the wrong way. Using another avalanche survival tip, I intentionally drool saliva out over my lips. Gravity pulls the spittle back down my cheek, and I feel it ooze toward my right ear. The technique works; I know I'm still facing up.

I struggle to wiggle anything—a hand, a foot. Nothing. Suddenly, a wetness warms my crotch, and I realize I'm peeing. In total fear, I'm peeing. A flash of shame passes over me because I think it means I'm weak. But a survival voice in my head screams like a drill sergeant, *It doesn't matter! It's just your body getting ready to fight. So fight, damn it!*

I try pushing my chest up again, until my torn abs protest.

My God, I'm really stuck. I'm covered and I'm stuck.

I don't feel wounded—no broken bones, no crippling pain, no gushing blood. How, I wonder, could I have fallen that far and not be wrecked? My God, I think sadly, Gloria was right: I'm going to die on a mountain. I figure I have enough air to last maybe ten minutes. But what if it's longer? Just gasping away and waiting for the end?

The reality of it all is overpowering. I'm not badly injured; I feel like I could stand up and walk away. But I'm going to die anyway. There's some air in the void around my face, but it won't last. I almost wish I were more hurt so that I would go faster. I can think clearly, I can feel my whole body. But I'm going to suffocate slowly.

This is a bad way to go. I wish I'd been killed in the fall.

Death will come in ten minutes if I'm lucky, maybe twenty minutes if I'm not. It doesn't seem fair. I push again. Still nothing.

Get out before it freezes. Sit up. Get out. I can't breathe.

I pant for air, but my exhaled breaths bounce off the icy surface lining my small air space and flow back across my wet face.

I'm running out of air. Maybe this is it.

I try to accept that my life may end here, alone. With loving parents and a great wife, I have had a good life. I tell myself to remain calm, to face what happens, not in terror—I have never lived that way—but in peace.

Ride it out. Ride it out as best you can, all the way to the end, the same way you've lived your life.

But I don't want to die. I want to live.

LETTING MY MIND drift away in fear makes me lose my focus on keeping the snowball safely off to one side of my mouth. The slippery chunk slides farther back and blocks my airway for an instant. Reflexive gagging shoots another surge of adrenaline through my veins and a pulse of fight back into my heart.

I remember an old adage from the martial arts classes I took years ago, before I became a climber: "Focus your power." So instead of trying to push all over, I concentrate on my strong arm, the right one. I imagine all my power flowing to my right arm, and I shove. I feel something heavy—an ice chunk the size of a cinder block—shift off my forearm, and my right hand bursts out of the snow above me. Waving my hand about in the air, I sense openness and freedom.

I desperately grope around with that hand, sweeping the surface, and I can hear crunching through the snow above my head. My fingers brush against our rope. When I realize I can push aside the loose snow on my face, I frantically start thrashing at the mush, shoving handfuls of it away.

The air I'm breathing grows stale.

I can't breathe. Hurry up! Faster, faster!

I'm digging, making progress—stay calm.

I feel like I'm the third person in the conversation, the mediator who has to balance the emotional and logical voices, who has to decide who is right each second. It is a strange thing, this battle of wills between the voices. I am buoyed by their resilient tone, and a spark of hope flickers in my heart. Maybe I can make it.

My gloved fingers scratch furiously at the frozen debris around my face. As I dig deeper toward my head, the crunching sound grows louder. I feel the slop above my right eye move. I paw and grasp, and my hand sweeps across my eye. And then it is clear, and I can see up a little tunnel through the snow and make out a hand in the gloom. I am so disoriented that at first I don't realize it's my own hand in my own purple glove.

Dense, cool air flows down the foot-long snow tunnel and settles on the wet skin of my right cheek. I dig the hole wider, reaching my nose and then clearing off my mouth. Desperate to breathe freely, I make a one-finger sweep of my own mouth and pluck out the cursed ice ball. Finally, I can take an unconstrained breath. I suck in a bunch of rushed gasps, blood ringing in my ears. My eyes dart back and forth as if I'm a cornered animal.

My heart slams hard and rapid against my sternum.

Bring it down. Bring it down.

The grip of fear is tightening. I try calming myself—I'm not going to suffocate. I can last an hour under here, but I've got to get out of the snow before it sets up and I'm stuck for good. Fumbling around, I grab handfuls of snow, tossing them behind me, one after another, as quickly as I can. I'm in a race, and if I lose, I die.

"Mike!" I scream.

Probably only a couple of minutes have passed since I plunged through that snow bridge, dragging Mike into the crevasse behind me. In the terrifying moments that followed, I was so occupied with trying to gulp in air that I hadn't thought clearly about my partner, my friend. Wondering where he is, I figure that since he fell in after me, he's got to be on top of the snow.

"Michael!" I yell again.

Thrashing around with my right arm, I hit his plastic climbing boot, knocking it sideways in front of the tunnel above my face.

He's on top. Thank God.

My eyes feel very wide open, as if someone is pulling back the lids—and a flurry of screams erupt from my mouth.

"Michael, get up! We've landed and we're covered with snow. Jesus, get up and dig us out. Get up quick!"

My words reverberate between the frozen walls, but I hear no other sound.

"Mike, we fell in, we fell in, I'm buried," I shout. "Dig me out."

I hear a muffled moan. I think for an instant it's muted because the snow is jammed up next to my ears, so I call out again.

"You gotta get up," I yell as I shake Mike's foot to rouse him.

I hear another moan. Maybe he doesn't know where I am. Still buried to my chin, I wave my free arm wildly, until it bumps into Mike's calf.

"Mike, I'm right here," I yell in desperation. "Michael, get up! Dig us out before it freezes up!"

For a moment, I believe Mike is merely stunned. But his leg doesn't move. Then I realize he's probably hurt, bad. He can't hear me, or he doesn't understand what I'm saying, or he can't move. He can't dig himself out—or me. I have to get out myself, and I have to help Mike.

I feel an incredible weight settle onto me, the burden of sole responsibility for our survival. I moan as the emotional side of my brain comprehends what my logical side has already realized.

Furiously pushing snow with my right hand, I widen the hole around my face. A minute passes, and I uncover my neck. I am making some progress, but an inner critic in my mind lashes out:

You're digging too slow—you're never going to get out.

Mike's breathing is slow, labored. My first-aid training kicks in, and I remember that words of encouragement can sustain someone badly hurt.

"I can't get to you yet, Mike, but I'm trying," I yell. "I've gotta dig out. I'm coming."

TOSSING A HANDFUL of snow over my shoulder, I realize it is falling down behind me, but I don't know where or how far. Clearing away more snow from around me, I am still buried from the chest down. My head and right arm protrude from the snowy floor of the shallow depression I have dug around myself. It's been five or ten minutes since we fell in, so my eyes now focus better in the near darkness. I can make out Mike's other boot on the opposite side of my snow basin. His feet are pointed toes down, on either side of my head, and I assume he's facedown, with his head positioned way down near my feet.

Staring at the sole of his boot, I grab his ankle and shake it.

"Michael, wake up!" I plead.

I hear a single moan.

Then Mike's breathing grows raspy. I have never heard this sound before, but it horrifies me to my very core.

"Michael! Michael!" I scream.

I know now that he is on the edge, and I try to keep him going.

"Breathe, Michael, breathe!" I shout.

It occurs to me that if I dig out my left arm, I'll be able to uncover myself and more quickly get to Mike. Fumbling around in the near darkness, grabbing handfuls of snow, I find an ice ax. I use the scoop-shaped adze on the ax's head to dig faster. As the basin around me gets wider, Mike's feet flop down near my face, so I have to move my head to dodge his boots, as well as my own swiping ice ax.

All the while I try connecting with Mike, to keep him sucking in breaths.

"Come on, Michael, breathe!" I shout. "Breathe! Hang in there!"

Finally, I extricate my left arm from the snow. Frantic, I try to sit up, but can't.

I hear his sputtering breath. Then an exhaling sigh. Then: silence.

I freeze, staring straight ahead. Eyes wide, I remain motionless, listening. Clutching the ice ax in mid-swing, I realize I'm holding my breath.

Maybe he's just between breaths. Maybe I can't hear him with all the snow crunching around my ears. Quiet!

I wait three, four, five seconds, and I know he's really not breathing.

"Mike!" I scream in a rising pitch. I grab his calf and shake the hell out of it. Through his climbing pants, I pinch his calf hard, trying to get a reaction. Nothing.

Panic clutches me, and I thrash violently at the snow, trying to break free, trying to get to my partner. In frustration I punch the snow pile.

"Mike!" I screech again, my shrill voice cracking.

I open my hand and let the ice ax go. I sense it slipping past my right ear and disappearing into the blackness behind me, far from reach. A critical voice in my mind hisses, *Stupid move.*

I try again to sit up. But something holds me back: my helmet. It's caught on something behind me, probably my pack. I pull hard on the chin-strap buckle to loosen it. I yank the nylon strap up over my nose, and as it drags across my face, I feel stinging pain—I must be cut up. When I let go of the strap, my helmet falls behind me, and I hear it bounce away. *Clunk. Clunk.* Silence. *Clunk.*

I sweep aside mounds of wet snow with both arms, digging my way laterally toward Mike's head, which is still out of sight and out of reach. I can now see along the backs of his legs up past his knees. My fingers hook on something as I dig, and when I pull, I snag the brim of Mike's helmet. Touching his helmet confuses me, because it should be on his head, which is way down near my feet, not up here, next to my chest.

I dig again, and on the next scoop, I hit Mike's sunglasses. Mike's head seems to be here near my chest, facing upward. But that can't be as his feet are here too, but facing downward. I brush aside loose snow next to his sunglasses and see Mike's cheek. Relieved to have found him, I clear more snow off his face, but I'm still confused as to how both his head and his feet are up near my chest.

Then I understand.

Mike is on his back, facing up. His legs have been bent way too far up toward his head. So far that his feet are just behind his ears. He's folded over.

I brush more snow from his face, and his head flops gently to the left side, toward me.

I reach into his mouth, pulling out a bunch of snow. I start to do it again, but I fear that I will make him vomit and choke, so I make a baby sweep with one finger.

"Mike! Mike!" I scream.

I grab his cheek, pinching and twisting the flesh as hard as I can, giving it everything I have. Pain is a powerful thing, and humans—even ones knocked out or on the edge of death—respond to it.

Nothing happens.

I rip a wet purple glove off my right hand and reach to his neck, checking for a pulse, but I feel nothing. My fingers shake against my friend's neck.

This can't be real. This can't be real.

CHAPTER 11

▲ ▲ ▲

EVERY SECOND THAT ticks by, the chances that I can save Mike—or myself—drop perceptibly.

A little light filters through the gloom, and I can see some details. Mike, doubled over on top of me, is in big trouble.

With Mike's head on my chest, and me still trapped behind and beneath him, I twist my upper torso and crane my neck sideways to look at his face. I detect no movement in his lips, nose, or cheeks. Tucking my face close to his, I feel for his breath against my cheek while I stare down at his torso. I pray to see his chest rise or feel his puffs of life against my wet face, but my spirits sink further as I detect nothing. Again I place my fingers on his neck and press, trying to find a pulse, but my hands are so cold from clawing at the snow for the last few minutes that I don't know whether to trust the fact that I feel only stillness.

Random loops of our climbing rope arc in and out of the snow, snagging my arms and hampering my movements. Claustrophobia grips me as I tussle to maneuver while still buried to my sternum in our cramped little snow pile. Mike faces up with his legs doubled up toward his face, in a hyperextended pike position. His feet dangle up by his head and by my head. One of his boots sticks in my face, next to my ear.

I know I must move his legs out of the way so I can reach his mouth and nose to breathe for him, but the thought scares the hell out of me. What if he has a spinal cord injury?

I realize I don't have any choice—I've got to try to breathe for him, and the only way I can get to his face is to flip his legs out of my way. If I don't breathe for him, it won't matter if his spine is damaged.

I grab both of Mike's legs and push them upright into the air, away from me, closing my eyes and turning my head away—I can't stand to see it. Trying to lessen the impact, I grasp the loose nylon fabric of his climbing pants and ease his limbs downward. When the snow encasing me to my belly won't let me stretch any farther, I open my hands and let go. Mike's legs flop over to a normal position and his boots plop softly into the snow on the far end of the ledge. The thought of what I may have just done to my friend forces a small gurgle of horror from my throat.

Now I can easily get my face to his. With my right thumb and index finger, I pinch Mike's nose closed. I open my mouth wide and seal it around his. I blow a puff of air into him, but it shoots right back out, as if it didn't go very far.

Oh God, he didn't use it.

I tilt his forehead back a little and lift his chin, then give him another strong breath. I get more air in this time, and it seems like the air goes in deeper. When I pull my head back, I watch his chest and see it drop down: good. I got air in and it flowed back out. But it feels as though I'm just blowing into a balloon and the air is escaping as soon as I pull my mouth away.

I puff into him again. This time I just retract my lips and remain stationed right over Mike's mouth. When the air rushes back out, it flows right into my mouth and nose. We are truly sharing breaths. In our shared air I taste and smell a slightly sour odor. Is it me? Is it him? Doesn't matter. It is us.

I HAVE TO start chest compressions. Mike's head rests on my chest, and I'm basically behind him, fighting the ice wall and the snow pile to position my left arm. I torque my shoulder, hover my left palm over his sternum, and push down hard with the heel of my hand. But with Mike resting on the layer of loose snow that's trapped between us, it feels like all I'm doing is shoving him down deeper into the slop. It doesn't feel as though I've compressed his chest enough to force life-giving blood through his body.

I know that I should be compressing with both hands, but I can't. Our bodies are a tangled mess. Since I am trapped below him, I simply cannot get above him to do compressions the way I have been trained to. I'm forced to reach around from behind him and lift my left arm above us both just to get one hand over his heart. I can't twist my body any farther or stretch my right arm high enough over Mike's head to reach his chest with my right hand. Getting one hand on him just above the sternum is all I can do.

With the next compression, I again mostly just shove him deeper into the snow jammed between us, and I feel Mike get pushed down against my body. I realize that since I'm trapped behind Mike's back, I can support him from below as I simultaneously press down from above. I sort of puff out my rib cage, wiggling so Mike's shoulder blades are squarely against me. Now I press down with my left hand on his sternum while thrusting up my own chest against Mike's back to support him, almost like sandwiching him between my open hand and my body. With me reaching around him from behind, it's sort of like performing a one-handed Heimlich maneuver.

It works better. His chest recoils, and I can feel that I'm actually doing some good. I get in another solid compression, and then switch back to breathing.

I blow a breath into his mouth, and seek some sign that he's responding. Seeing nothing reassuring, I do CPR again, and again. I had hoped that after just a few cycles, Mike would recover, wake up, and everything would be fine. None of that is happening.

It's not working.

I settle into a pattern: compressing his chest as hard as I can, cradling his head and pinching his nose with my right hand and blowing air into his lungs, and sweeping away snow with my left hand.

Compressions. Breathe. Sweep.

As I move more snow away from me, I become slowly able to sit up a little farther. Working my way out of the snowbank, I rise a bit higher above Mike, and I'm able to give more forceful compressions. But I can still get only one hand on his chest, because my right arm is still torqued and trapped behind Mike's head.

During all this action, I accidently knock off his sunglasses. I do not want to look right at Mike, but I need to. Although my training dictates that I study his pupils, I try hard not to actually stare into my friend's eyes, into his being.

Clinically, I note that his pupils are fixed. To test their reaction, I cover his open eyes with my right hand for a few seconds, then pull it away to see if the pupils respond to the shaft of sunlight stabbing down into the crevasse.

They don't. I shudder.

Maybe they're not responding because it's so dark in here. Keep going.

I see what looks like bruising behind his left ear and along his jawline. That's a bad sign, but I continue CPR. As I struggle to revive Mike, I begin to understand what is happening, though I don't want to accept it. It's been a while since I've heard or seen any sign of life from Mike. I'm losing him.

Compressions. Breathe. Sweep.

A blast that sounds as if it's from a rifle pierces the air, and instinct warns me that ice or snow has ripped free far over our heads and is screaming down through the crevasse. I lean over Mike's head to protect him from the falling debris—just as the professional rescuers showed me on Longs Peak last year—and throw my hands above my head. A snow slab whistles by just past our feet, crashing somewhere far below us in a thunderous explosion. Two seconds later, snow dust billows up from somewhere below and settles around us.

The near miss unnerves me, but I realize that more light is now streaming into the crevasse. I can see more clearly, so I slide my hand in front of Mike's eyes, blocking out the light. A new wave of sadness sweeps over me after I move my hand out of the way and confirm that his pupils don't react. My training tells me that I'm supposed to continue resuscitation until I'm either relieved by another rescuer or the patient is declared dead by a doctor. But those things won't happen—I'm the only one here. I don't want to quit. Not on Mike. It's not working, but I mechanically continue the CPR fight.

However, I also know that I can't prolong this exhausting effort forever. At some point, I have to stop, and I have to escape the snow before it locks me in. The tension between needing to continue and needing to stop tears at my heart.

Finally, I check for a pulse again and glance at his lips; they look blue. I move my hand in front of his eyes, and again I get no response.

"I think he's gone," I say to myself quietly.

I stop CPR, staring at Mike for about ten seconds. Nothing changes. I hope, illogically, that he'll take a breath. He doesn't.

Dumbfounded, I lift Mike's gloved hand off the snow. When I let it go, it flops limply back down.

I GENTLY LAY my head down on his chest and rest my arms across him, shaking with fear. Tears well up at the corners of my eyes.

If you let that come up, you're going to die down here.

I fight to force emotion back. I stare ahead, numb on every level, unable to move.

A voice inside my head pulls me back, shaking me from the shock—a desperate voice of survival, half emotional, half logical.

Dig. Dig out of the snow. Get out before it freezes up.

I pull my right arm out from behind Mike's head and furiously paw at the snow with both hands. I don't have the ice ax—I dropped it—and I'm momentarily angry at myself for that. A jolt of alarm hits me as I realize the consequences if I don't get out before this slurry freezes.

My breath bursts out in heavy wheezes. I dig madly and manage to get down to about my waist. Finally, I can move enough to loosen my pack's shoulder straps and waist belt and wiggle free.

Logically, rationally, I know I should keep digging to gradually free myself from the grip of this icy debris. My gut reaction, however, is to just wrench myself loose. I panic and try to push out of the snow all at once. But I'm stuck fast. It's like being buried in the sand at the beach.

"Slow down and dig," I say in a sort of lecture to myself.

I scratch away some more, and get down to my thighs. Mike is crammed in next to me, rope and gear are tangled all around us, and I'm so oppressively confined I feel like I might completely lose it.

I try to push free again. Nothing. I try yanking my left foot free, but all I manage to do is hyperextend my knee, causing a grotesque stab of pain.

I resume digging, and as I move the snow around, I realize that Mike has slid away from me a little. I don't want him to slip off our snow pile, so I grab the back of his jacket with one hand. His chest is squishing me against the left ice wall, and I know that digging myself out would be easier if I could sit him up for a minute. I stop and think about it. Part of me is worried about aggravating what I am sure is a serious spinal injury. Another part of me admits that any such worry is moot now.

"He's gone, and it's not going to hurt anymore," I mutter to myself sadly.

So I push him upright, which takes a lot of his weight off me and gives me more room to move. I clutch a handful of his jacket in my right hand while I dig with my left, and after a couple of minutes I manage to get my left foot free. The increased freedom is intoxicating, and in a rush I try yanking my right foot out. I feel my knee strain, so I stop pulling and dig some more.

I switch hands and hold Mike up with my left hand and dig with my right. Once I excavate to my calf, the weight on my lower leg lessens, and suddenly I can pull my right foot out of the snow. Elated, I watch my boot emerge from the hole, and relief washes over me. I'm out.

I lay Mike back down. Now that I am free and poised right above him, I realize that I'm in a better position to perform CPR. Somehow, I think, it will all be magically different this time, even though it's been five or ten minutes since I stopped.

I hunch over Mike, resting on one foot and one knee. With my fingers interlaced and both arms straight, I start giving strong compressions. I pause after every few pushes and blow air into his mouth. Nothing changes, but I continue, hoping for a miracle.

I keep going, though the work tires me. My calm, logical inner voice urges me to stop.

"Look at the medical signs," I softly say to myself.

Finally, I persuade myself to stop. Stopping the second time is harder. I know for certain that I will not try again. Mike is gone.

I lay my head down on Mike's chest again, bewildered, unable to comprehend what has happened.

KNEELING OVER MIKE, I stare at his rumpled jacket, unsure of what to do. A question rings loudly in my mind: *Where are we?*

I stand tentatively to look around. The crevasse walls are about two feet apart here, and they rise high above us on either side. How far, I'm not yet sure. I know on every level that I am in a desperate situation.

Leaning to the right, I stare over the drop-off behind Mike's head. I see the crevasse disappear into nothingness dozens of feet below us, and it's as if we're on a snow pile maybe seven feet long that holds us aloft between the ice walls. Mike's feet dangle off the far end.

I look laterally along the crevasse's length, hoping there is a way to simply walk out the end of it, but it stretches for around a hundred feet in the up-mountain direction, then vanishes into darkness. I turn the other way, down the mountain: After about two hundred feet, the crevasse shows no signs of ending.

Maybe twenty to thirty minutes have passed since I took that awful step on the glacier's surface and the snow beneath my feet collapsed. I know I have to look up and see how far in we are, but I'm scared. After stalling for a moment, I gather the courage and raise my head, determined to get a firm physical understanding of just where we are trapped. All those summers working with my father's painting crew, estimating building heights and calculating the rigging we'd need, come back to me.

My eyes travel up the frozen walls, first dark gray, then dark blue, then bluish white near the top, reflecting splotches of light. I figure it is almost eighty feet up to the sunlight flaring through the hole we punched in the snow bridge. The walls above me climb up at about eighty degrees until the crevasse is eight feet wide; then the ice walls go dead vertical; and then, higher up, they close back in toward each other in an overhang.

Oh my God.

The full depth of our predicament settles on me like a great weight.

I stand awestruck, staring up at the underside of the snow bridge that spans the crevasse. In places, the frozen veil is so thin I can see light filtering right through it. Being way down in this dangerous dark hole, it is as if I am looking out from the belly of a beast, its jagged white teeth interlocking above me.

"Oh, we're in trouble," I hear myself say out loud. "We're in big, big trouble."

STUNNED BY THE overhanging walls arching above us, I look beyond the edge of our snow pile. If we're on the bottom of the crevasse, there should be a snowy floor just below us instead of that black drop-off I see. I'm confused. What did we land on? Why is there so much dark space beneath us?

I kneel down and scan beneath our perch, and it's just as if I'm on a platform, bent over and peering underneath it: We're on a ledge, and there's nothing below us but frigid air. As I stare at the ledge's underbelly, I realize that our perch is composed of my green Gregory backpack jammed against an ice slab the size of a coffee table. The ice slab must have fallen down here long ago and lodged, leaving a gap just about the size of my pack. When I plummeted down here, pack first, I landed right on that narrow gap. In essence, my backpack corked between the crevasse wall and the ice slab. If the slab hadn't been there, or had been a different size, or I had fallen a few feet to either side, the alignment of pack and ice slab could not have happened. Instead, I would have plunged down another five or ten feet, until I corked, permanently wedged between the unforgiving crevasse walls.

I sit upright, stunned as I realize how lucky my landing had been. It's hard to believe what I have just seen, so I bend back down to look at the ledge's underbelly again. The shelf is partially supported by snow crammed in between my pack and the ice slab. At the far end of the snowy ledge, Mike's boots dangle down into space. It hits me that Mike and I are precariously perched on a makeshift platform of unknown strength and longevity. If anything gives way, we'll plummet deeper into the narrow crevasse—something I'm sure I won't survive. We need an anchor, quick.

Mike and I always carry enough climbing gear on our hips to set an emergency anchor. An ice screw, snow fluke, rescue pulley, carabiners, and slings always dangle from my waist, and from his. I stand up, unclip an ice screw from my harness, and grab Mike's ice hammer—the only tool visible in the jumble of gear around us—and start pounding the screw into the wall. The blows echo dully in the cavern, but after a few swings it's set deep enough for the teeth to grab. Then I stick the tip of the hammer's pick into the eye of the screw and use the hammer as a giant lever, twisting the metal ice screw deep into the concrete-hard ice. The screw screeches with each twist, but after a few minutes it's well set. I fish around and find my end of the rope and tie a figure eight on a bight into it, snap a locking carabiner onto the screw head, and clip into the anchor. I'm safe.

I fumble around some more, looking for Mike's end of the rope, and once I find it I tie a similar knot and clip Mike in secure with two biners. We are both tied into the same screw.

That screw will keep us from sliding deeper into the crevasse if the snow ledge gives way. It will give me a chance to save myself, and this way I won't lose Mike's body deeper in the slot. He's gone, but I still have to watch out for him. We're still partners.

I've taken a first, tentative step by anchoring us. It feels good to have grabbed some tiny bit of control in this impossible situation.

Hardly believing that this snow shelf is really as precarious as it seems, I unzip the one pocket on my pack that's accessible, and find my red-handled jackknife and headlamp.

When I snap on the lamp, its beam cuts through the darkness, and for the first time, I can truly see what we are up against.

Below me, the lower reaches of the crevasse come into view. Thirty or forty feet down, the walls converge to within a few inches of each other. I can't see the bottom. From the glacier's surface eighty feet above, down past me, to as deep as I can see, the total crevasse depth is about 120 feet. Sensing that yawning chasm below us, I realize I can't take any chances, so I reach for another ice screw on Mike's harness. After I beat and crank it into the wall, I clip us both to it as a backup. If I am to have any prospect of getting out of here, I can't make any mistakes.

As I look down, I realize we could lose all the gear, so I tie both packs into the screws, too. This makes me consider the loose gear on and in the snow pile that is our ledge. I dig around, recovering a few stray items, and carefully clip them all to me or the ice screw. I'm going to need every piece of gear we've got to survive this— dropping anything deeper into the crevasse isn't an option.

Looking up to the sunlight—to the surface—again, I have no idea what to do. The only thing that comes to mind is to yell for help.

"Help! Help!"

My shouts echo around the slot, unsettling me. I hear the fear in my own voice, and it loudly demonstrates just how scared I really am.

Yelling isn't doing any good. Start taking care of yourself.

Meltwater drips constantly from the sun-baked snow bridge above me. I'm already soaked.

I struggle to organize my thoughts: Put warm clothes on. Strap on your crampons. Yell for help. Don't yell for help. Get in the sleeping bag. Clip into the ice screw again. Put on more clothes. Eat. Check on Mike. Don't stumble off the ledge. Look for an ax. Jam another screw into the wall. Scream for help some more. Blow your whistle. Find your helmet. Drink.

"Hypothermia," I hear myself say aloud.

It's a sign, I figure, that the intuitive side of my brain has identified the primary concern I must deal with now. I look down. Mike's pile jacket sticks out of his pack.

"I'm not wearing that," I say, instinctively recoiling at the thought of putting on my dead partner's coat. "I'll put on my own clothes."

I'm standing on snow and partially on top of my pack. Reaching down, I grab the pack's handle-like haul loop between the shoulder straps. I give it a strong upward tug. Bad move—I feel snow shift beneath my feet, and a chunk of our ledge calves off. Our tiny, suspended island of comparative safety just shrank.

Stop! Stupid!

It is a dangerous reminder that my pack is not just crammed into the snow; rather, it's a key structural underpinning that holds our weak snow ledge together. If I had succeeded in pulling the pack up, the ledge would have collapsed and left me, Mike, and the gear hanging in space from the ice screws.

I drop the pack strap as though it's electrified. One moment's inattention almost made everything much worse. Now what?

I have to get to my clothes and my other gear, but I can't pull out the pack. From the top side, I can't reach the pack's main compartment, so I decide to cut through the pack to get at my stuff.

I fold open the jackknife, kneel down, and poke the knife tip into the pack's taut side. The blade easily slits through the forest green nylon. It's almost as if I'm outside my own body, watching someone else. I realize how deadly serious this is.

Working carefully, I try not to drop anything. I pull out my heavy expedition jacket, but I can't safely grab my fuzzy pile pullover—tugging on it, I fear, will cause my pack to collapse and our perch to fall away. I look again at Mike's blue Patagonia pile sweater, crumpled in the snow, and I momentarily hesitate to put it on. Recognizing I need all the warmth I can get, I carefully peel off the sopping-wet Gore-Tex jacket I've been wearing, pull Mike's sweater on, slither into my expedition jacket, then wrestle my soggy shell jacket back on. For more warmth, I yank my red pile Marmot hat onto my head.

I already have on two pairs of pants: a polypro pair underneath and a Gore-Tex shell on top. I want another layer, so I reach carefully into my flayed-open pack and work a pair of pile pants free. They should go on underneath the shell pants I'm already wearing, but that means first taking off my harness and disconnecting myself from our anchor. No way am I doing that. I'll just put the bulky pile pants on over my shell and harness. I undo the side zippers so the legs will fit easily over my boots. I step into them with little trouble, but for some reason I can't get the pile pants zipped up.

My hands shake.

Breathing slowly, I try to calm myself enough to zip up the pants. But I have to stop, unable to finish. I look down at my pack: The top where I cut it is wide open over the gaping crevasse, and I realize gear may fall out and plunge away from me.

I blow out another breath and am finally able to get my pile pants zipped.

Reaching down, I stuff the protruding gear back into my pack. Then I partially close the ragged opening by using a carabiner to clip two gear straps across the wound.

With me now dressed as warmly as possible, and the remaining gear secured away, I pause. I wonder why my brain settled on hypothermia as the most important of all the concerns rushing by me, and it quickly makes sense: If I get hypothermic, I'll shut down and die. I realize that I must trust my inner voice.

I've dealt with my own warmth as best I can, so it is on to the next priority. But what?

"Climbing gear," I say aloud.

I am thinking now. I am shocked and weakened by what has happened, numb with sorrow over Mike's death, but my climber's instincts are kicking in, so I ask myself a question: Can I climb this?

I stare at the walls for a minute. I've never been able to lead any sustained ice steeper than seventy degrees in my life. Far above me, both walls are ninety degrees and even overhanging. And there is more. As I face down the mountain, with my left hand on one crevasse wall and my right hand on the other, I realize I have only one shot. That is to go up the wall on my left. The reason is simple: It leads directly to the hole I crashed through. The wall on my right leads up underneath the snow bridge, which sticks out a good eight feet—like a gangplank protruding from the deck of a ship. That means that if I ascend the right-hand wall, I'll have to dig through the unstable snow bridge to get out.

No way.

The left wall is my only chance, but there's a big problem: It turns vertical quickly, then, about twenty feet from the top, juts out about three feet in an overhanging ice roof. If I make it that far, I'll have to fight my way past that overhang. It'll be like climbing up a sixty-foot wall, then three feet out beneath the horizontal ceiling, and then up another twenty-foot wall. The only good news is that the ice-wall section above the ceiling doesn't appear as steep—maybe eighty degrees.

"See," I say to myself meekly, searching for some positive in this mess, "maybe I can climb that last part."

My trickle of confidence erodes as I keep looking up and realize that the last section is plastered with scary-looking chunks of rotten debris—the dollops of snow and ice that had slapped my face as I ricocheted between the walls.

Postponing any commitment to try climbing, I yell again. Between shouts, I wonder if anybody is coming, if anyone saw us fall in.

"Help! Help! Help!"

I want someone to save me, to make this scary situation just go away. If someone else solves the brutal difficulties, then I won't have to.

"Help—down here!"

I sense the crevasse walls grabbing my shouts and swallowing them.

I close my eyes, trying to picture where we were before the accident. I remember seeing a rope team far below us, but they were headed down, and thus not looking back uphill at us. I think about those two guys we'd passed, but I figure they were at least three hundred feet above us, and around the corner of an ice block. If I couldn't see them, they couldn't see us.

Nobody saw us fall in. I understand that with no one coming for us, to escape I will have to climb up the overhanging ice wall.

Doubt flares in my mind. I survived the fall and I dug myself out and I'm not hurt bad. I'm not going to get myself killed trying to climb something I know I can't. I'm going to stay here until someone comes to get me.

What if no one comes?

Mike and I had filled out little cards at the White River Ranger

Station to register our climb, but as I think it through, I realize it will be a day before anyone will consider us overdue. Even then, on such a big route, the rangers might wait another day in case we're just slow.

Once the rangers decide to search, I figure, they'll start at the base of the Liberty Ridge, on the other side of the mountain. They'll follow our footprints up and over the top, if they can; then they'll lose our tracks among all the other climbers' prints. Maybe, eventually, they'll narrow their search to this glacier. Then maybe they'll start looking inside crevasses. But there are hundreds of crevasses on this glacier, maybe thousands. It will be two or three days before a serious search starts, and probably another two or three days before they look in this hole, in this crevasse—if ever. Five days, maybe six until they might get here. I wonder: Can I last that long down here?

I have a pan, a stove, and a pint of fuel. I have a little food I can stretch. With two sleeping bags, maybe I can place one inside the other and hunker down.

Summoning a decade of climbing experience, I assess my odds. My gut tells me that the supplies might last three days, maybe even four. Maybe.

I try imagining what waiting down here will be like, and immediately recognize that there's no way I'm going to live a couple days.

I'm soaking wet, shaking, exhausted . . . when it gets dark in here tonight, what's going to happen?

I know that nightfall will bring bitter cold. The crevasse might shift, or close shut with me in it. And tonight it will get dark—very dark. I sense that I am already teetering on the edge physically, emotionally, mentally, and spiritually, here on this terrifying ledge with the body of my good friend just inches away. I won't last through the night down here.

If I am still in this crevasse when darkness descends, I will not be alive when the sun returns.

I look at my watch. It is just after noon. I figure I have nine hours of sunlight up on the surface.

My only chance is to climb.

CHAPTER 12

▲ ▲ ▲

I GLANCE DOWN at my pack, crushed against the frozen crevasse wall. Thoughts swirl through my brain, rushing at me as I try to figure out what I need, what to do.

"Crampons," I hear myself say, and I crouch down and make out the spiky black frames inside my pack. I immediately feel a mixture of relief and fear—I'm glad they're inside, not clipped to the outside and jammed against the frozen wall, where I might not be able to reach them. Without my crampons, there's no hope of climbing out. But I'm also scared that one wrong move will send them tumbling out of my grasp and into the depths, sealing my fate.

Moving with the care of a bomb-squad technician, I reach into the pack, wrap my fingers around the crampons, squeeze hard, and pull them up to my chest.

In an instant, a be-careful-what-you-wish-for realization sweeps over me: Now that I have them, I'm going to have to use them.

I ignore the anxious feeling and delicately step into them, one at a time. The affirming sight, solid sound, and reassuring thump of each crampon's heel lever snapping to my boots eases my tension. After buckling the safety straps around my ankles, I release a long, slow breath. The crampons are on me now, and I'm a step closer to being ready to climb. I question whether the walls of centuries-old ice are too hard for my front points to penetrate. I kick once, and the spikes protruding from my boot's toes bite into the ice a half inch— the wall is hard, but not as unforgiving as I feared. It's climbable.

My eyes travel up the steep walls of the crevasse again. As I ponder trying to climb out, doubt swells in my mind.

You've never climbed anything like this in your life. What makes you think you can climb it now, all beat up and scared? Without any mistakes? If something goes wrong, you'll wind up at the bottom of this crevasse. Alone. Corked. That's where you'll stay.

I have never led or even followed anything this steep before. But logically I know I have only one chance, and that is to act.

You should climb out now, while you still can.

Emotionally, I still can't accept the idea.

But if I try climbing out now, then I take the huge risk now. I'll just wait and take the risk tomorrow if I have to, but I'm not going to take it now if I don't have to.

I recognize what's going on: Part of me is trying to talk myself out of climbing, to avoid the risk and the commitment. Another part of me, meanwhile, lays the situation out bluntly:

You won't be able to climb tomorrow. Either the ledge you're standing on will collapse, the snow bridge above will fall on you, your spirit's going to be crushed, or something else will happen. If you wait until tomorrow, you won't be able to climb out. If you're going to get out, you have to do it yourself. Today.

I recoil from the brutal analysis. I don't want to climb this myself. I can't. I won't.

What I really want, I suppose, is for someone else to come along and solve this for me, to throw a rope down, to rescue me. I hear my voice again. This time, the words tumble from my mouth in a flat tone, disembodied. It's like I'm listening to someone else talking. Out loud I say, "You're totally alone."

Hearing the blunt truth aloud is terrifying. It's as if I'm in another world. Thoughts of Gloria pop into my head—I can see her in my mind, her auburn hair, and in the waking vision I sense other people with her, too, my family and friends. Their proximity makes longing well up in my chest. The thought of never seeing them all again is too much, so I look away. My eyes settle on Mike, at my feet. The emotional grasping gets slapped hard by the unforgiving physical reality right before me.

Standing in place, I shuffle my feet about aimlessly. I don't want to climb these walls. Anything would be better than that. I consider trying to stem sideways, out toward the down-mountain end of the crevasse; I could bridge myself like a big X between the two ice walls, putting one foot and one hand on each side and using oppositional forces to hold me up. In this way I could crab my way laterally and straddle the crack all the way out. But I realize I don't have enough rope to make the far end—the slot stretches sideways two hundred feet or more and vanishes into blackness. Besides, I might go all the way to the end and be stuck there, in a worse jam than I'm in now. Traversing sideways down-mountain won't work.

Traversing the opposite way, in the up-mountain direction, is no good either. That will only take me deeper under the glacier, and that is certainly no solution—somewhere that pulverizes bedrock to dust is no place to head toward. I concede that there is no easy way. The only way out is straight up.

I have no more vague alternatives left to offer myself. Only the awful truth remains, and it is painfully clear. I have to climb out of here myself.

My crampons are on my boots—a good start. I look down at my pack and see a nylon ditty bag that holds the rest of our ice screws and hardware. It hangs partially out of the hole I cut in my pack. I realize that, as with the crampons, if the hardware drops away, any hope of climbing out vanishes. Crouching down slowly, I focus on making my moves surgically sharp. I hear Dad's voice echo in my mind: "Do it like ya mean it."

When I get about six inches away, my right hand flashes down, grabbing the yellow sack as if I'm seizing a wild air hose. I close my eyes in fear and pull the bag close to my chest and hug it for a second.

One by one, I pull gear out of the sack and rack it on a sling looped over my shoulder and head. I realize I have only the two ice screws in the wall and four around my neck—that's it.

We have a seventh ice screw, but one of the teeth is broken, and it's in an outer pouch of my pack, on the underside of the ledge, tantalizingly close and out of reach at the same time. I think about trying to get to it but decide that one more broken screw isn't going to make a difference.

Methodically sorting the gear, I rack it as I would if I were leading any climb. Extra biners in the front, the ice screws next, and in the back, the hardest place to reach, the items I likely won't need: the two camming units. Maybe I can work them into an ice crack.

As I crane my neck to study the walls again, my climber's mind whirs, trying to analyze the choices. Logic, experience, and gut instinct sift the variables, searching for the easiest, safest, most successful way to escape. I reconfirm that I have to climb the steeper wall, as it leads directly to the existing hole through the snow bridge. I shake my head at the irony. Damn!

The crevasse is only a few feet wide for the first twenty feet over my head. I can probably stem my way up between the walls and make fast progress until the spread grows too great for my legs to span. That will help launch me up the lower wall; above that, perhaps I can aid climb. By relying on the gear to advance when it gets really steep, maybe I can work around my inability to free climb overhanging ice.

But, really, I've hardly ever aid climbed before. I've done only a little, on warm rock in Yosemite and Montana, well protected by a partner holding my top rope.

That measly experience sure doesn't qualify me for this. But I know the principles. Maybe I can figure it out.

Dredging my memory, I scrounge up aid-climbing tidbits from stories I've heard, manuals I've read. Like when starting a new rigging job with Dad, I compare the gear I need against the gear I have.

To aid climb well, I definitely need aiders, the ladderlike slings with five or six steps that I could scamper up after clipping them to an ice screw. I need at least two aiders; I have none. Scanning my rack, I see that I do have an assortment of simple nylon slings. I'll have to make do, dangling slings of various lengths from each ice screw placement and standing in them as best I can. It might work.

As I consider my options, Gloria, my dad and mom, my climbing buddies, and my sisters make cameo appearances in my mind. I remind myself that it's just me, that I am alone. If none of those others can do anything physically to help me at this moment, I just can't think about them now.

But I can't stop thinking about Mike. My friend lies at my feet on this tiny ledge. It's so cramped that I stand next to his shoulders, the edge dropping off immediately to my right. I scoot back a crowded inch to avoid pressing against him. When I recognize that I haven't been looking at Mike much, and that I'm trying not to think about him, an ugly pang of guilt hits me. Instinct tells me, though, that this is okay, that I have to focus on getting out of here.

Finally, I finish racking the gear. I have ten short slings, two long slings, three Prusik cords, a belay/rappel device, and two cams. I wish I had aiders to hang from or mechanical ascenders to scale the rope. I smirk a bit when I hear an old line of Dad's run through my mind: "Wish in one hand, crap in the other. See which fills up first."

For ice screws, I have the four on me, plus two already in the wall. Maybe I will pull one of those two anchor screws and take it with me. Leaving just one screw for our bottom anchor is incredibly risky, but having a fifth screw up on the wall will really help.

It's not nearly enough, I know—with twenty ice screws, aid climbing out would be feasible. I could just crank one in every four feet, clip a biner to it, haul myself up to it, and steadily work my way up the eighty-foot wall. But I don't have twenty ice screws. I have six.

Worse yet, I know that my supply will dwindle fast, because as I climb, I'll have to occasionally leave gear behind in the wall, to protect me in case I fall. Then, when I run out of gear, I'll be forced to lower myself back down over the same section to retrieve some of the screws and biners to use again higher up. Once I have the gear back, I will have to reascend the dangling rope over the same ground to regain my high point. For every foot of gain, I will have to go up, then down, then up it again. Aid climbers call this "leapfrogging the gear," and it's done only in desperate situations, because it is slow, exhausting, and dangerous. Hauling myself back up the rope with jury-rigged friction knots will be ridiculously hard. But it's all I can do.

The rack now sorted, I move on to my next big need. I have to have an ice tool in each hand.

Back near the surface, when I shot through the collapsing snow bridge, I had an ice ax slung from my right wrist. Now it's gone. My ice hammer is strapped to my pack, crushed impossibly between the ledge and the crevasse wall. I can't get to it. I have Mike's hammer, but that's it.

I look about our tiny ledge but don't see Mike's ax. Dropping to my knees, I paw through the dense snow. Nothing.

A sickening feeling grabs my stomach as I remember. I had an ice ax in my hand when I was digging out of the snow—Mike's ax. But I dropped it over my shoulder in a panic when Mike stopped breathing.

Mike Price soaks in a desert sunset in western Colorado during a stop on his way to Utah, where he was headed to teach an Outward Bound course. *Courtesy of Deb Follo Caughron*

Andy Thamert, *left,* and Mike ski across a glacier in the Yukon during the thirty-seven-day adventure they experienced with two other friends. *Courtesy of Bob Jamieson and Andy Thamert*

Mike sits outside the tent and writes in his journal near the end of the Yukon trip. *Courtesy of Bob Jamieson and Andy Thamert*

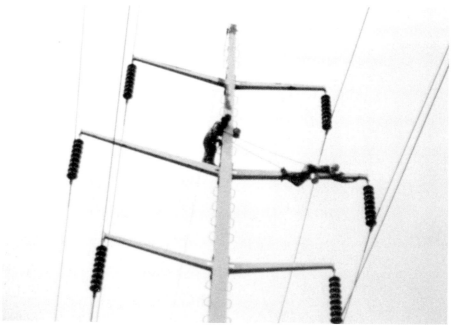

Another painter holds my safety rope as I stretch out to paint the end of an electrical tower arm in 1982—work that prepared me for my life as a climber. *Courtesy of Jim Davidson; photograph by Joe Davidson*

I stand atop the summit of Maine's Mount Katahdin in December 1985, one of my early experiences with winter climbing. *Courtesy of Jim Davidson*

Daryl Miller, Jeff Bopp, Pat Rastall, and Scott Anderson flank me as we ham it up on the summit of Argentina's Aconcagua (22,834 feet) in January 1987— my first high-altitude peak. *Courtesy of Jim Davidson*

Liberty Ridge cuts directly up the center of this photograph, reaching the Liberty Cap. Our ascent route and our three bivouac campsites are shown. At left is the true summit of Mount Rainier (14,410 feet) and the beginning of our descent route down the Winthrop and Emmons glaciers. *USGS*

A series of crevasses cuts across the lower Winthrop Glacier behind me on our first day of climbing on Mount Rainier. *Courtesy of the Price family; photograph by Mike Price*

Liberty Ridge looms above me as we begin crossing the Carbon Glacier on the first afternoon. *Courtesy of the Price family; photograph by Mike Price*

Mike tightens his crampons on the second day of our Mount Rainier climb. *Courtesy of Jim Davidson*

Mike sits tethered to an ice screw after we woke up on a little shelf perched above the Liberty Wall—a bivouac spot we found in the darkness our second night on Rainier. Beyond his toes, the Carbon Glacier stretches out 7,000 feet below us. *Courtesy of Jim Davidson*

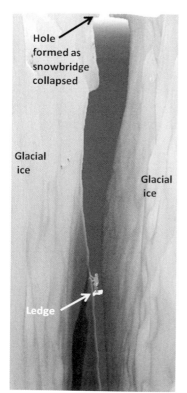

Hole formed as snowbridge collapsed

Glacial ice

Glacial ice

Ledge

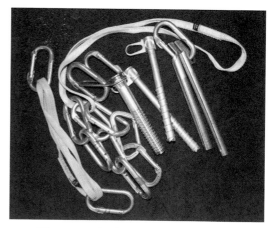

These are the ice screws and some of the carabiners and slings that I used to climb up the crevasse wall. *Courtesy of Jim Davidson and Kevin Vaughan*

This cross-section illustration of the crevasse, drawn approximately to scale, represents the challenge I faced—climbing eighty feet of vertical and overhanging ice to reach the glacier's surface. *Courtesy of Jim Davidson*

I knew I'd been through something that would indelibly impact my life, and I knew I'd never want to forget how it affected me when I snapped this self-portrait early on the morning of June 23—less than forty-eight hours after the accident. *Courtesy of Jim Davidson*

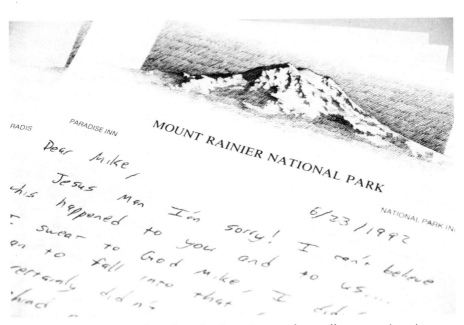

RADIS   PARADISE INN   MOUNT RAINIER NATIONAL PARK   NATIONAL PARK IN

Dear Mike,

Jesus man I'm sorry! I can't believe this happened to you and 6/23/1992 I swear to God Mike, I us... on to fall into that did - certainly didn't had

Two days after the accident, heartbroken, I poured out all my emotions in a letter to Mike that I wrote just before leaving Mount Rainier. *Courtesy of Jim Davidson and Kevin Vaughan*

Winds ruffle prayer flags as Prem Lakpa Sherpa and I toss blessed rice toward the mountaintops during our *puja* for Mike's spirit in Nepal's Khumbu Valley at the base of Mount Everest. *Courtesy of Jim Davidson; photograph by Gloria Davidson*

In the years after the Rainier accident, I returned to climbing icy mountains and embraced all that it brings to my life—in this case, a frozen face on Denali Pass (18,150 feet on Denali, Alaska). *Courtesy of Jim Davidson*

I move to the edge of the shelf and look down, my headlamp throwing an eerie light into the darkening fissure below me. About eight feet down, I see a thin, wispy snow bridge stretched between the walls. The missing ax rests on it, standing on its head, its handle sticking straight up and leaning against the right wall. If I want that ax, I'll have to go down there and get it.

I close my eyes and tilt my head.

I can't believe this.

To have any hope of climbing, I must have that ax. No one can climb an overhanging ice wall with just one tool, no one. To go up, I'll have to first go down.

I'm not going down there. I'm not!

Remembering my hammer wedged tight between my pack and the wall, I think, *Maybe I should just cut all the way through my pack and get the hammer instead.* I pull out my jackknife, prepared to cut ruthlessly, but stop myself. If cutting and emptying the pack makes it smaller, our ledge would probably collapse, leaving Mike and me dangling from our anchor screws. If that happens, I figure, I'll die.

I slowly fold my knife shut, resigned to defeat.

Well, that's it then. I'm stuck here. Maybe I should try to last long enough for them to find me.

I think again about hunkering down, about the stove and the bits of food left, and I wonder whether I can last that long.

But I know that waiting several days is not an option. When the sun sets tonight, if I am still down here, I will die. I have already made that determination, yet it is as if I am still seeking a way to not climb, to find something—anything—to do, short of going deeper into the crevasse and getting that ax. I look down again. My headlamp burns through the gloom and illuminates the ice ax. I see the blue handle and the metallic gray pick. The tiny snow bridge it's landed on looks thin; it could collapse at any time. Next to the ax, the walls press close, a narrowing trap ready to slam shut on me if I dare go down there. Then, I remember *Touching the Void,* by Joe Simpson.

The first time I read the epic climbing survival book I was up all night, devouring it in one sitting, captivated by how he barely survived a climbing disaster on 20,813-foot Siula Grande, in Peru. Joe, a brilliant British climber, suffered a horribly broken leg during the descent, and had to be lowered thousands of roped feet by his partner, Simon Yates. After Simon had lowered Joe over a cliff at night, the two men became trapped, Joe dangling in midair, Simon fighting to stay in a seat he'd carved in the snow that was slowly collapsing. Ultimately, Simon was forced to cut the rope, dropping Joe into a crevasse; if he hadn't, they both faced certain death.

Presuming Joe to be dead, Simon hiked off the glacier. But Joe wasn't dead. Still alive, he was stuck fifty feet down in a crevasse, alone, in the darkness. With no one coming to get him, he had to go deeper into his crevasse to find a way out himself or die. The similarity of my crevasse entrapment and of having to go deeper into the slot in some long-shot attempt to maybe escape upward both make my situation feel similar to Joe's survival fight. Like him, I have only myself to rely on at this moment.

His climbing route out was easier than mine, but I'm not hurt bad, the way he was. So, basically, we're even, I tell myself. If he did it, I can, too.

I'm going to go deeper into the ominous crevasse. I am going to face my fears, wrap my arms around them, and pull them close, just to get that ax and have a chance to live.

I START SORTING the rope system so that I can rappel down. Using a long sling, I clip directly into the anchors so that I'm secure while I untie from the rope. But my figure-eight knot tied into the rope's middle is iced over. I poke, pull, and tease the frozen knot but can't get it undone. Using my teeth, I loosen it some, but it is still locked up. It is more than just the ice; the jerking force of my fall must have cinched the knot extra tight. I decide to pry open the knot by using a tool on my jackknife—not the main blade, though, as it might cut the rope. I swivel out the usually useless file, with its dull, stubby end, and start prodding. It works, and soon I undo the knot.

I have now freed up about 110 feet of rope. The rope's remaining fifty-five feet stays tied to Mike on a locking carabiner connected to his harness. I have plenty of rope for my short rappel down to the ax. I connect a new anchor sling to our two screws and equalize the sling to distribute my weight evenly to both anchor points. After clipping a locking carabiner to the extended anchor sling, I tie the end of our climbing rope to it, then thread a curled bight of that rappel rope through my friction belay device. I am almost ready to rappel, to lower myself deeper into the beast's throat, to recover that ax.

A brief nightmare emerges: I see myself down there, reaching for the ax, and then, at that exact moment, it slips away, skittering irretrievably into the depths. If that happens, it's all over. The vision reinforces one overriding thought in my mind: *I'm going to have to be very careful about this.*

From my hip, I pull off a Prusik cord, a knotted loop of thin line that I will wind around my climbing rope and then tether to my harness. The wrapped Prusik knot will slide along the climbing rope when there's no pressure but will cinch down under my weight if I fall, stopping me. This will give me a backup during the rappel. I wrap the six-millimeter cord around the rope in a curling French wrap technique Mike taught me. He had always said it produced more friction than a standard Prusik hitch. I am relying on my experienced partner's advice, and I find reassurance in that.

I double-check the knots, the rappel setup, and the anchors. I double-check my harness and my Prusik cord, then check them again. I can't afford any mistakes. I squeeze my right hand, the one I'll use for braking, hard around the rope and tug to make sure I have rigged myself securely.

Letting some rappel rope slip through my brake hand, I ease backward off the ledge, pressing my cramponed boots into the side walls in a stemming move, and begin lowering myself deeper into the slot. I feel very vulnerable leaving the only secure ground I've got, the only quasi-safe place down here.

As I descend gradually, my head drops below the underside of our ledge. Above me, my twisted green pack is jammed tight between the ice slab and the frozen wall. I am shocked to see how my pack was the perfect width to cram solidly against the slab, just preventing my shoulders from corking between the ever-narrowing ice walls. Each exhalation of mine jets out warm air that turns foggy in the moist, cold chasm.

My bobbing headlamp lights up the mini clouds, so that they seem to glow from within. The sharp illumination of the light beam makes the region beyond even more dark and threatening. When I descend another two feet, the crevasse becomes too narrow for my shoulders. I have to turn sideways to squeeze in deeper. With one ice wall pressing against my chest and the other right at my back, the claustrophobia makes me sweat.

Every inch I descend, the black walls squeeze in tighter. If the glacier slips or lurches right now, I will be crushed to a pulp.

Blackness leans heavily upon me from both sides. I keep moving my head about to illuminate the area around me, in an effort to drive back fear. But even the light beam plagues me—when it hits the slick walls, it reflects harshly into my eyes, making the constricting space around me feel even more confusing and menacing.

For the last foot, I slow my descent to a crawl, then stop with my cramponed boots dangling mere inches above the crusty snow shelf holding the sacred ice ax. The handle is just three feet from me, but I can tell that the snow ledge is maybe an inch thick and as fragile as glass. I can't step on it.

My stomach muscles clench tight as I hang motionless in my harness. I hover above the ax, making a plan to grab it while still holding myself on rappel.

I wind the dangling end of the rappel rope twice around my right thigh in a friction wrap to make sure I don't slip down. Reaching out with my left hand and leaning over, I stretch out sideways, nearly parallel with Mike, who lies on the ledge about eight feet above me. The icy walls press tight against my chest. Using the only caving trick I know, I force a breath from my lungs to shrink myself. I lean over farther and reach down deeper. My purple-gloved hand moves close. Delicately I close my hand around the handle.

Squeezing the precious ice ax handle with my left hand, and locking off the rappel rope with my right, I have no free hand to pull myself upright. I hook the crook of my left elbow behind the taut rappel line above me. With this as leverage, I grunt and heft myself vertical.

As I pull the ax to my chest, I hug it for a moment, then clip it into my harness with two carabiners snapped onto different spots.

No mistakes.

I glimpse my battered orange helmet a few feet farther down, the brim broken off. For a moment I ponder heading down to get it, but recoil at the thought of going deeper. I decide to leave it. I push myself back up with a scissors-kick motion off both walls.

As I wiggle up, I pull the now slack rope through the belay device at my waist to keep myself tight. Chunks of snow drop around me as my bouncing rappel line saws at the end of our snow ledge. Though I am moving closer, I worry that the ledge will collapse before I get there.

It holds.

Fifteen minutes after I'd left, I step back onto our tiny shelf, fighting to catch my breath. I feel a wisp of reassurance being back with Mike. Recognizing the twin achievements of retrieving the ax and returning to our ledge lifts my spirits a bit. My neck tingles as I sense the dark, frozen walls hanging far above, waiting for me. But I refuse to worry about them for the moment. I need to bask a little in the idea that some progress has been made.

Bent over at the waist, panting, I'm staring at Mike's chest; I turn my head to the right and look into his face. Though I feel uneasy looking at my dead partner, the successful ax recovery feels like an important step forward to share with my friend. At my side, I pat the precious ice ax. With Mike's ax and hammer, I have two ice tools.

At least there's a chance to get out now, Mike.

CHAPTER 13

▲ ▲ ▲

NEARLY AN HOUR has passed since that awful moment when the snow bridge ruptured beneath my feet, and now a new fear arises: There's something wrong with me physically. The worry bursts into my mind after I hack phlegm from my throat, spit, and see a red-black clot hit the ice wall. Bright red blood drools down an inch, then freezes in place.

Frightened, I spit again. More blood, this time all fresh—no black clots. I don't know where it's coming from, so my first-aid training rattles off possibilities, all of them scary. Stomach? Liver? Lungs? I inhale deeply and shove the breath out hard—lungs seem good.

I realize I haven't properly assessed my own medical condition. Reversing the traditional exam order, I reach toward my feet and begin a toe-to-head check. I'm certainly not taking off my boots down here, so I just wiggle my toes and push on the rigid plastic boot tops. Both feet feel fine.

I get to my ankles, probing hard with my fingers. No pain or protruding bones—so far, so good. I mentally check another box off the examination list and move toward my shins. But what if I find something?

It's an intriguing question, and I stop my assessment to think it through. If something's really wrong with me, what am I going to do? Our first-aid kit consists of Band-Aids, gauze, ibuprofen, and white athletic tape. For minor wounds I can improvise with other materials, but there's little I can do for serious problems or broken bones. If I discover a major injury, I can't fix it—maybe it's better not to know. Hurt or not, I have to try climbing out of here.

Though I haven't solved the mystery of my bloody throat, I no longer care. To prove this, I gurgle up more fluid and spit angrily through pursed lips. Dark droplets spray the ice wall.

I keep conjuring an image of myself dangling frozen on a climbing rope. It's all too awful, and I feel overwhelmed. Mike's gone, I'm hurt, and I must face this impossible situation. It's so damn scary it seems unreal. Maybe it isn't real.

I consider the possibility that I'm actually still trapped under the snow, dying. Maybe the air is all gone, and I am just spending my last oxygen molecules wistfully concocting some self-soothing, implausible flight to life.

Maybe I'm already dead.

No. I'm terrified and apprehensive about everything. I don't think I would feel this scared if I were already gone. And when I tilt my head to the left in a self-induced pain check, fire shoots up my neck and my left hand tingles uncomfortably. You can't feel pain if you're dead, so I must be alive. This must all be real.

THE GEAR RACK is sorted, and I have Mike's ice tools now. I am clipped safely to the anchor screws with a sling. I stare at our supple yellow rope, trying to figure out how I can use it to protect myself during the climb out. Thoughts of climbing bring thoughts of belaying and, with them, a sober realization: There's no one here to belay me.

It's an enormous obstacle. And then it hits me: I'm going to have to self-belay—something I've never done before.

I try imagining how a self-belay system might work, having only ever seen it in books. One end of our rope has to be anchored at the bottom. The other end has to be tied to me so that I could, theoretically, climb out its full 165-foot length. But I can't quite envision how I will rig it to hold me tight on belay while still feeding out slack as I ascend. I review the tie-in options I know, but none seem right. Since I was fifteen and Dad steered me toward the Concord library's adventure literature, I've had a voracious appetite for mountaineering books. My mind flips back through snippets and half-remembered diagrams from all the climbing manuals I've read. Mental pictures pop up from a decade of tent and campfire gatherings with other climbers—snapshot images of rope tricks, tips, and knots.

My hands unconsciously fiddle with a rope strand as I recall various knots. Old standards like the bowline, figure eight, and square knots aren't helpful. I could never remember how to tie a sheepshank—God, I hope that's not the one I need; if so, I'm screwed.

I need a knot that can move along with me as I climb. A basic Prusik loop wrapped around the main climbing rope, like the one I used earlier on the rappel, could serve as a sliding friction knot. With the other end of that Prusik loop clipped to my harness, it would serve as a short leash, attaching me securely to the main rope. I figure I can scoot the Prusik loop up the rope with me, steadily increasing the length of climbing rope between me and the bottom anchor screw. But if I fall, the Prusik should cinch down tight and hold me. This will provide the adjustable self-belay I need.

I know I'm right; now I just have to determine exactly how to rig this rope system through my ice-screw protection. I picture it one way, then another. Each time I think a few steps ahead, I get confused.

Pressing my forehead against the crevasse wall, I close my eyes and search for the answer. Frustrated, I gently tap my forehead against the hard crevasse wall. The ice burns my skin. Suddenly, I open my eyes, realizing I can practice on the two ice screws already in the wall. I can tie one end of the rope to the bottom screw, run it up through a biner on the second screw, and then rig and test my self-belay system.

To do all this I need to free the climbing rope from Mike's harness. First, I have to secure Mike to the wall with a piece of webbing—I can't let him fall in. I scan the gear and glimpse a bundle of half-inch pink webbing about twenty feet long. Mike always left it untied to use as an adjustable anchor sling. At times it snagged, annoying me, but Mike liked it.

I attach one end to Mike's harness and tie him tight to the ice screw, letting the excess webbing dangle loose. The rope remains tied to him by a figure-eight-on-a-bight knot into the locking carabiner on his harness. The easiest way to disconnect it is to unclip the carabiner, but the locking screw gate won't budge. Yanking my gloves off for a better grip, I feel frigid aluminum bite my skin when I grab the biner. I twist and pull, but it's jammed.

Figuring it's frozen, I warm the biner between my shaking hands. I pry and push, pull and jerk, but nothing works. I even smack the knurled locking sleeve of the carabiner with the ice hammer, trying to knock it loose. Nothing.

Unable to open the biner, I figure I'll just cut the rope off it.

I pull out my knife, snap open the blade, and reach for the rope, then stop short in a wave of panic.

What are you doing?

Before I cut the rope, I had better think it through. There is 165 feet of rope. Mike is tied in about one-third of the way from one end. If I cut it at his harness point, I'll have about 110 feet of rope left, but that might not be enough. I double-check my wall-height estimate the way Dad taught me, mentally stacking imaginary people, one on top of another, until they reach the snow bridge's roof. It's roughly eighty feet to the crevasse lip, give or take. But what if zigs and zags demand more rope? What if the climbing or rappelling requires me to double up the rope? Then 110 feet might not be enough. No, I shouldn't cut the rope.

If I can't get the rope off Mike's carabiner, I'll just remove that biner from his harness. After unthreading Mike's waist belt, I easily free the locking biner from that half of his purple harness. Then I re-buckle the waist belt so that Mike remains clipped to the anchor.

But the jammed carabiner is only partway off Mike—it's still clipped through his harness's leg loops. There's no way to unthread his permanently sewn leg loops, though, so the biner and rope are still stuck to Mike's harness. This is a serious problem. I resume struggling to open the biner, on my knees, hunched over Mike, with my shoulders barely able to fit crossways in the narrow crevasse. Every time I lift my arms to put some muscle into my efforts, I bump against the ice. I curse the tight space and jab an angry elbow at the wall behind me.

Since I can't detach the carabiner from his leg loops, I realize that I'll have to cut the loops off the biner. The thought startles me—slashing through his harness seems almost evil, as if it somehow desecrates our partnership or says that I am willing to put him at risk to save myself. Good Lord, what if I don't live through this and someone finds us both dead, with part of Mike's harness cut through? Will they think I did something murderous down here? I'd rather give up and die here, stopped short by one stuck carabiner, than risk anyone thinking that. I soothe myself with the thought that I'm not really putting Mike at greater risk; he's still anchored in by his waist belt.

I double-check Mike, running my hands and eyes along his sling. He's secure. Reassured, I dig my jackknife from my parka pocket and flip open the small blade. I puff out a breath to steady myself, then pull the blade across the central tie-in point of Mike's purple leg loops. A second swipe with the knife finishes the job, and the rugged webbing flops open.

I pull the biner straight out the opening I just cut through the central attachment loop. With the carabiner off his harness, at least the entire rope is free from Mike. Now I need to get the biner off the rope. I stand to give myself more room to fight it. Though I apply more strength, it's still stuck. Agitated at this continuing roadblock, I lash out angrily: "Man, I want to talk with the idiot who designed this stupid thing."

Rather than struggling further to open the jammed biner, I realize I can instead just untie the knot from around it. But the fall cinched the knot so tight that it's almost as dense as a baseball. Using fingers and teeth, I push, prod, and pull the tightly bound clump of rope. Frustrated, I fight it, but it won't budge. Figuring there might be ice freezing it shut, I stuff the knot partway into my mouth and exhale forcefully onto it for a few minutes. Dirt and aluminum dust from our gear leave the rope tasting like a dry soda can. I gently chomp my teeth on the knot and feel it soften. Taking it from my mouth, I work at all four strands forming the knot, making slow progress. I pull two strands in opposite directions, as if I'm prying open elevator doors, and the stubborn knot yields at last.

Finally, I pull the fifty-five-foot end of the rope all the way through the loose knot, freeing it from the broken carabiner. I glance at the stuck biner—it's useless now, and I think about tossing it away. But instinct urges me not to. I took it off Mike, so it's important now. I open the right chest pocket of my parka and drop Mike's biner inside.

Still a little shaken at how close I came to mistakenly cutting the rope, I'm thrilled to have the whole 165 feet back, undamaged. Reclaiming our rope while still keeping both of us anchored gives me some confidence that I'm working all of this through. Now that I have the rope free, I tie one end to my leg loops and waist harness. At the other end, I weave a figure-eight-on-a-bight knot and clip it to our anchor screw with a locking biner. I wrap my Prusik loop around the climbing rope just a few feet up from the bottom anchor and clip the loop back to my harness with another locking biner. The rigging is almost ready, but I still need to test my first ever self-belay system before my life depends on it.

I reach up and clip my climbing rope through the upper anchor screw, as if I had just led a short section of wall. Sinking my body down, I slowly settle my weight onto the Prusik-held rope. The friction knot clenches tight, and my 170 pounds stretch the skinny Prusik cord and climbing rope taut. I flick the tensioned lines, and watch with satisfaction as they vibrate and stop. When I lift my feet off our snow ledge, my suspended body slumps against one ice wall.

My system holds.

NOW MORE THAN an hour has passed since Mike and I crashed through the snow bridge. It is almost time to climb. Trying to envision myself making it up there, I keep glancing high above me in the crevasse. The upper chamber glows iridescent blue, as if some alien light emanates from the ice itself.

I've decided to leave only one ice screw as the bottom anchor and take the other. Remembering that the upper screw felt weaker when I placed it, I strip off the biner. Sticking the ice hammer's pick into the screw's eye, I twist it back out of the wall. The threads squeak in protest against the dry, hard ice. Once the screw is out, I blow the ice core from the middle of the hollow tube. Now I have five ice screws with which to climb—not nearly enough, but better than four.

Since we've been down here, chunks of snow and ice have crashed around us, and I know I need a helmet. But mine's deeper in the crevasse, broken. I briefly consider going back down again to get it, but I shudder at the work, and the time, and the fear it will involve. What if something goes wrong this time and I don't make it back to the ledge safely?

I could wear Mike's helmet, but taking it from him feels sacrilegious—that's his, not mine.

However, Mike and I had always agreed that on the mountain, there was no "yours" or "mine," only "ours." We always pooled our resources—food, water, clothing, carabiners. It didn't matter if one of us dropped something, or the other guy broke something. We're in it together. We just split the cost after we got home; paying with beers and burgers was the preferred settlement method.

Still, taking Mike's helmet feels like stripping him naked. I think briefly about hoisting him up as I climb but quickly toss the idea aside, torn between knowing that I can't take him with me and wishing that I didn't have to leave him behind.

My mind roils. The only thing I can do for Mike now is climb out and tell his family what happened to him, and get him off the mountain. I have to make it out, and wearing Mike's helmet will improve my chances.

With that thought, my resolve gets stoked a bit higher. Before I lose the courage to act, I reach down, fiddle with the strap on Mike's blue helmet, and pull it off him. I grit my teeth, grab the chin strap, and cinch the helmet down hard onto my head.

Reaching down again, I gently set Mike's sunglasses back over his eyes. I snug his gloves fully back onto his hands. I look over his waist harness and anchor sling—they're good. Again I inspect that lone ice screw in the wall that will keep Mike from plunging in any deeper and will also be my bottom anchor. I like it that we are both tied into the same screw.

It will work for both of us, or it will work for neither of us. We're still in this together.

I PLAY WITH the gear, stalling—the way I sometimes do when I face something scary. In these situations, Mike always urged me on, infusing me with an empowering energy in moments of uncertainty. We'll be on the rock, and it'll be my turn to lead, and I'll hesitate, afraid it's too much for me, fiddling with the gear, buying time. Mike will sense this and move to cut it off.

"You can do this pitch, Jim," Mike will say. "Get up there."

"You wanna take it?" I'll ask, hoping the answer will be yes.

"No, no—you take it," he'll insist.

When Mike says I can do it, that means I can.

Before I leave, I decide to tidy up the ledge a bit. That way there will be less gear to snag the rope. Besides, if I don't make it and someone finds us, I want them to know that we kept it together as best we could, for as long as we could. While stuffing some loose gear back into my pack, I see Gloria's black Ricoh camera dangling halfway out, ready to take a ride into the depths, but I don't care. It's as if I'm spiting the camera, as though it has something to do with my predicament. It's stupid, but I realize this is an important step for me because it shows how little I care about physical stuff. I am ready to leave it all behind.

Pulling myself together, I push the camera back into my pack, then wonder if I should take a picture of myself in the crevasse so that if I die someone might find it and know that I survived the fall, that I tried to save Mike. I also have a notepad—maybe I should write something to go with the picture. It's suddenly important to me that I make sure that someone—anyone—will learn my fate if I don't make it out alive.

Immediately, I realize that self-doubt is the wrong way to go. I need to believe that people are going to know what happened to us because I am going to get out and tell them. How well we climbed;

how incredible the summit was; how the glacier opened beneath my feet and swallowed us; how hard I tried to do something for Mike.

How he died.

Explanatory notes and photos in case I fail might enable a lack of commitment in me. This realization steels me. No pictures. No note. If I die on the rope, hanging off the frozen crevasse wall, maybe whoever finds us will figure out what happened. Regardless, I'll keep climbing until I make it out and get us both found or I die trying. It's that simple.

For the first time, the concept of climbing out of here begins to feel right, natural. I think again about what I should take with me. Gingerly, I reach through the gash in my pack, considering what I might need: the food bag, the stove, my sleeping bag, and more. But I am foolishly selecting gear as though I'm setting out on a cushy overnight hike—not trying to scale a frighteningly steep, nearly impossible ice face.

I realize that I can't take all this crap with me. I'll be lucky if I can climb this wall at all, let alone lug along equipment. If I don't get out of here today, I'm not going to need this gear anyway.

I decide to secure the gear in case something goes wrong; at least then I'll have something to come back to. I can't stand the thought of hanging from the rope, unable to get out, with nowhere to go. So I'll leave most of the gear clipped to the anchor and take the bare minimum with me.

I grab a pair of thick mitts and stuff them inside my jacket, along with a red balaclava I can wear to keep my head and neck warm. This makes my jacket bulky, though. I can't climb like that, so I seize my blue sleeping bag sack and decide to haul it along behind me with a few things in it. Into the empty sack go the extra mitts and the balaclava. A quart of water. A pair of dirty but dry socks.

I realize that if I make it to the surface I'm going to need snow protection to anchor myself when I get there. I grab an aluminum snow fluke and drop it in. The stuff sack weighs three or four pounds, and I clip it to the back of my harness with a biner. I'm getting closer to the moment when I will leave the ledge.

With a pat to the chest pocket, I confirm that my red-handled knife is inside my jacket. I think about carrying the knife with the blade open in case I need to cut the rope, so it'll be ready a half second quicker, but I immediately discard that dangerous idea. I press my sternum and am comforted when I feel my medal dig into me.

I'm almost ready, but at the thought of actually leaving, I nearly crumble. I'm a fraud. Assembling all this gear, I've only been acting like I am going to climb out. Part of me will not yield, though, and struggles to beat back my fear. In my mind and heart, I realize I'll get out only if I believe it, only if I am confident that I can make it to the top. To keep busy while I recover my plummeting confidence, I slowly pick through a small ditty bag of miscellaneous items in my pack.

There, I see my sunglasses. If I pull myself onto the surface of the glacier today, the sun will blaze blindingly on the white mountainside. To prove to myself that I intend to make it out before the sun goes down, I grab the sunglasses and drop them into my left chest pocket.

Yes! Now you're acting like you're getting out of here today.

I resume mining the ditty bag, searching. I see the National Car Rental key chain, with the keys to the car. It's crazy, but I tell myself that once I get out of this slot, I'm going to drive back to Seattle, get on a plane, and go home. I stuff the car keys in with the sunglasses, then zip the pocket shut. My right hand pats the lumpy pocket twice, and the stiff plastic gently pokes my chest.

After I get out, I'm going home.

And then it hits me: If I want to see Gloria again, I better keep acting like I'm going to get out.

IT'S TIME TO go.

I look down at Mike, and I have the strong urge to say something before I leave—something important, something meaningful. I am almost overcome. I kneel next to Mike's body, look sadly toward his eyes hidden behind sunglasses, and begin talking to him in my head. No words leave my mouth—the only sound is in my mind.

I don't want to go, Mike... I'm not supposed to go... I'm supposed to stay with you... We're partners, and we stick together... But you're gone now, and I'm the only one left... If I'm going to keep living, I've got to get out of here... That means I have to leave you... I'm sorry. I don't want to leave you, but I've got to... If I'm going to get us found, I've got to get myself out of here, but that means I've got to go and I can't take you with me... So you're going to have to stay here for now...

My hands shake, and I press my eyes closed, fighting to pinch off the tears. Tentatively, I touch the sleeve of Mike's jacket. Unconsciously, I blow out rapid breaths, one after another, as I subdue the urge to cry.

I know leaving is the right thing to do, but it feels so wrong. I stand, my head still bent forward. I'm looking down at the jumble of rope lying on the snow. Suddenly, I fear that the rope will tangle around the gear or even Mike after I leave the ledge, stranding me halfway up the wall, unable to ascend or descend, possibly yanking hard on Mike—bad for him, dangerous for me. I don't want to hurt him. I know that I'm facing a messy climb, that chunks of snow and ice will rain down as I scale the crevasse wall.

I realize that if I cover Mike with his sleeping pad, it will shield him from falling debris and will also provide a safe place for the remaining rope while I climb. I pull out his rust-colored Therm-a-Rest pad, unroll it, and cover him from his head down to his shins. His boots stick out from the far end.

Carefully, I begin stacking all the slack rope on the stretched-out pad. When I drop the first few coils on the foam surface, they drum out muffled thumps. The sounds fade as the rope pile builds on the mattress. These neatly flaked coils mean the rope should feed out smoothly as I climb. Knowing that the pad will protect us both soothes me anew.

It's so strange down here. One moment, I'm a meticulous climber, rationally clicking off the list of things I must do to give myself a chance. The next, I'm a grief-stricken friend too overcome to do anything but stare at the rope-covered pad, transfixed.

Rationally, I know I need to rally myself for the climb. But in this moment, I'm not rational, and in my head a battle erupts between confidence and doubt, the same one that has raged since the moment I landed on this ledge and a frozen slurry of ice and snow buried me alive. The negative thoughts send my courage draining from me as if it's liquid and I'm a fractured vessel. A cold wave sweeps from my head down toward my feet. It is as if heat and courage are leaking out of me and into the crevasse vacuum below. A few moments ago, positive emotion had grown inside me like heat rising from my gut. This is the exact opposite.

I stare at my feet, wondering for the hundredth time whether I have the courage to even try. It takes every fiber of my spirit to fight the urge to cower and hide—I have to be strong, I have to take action.

Then, in my mind's eye, I clearly see Mike's face several feet in front of me, off to the right. He scowls at me, a hint of irritation on his face.

"Come on—climb!" he shouts. "You have to try!"

He's not yelling because he's mad at me. I realize that he's yelling to psych me up. He's yelling because he wants me to get out of this frozen chasm.

"Go! Go now, before it's too late. Don't wait any longer! Get out of here while you still can! Climb!"

I know that Mike is physically gone, but his face is so clear and his words so stern that I know he is here and he is serious. Mike is perturbed that I might not even try, and so he is trying to push me into action. Looking up at the wall, I consider my first moves. His face softens into a grin. My partner senses my resolve returning.

"Yeah, that's it," he says more softly. "You can do it."

Adrenaline rushes through me.

I FACE THE left wall, a sense of upward momentum pulsing through me. It feels as if there's a hand on my back, pushing me, while at the same moment I summon my own willpower. I try latching onto the energy building around and in me, raising my right arm high, pumping it slightly up and down in rhythm with the three slow breaths I suck in. I yell out and swing the hammer in my right hand hard. The pick smashes into the frozen wall with a spray of ice. In concert with this progress, a voice inside my mind shouts: *That's it!*

I plant the ax in my left hand just as firmly two feet above my left ear. One foot lifts off the ledge as I kick the front points of a crampon into the wall. Squeezing my biceps tight, I heft my chest up and shift my weight to the tool and crampon placements. Holding my body tension snug to stabilize myself, I smash my other foot forward like a soccer player and drive the front points of my second boot into the ice wall.

I have begun leaving the ledge. I hear Mike whisper in my ear:

"You're doing it, man. You're climbing."

THE CREVASSE WALLS are only two feet apart, so I rotate my right hip out and kick my right foot into the far wall. With my cramponed boots now on opposite walls, I can easily balance on my feet and save my precious arm strength.

Starting up the wall had built into such a huge internal obstacle that I can hardly believe I am doing it. I look down to verify that I'm actually moving up. Twelve inches below the soles of my boot sits the lumpy surface of the snow ledge. I'm really climbing.

Guessing that I can ascend well by stemming, I slide my Prusik knot eight feet farther along the climbing rope. This extra slack defines my next goal as I rush to resume my ascent. Clinging to my tools for balance and with my legs bridged across the gap, I alternately move each boot upward. Like a chimney sweep, I shift my weight back and forth, stemming up the wall until my eyes are level with my buried ice tool picks. I set one tool higher, then the other. Raise one foot, kick the crampon into the ice. Lift the other foot, then scissors-kick to push myself up. Nervous that I will tire and peel off, and probably more scared that I might lose courage and back off, I move fast.

When the slack disappears from my short climbing rope, I reach down with one hand to pull some more through my Prusik, letting out another six feet. I ascend quickly, getting myself into a good rest position, with one foot planted on each wall. I reach to the gear rack hanging from my shoulder and unclip an ice screw. The screw's name is a bit of a misnomer, because while these hollow metal tubes are threaded, I have to start them—and sometimes finish them—with hammer blows. With my left wrist still leashed to its firmly planted ice tool for security, I use my left hand to hold the tip of the screw against the wall. With the ice hammer clutched in my right hand, I beat hard on the screw's head. Once the teeth and threads bite the ice wall, I use my hammer as a lever to slowly crank the ice screw all the way in.

That done, I clip my rope onto the screw with a biner. I should be safe now, but I am still unsure of my jury-rigged self-belay system. I slide the Prusik knot until the other end of the cord snugs against my harness. I've got to test my system now; I can't afford to climb far up the wall and then find out the hard way that my improvised safety net won't hold.

I figure I can ease myself onto the self-belayed rope, but I'm also nervous that it'll fail, so I pull out a sling and hook one end to the screw, the other to my waist harness. If my Prusik knot fails, the backup sling will hold me.

I stretch up, pull my ax out from the ice, and sort of step off the wall, falling about half a foot.

Weighted nylon creaks and a loaded biner clicks against the ice screw's eye, but my system holds tight.

I feel a subtle confidence boost. I've taken a test fall—a small one, for sure—and the rope and the screw and Prusik loop did the job I had imagined they would. I'm calmer now. I have figured it out.

I look down: I am fifteen feet above the ledge. One-fifth of the way to salvation.

My watch says it's one-ten P.M. It took me more than an hour to get off the ledge, and I calculate that I've got at least seven hours of good sunlight—maybe eight. I'm climbing well. I make another move up, but the walls are spreading away from each other. With one foot planted on each side wall, I rest spread-eagled, the muscles in my groin stretched so far they burn. Momentarily, I glance down between my splayed legs at the yawning crevasse below me. I peer hard into the shadows back at the ledge, then stop myself. I should not think about the darkness down there, only about the light above.

I catch my breath, resting my aching left shoulder, and stare at the walls looming above me. I cannot stem up any higher—the gap has grown too great. I have to pick one wall and commit to it.

Even though I can see better from up here, my analysis is the same: If I climb the easier right wall, I face the dangerous task of chopping through the weak snow bridge to reach the surface. The left wall is vertical, then overhanging, and sports that protruding ice roof, but it leads right back to the hole, to the light.

I commit to the left wall. There is no going back.

CHAPTER 14

▲ ▲ ▲

I'M GETTING PUSHED off the wall. The ice is a hair steeper than vertical now, and it forces my chest back a bit, tipping me off balance. If I keep free climbing, using my tools and crampons, I might lose my purchase and fall, maybe crashing past Mike, maybe dropping all the way down until I'm corked. But if I can just make another move or two before I begin aid climbing, I can get a little higher before tapping my limited gear supply.

I am almost twenty feet above the ledge—above Mike. Every foot I ascend gets me closer to the sunshine, closer to the warmth. But it's a good-news, bad-news situation: The higher I go, the easier it will be to crank in the screws, but the easier it is to twist them in, the weaker they will be. I'm only a quarter of the way out, and already the ice is noticeably softer than it was down in the depths. Up toward the surface, the ice is rotten—that's why the snow bridge collapsed beneath my feet; that's why I'm in here.

When I hang from an ice screw to rest, the weighted harness bites deep into my thighs, even through three layers of clothing. Wiggling my hips momentarily eases the discomfort, but it makes the climbing rope jostle the screw holding me. Unsettled, I stare at the buried ice protection and wonder about its strength. I nervously scan the rope I hang from, no thicker than my pinky.

Tightly gripping the shafts of the two ice tools, I pull hard. Immediately I feel the weight in my arms. Fatigue burns through my already tired forearms, a fiery exclamation point on the challenge I face. Ice climbers call this "getting pumped," and if you can't get your weight off your arms, it usually ends in a fall. The pump is coming on fast. I know I have only a minute before I take a ride.

Fighting to stay calm, I kick the front points of my crampons into the wall. They sink a quarter of an inch into the ice—good enough. I stand up on the footholds, straightening my knees, and push my whole body up fifteen inches. Now I have to get an ax out and quickly resink it higher on the wall. Being bent backward by the overhang reduces my leverage and my ability to use my upper-body strength, so I can't get my ax to budge. The pick has bitten too deeply, and I wrestle it, desperate to pull it out of the ice wall. I yank harder.

Suddenly, it breaks free. The sharp metal edge of the adze smacks me an inch above the eyebrow, square on the helmet—Mike's helmet. The shocking blow knocks me off balance. I tip backward, ripping the hammer out of the ice wall. That's it—I'm falling.

My head smashes into the opposite wall, five feet away. Mike's helmet takes the impact, which shoves the dome forward, down over my forehead, and drives the brim into the bridge of my nose. I slump to a stop six feet lower, dangling halfway between upside down and sideways, swinging back and forth. Slings of climbing gear droop off me, jumbled around my arms and ice tools.

I struggle to right myself and then tilt the ill-fitting helmet back so I can see again.

Three feet up sits the single protective ice screw from which I now am suspended. I'm relieved that my screw and my Prusik loop worked just the way I hoped they would. Using my self-belayed rope system, I start pulling myself upward. Just then a low rumble echoes through the crevasse. A section of the snow bridge snaps off far above me and hurtles my way.

I scramble up closer to the screw, pressing myself against the ice, trying to make myself smaller. The collapsing snow sails past a good twenty feet off to my right, but even so it shakes me. I clutch the rope against my chest and hang on while I force myself to breathe rhythmically, waiting for the terror to pass. As my thumping heart slows, I think about my next move. I can't risk taking many more falls like that one. Even though clawing higher with my crampons and ice tools would help me conserve my limited climbing gear, such risky free climbing has to stop. It is time to aid climb.

Aid climbing means I'll have to sink an ice screw roughly every three feet, clip my rope into it, and hang directly off it. This is going to deplete my gear really fast.

God, if I just had more screws.

I started with only six, and I've already used two: one back at the ledge to give me a bottom anchor and to keep Mike secure, and the one I am now suspended from. Three days of alpine climbing have left them—and my picks—dull, but I'll have to make do.

To make the most progress, I reach as high as I can to place the next screw, struggling with stretched-out arms to get it started. Once it is seated, I insert the tip of my tool's pick into the screw's open eye and crank around and around until it is in deep. I clip my climbing rope to the screw above me and tighten the Prusik loop so that I am protected as I make my next move. I take a pink sling three feet long and half an inch in diameter and clip it to the screw as a substitute aider. With my left hand on a buried ice ax and the other on the screw's eye, I pull myself up and twitchily wiggle my right foot into the dangling aid sling. It is a struggle—the pointy tips of my crampons keep snagging on the floppy nylon. Finally, I work my bulky boot and crampon through the sling's small opening. Pushing my boot down, I stand in the loop, then kick the front points of my left boot into the wall for balance.

Grasping at the ice screw in the wall near my waist to steady myself, I fight to catch my breath. I have advanced up just three feet, and I'm wiped out. I rest, then start a new placement farther above. Repeating the same awkward process with ice screw, sling, and rope, I work my way up, and fifteen minutes later I have advanced another three measly feet. Between the free climbing earlier and this slow aid climbing, I am now about twenty-five feet above the snow ledge where Mike lies. I'm a third of the way out. I've got to make it before dark.

I SETTLE INTO a routine. One foot in a sling, the other foot kicked into the wall. One ice tool stuck in the wall, the other in my hand as I pound and crank my next screw in. I have the pattern down, and my pace quickens a little, but every step is a fight. The slings snag and the rope kinks. My gloves won't fit easily through the ice tools' skinny wrist loops. Then, after I finally wiggle and twist and shove them in, when I need to remove them later, they won't come out.

I set a new screw every three feet or so, using them up fast. My moves are getting sloppy, a little desperate, and I pay the price for that. As my gloved hand fumbles gear from the rack, a sling slips from my grip. I make a lunging grab for it but miss. As it slithers down my leg, I swing my boot, hoping to snag the webbing with a crampon point, but the deserter escapes, twisting as it falls into the darkness. I watch the lime-green sling spiral down, drifting just right of our ledge, floating past Mike's feet. I automatically project a silent plea to Mike: *Get it. Hook it with your foot.*

Then it drops into the throat of the crevasse and disappears.

If I have even one or two more slip-ups like that, I'll never get out. As I vow to be more diligent, I peer down at Mike, covered by the sleeping pad. My hacking at the frozen wall has already knocked snow and ice onto the pad, so I'm glad I put it there to protect him. But I am also struck from this perspective by how small the ledge is—two feet wide and about seven feet long. A few feet to either side and we would have missed it entirely. Of the entire length of the corridor that I can see, we landed in the only spot where we could stop without getting corked.

I notice something else: Already it seems a little darker down on the ledge than where I am now. I think that is a good sign—I am making the transition from the darkness up to the light.

I get back to work, executing my aid-climbing process again and again, fidgeting with cold, stiff fingers to work the Prusik knot up the ice-crusted rope. Finally, I reach a point about thirty-five feet above the ledge, probably forty to forty-five feet from the glacier's surface, and I place the fifth and final ice screw.

I am out of screws and I'm not even halfway up the wall.

I NEED TO descend and pull out my lower screws so I can use them again higher up. To get down there, I have to rappel off the top ice screw. Trusting my life to a single piece of pro is risky and unwise—if it yanks out, I'll plunge fifty feet to the bottom of the crevasse—but I have no other option. I feed a loop of rope through the tubular rappel device and attach it to my harness with a locking biner, leaving my mobile Prusik cord attached to the climbing rope as a backup. After double-checking my system, I slowly feed rope through the rappel device and descend back into the darkness I just fought so hard to escape. Giving back my vertical gain also feels demoralizing and counterproductive, like losing yardage in a football game.

I descend roughly fifteen feet to reach the first screw I placed. I twist it out of the wall, clean the ice core out of it, and clip it to my harness. I will need to leave an ice screw in the wall every fifteen or twenty feet to protect myself from a long fall. But I can't know exactly how much farther I have to climb, so it is tough to judge how many ice screws to leave in for protection and how many to remove for reuse higher up. There is no good answer, but I still need to make a decision.

I pull out three screws and leave three in the wall: the one I'm hanging from, my bottom anchor, and one in between as protection.

After pulling each screw I fight my way back up, kicking my front points into the wall, swarming up the slings, swinging my tools, pulling and pushing to regain the vertical territory I'd surrendered. With every precious foot recovered, I must work my Prusik back up the rope to keep myself snug and safe. The friction-producing knot is the key to my system, allowing me to move down or up the bottom-anchored climbing rope. But the clinching knot constantly seizes up on the wet rope in this frozen chasm, frustrating my progress.

Climbing the dangling rope in a slightly overhanging section, I push off the wall with one crampon, which sets me spinning. I twist slowly. I try ignoring it, but staring down into the twirling dark recesses of the crevasse scares me, and looking up at the snow bridge rotating over my head nauseates me. I wait until the twisting stops, recover my poise, and get going again.

Eventually I push and pull my way back to my high point. Three recovered ice screws dangle from my waist. It is now sometime after two o'clock. I am beat and want to rest again, but the thought of losing momentum scares me.

So I climb on, exhausted, sopping wet from the snow bridge's dripping meltwater. Soon I settle into a routine. I pull myself up, drive a screw into the wall, clip the rope in, and rest. Then I hang a sling from that upper screw, fight my boot into the sling's narrow loop, stand up in it as if it were a one-step aider, and rest. Set one tool higher, pull down on the screw above me, and hoist myself up a few feet. Once there, I clip my waist harness to the screw and rest again.

After three exhausting rounds of this, I advance a dozen precious feet up the wall and am out of screws. Yet again I will have to give back some of my advance to replenish my gear. So I lower myself down over the hard-won ground to retrieve two screws from below, then grapple my way back up. Leapfrogging the gear up the wall is working, but it's taking a huge toll on me.

My mind and body feel strong, confident, and fluid one minute, weak, hurting, and stalling the next. Each low point has the potential to discourage me. Summoning the willpower to rebound from each setback is wearing me out. I sometimes catch myself mentally checking out for a few minutes.

Every time I try to slide my crampons into the nylon slings that I must stand in, it is a little like trying to fit a foot into a stirrup on a galloping horse while wearing cleats. And the leashes on Mike's ice ax and hammer are too short for me. When I place the tools overhead, the leashes snap tight prematurely and restrict the natural arc of my swing, limiting my power, forcing me to smash the tools repeatedly before I get a solid stick. All these sapping issues coalesce into draining fatigue.

For reassurance, I poke my chest until I feel the pope-blessed medallion Gloria gave me all those years ago.

IT IS MIDAFTERNOON.

After my second round-trip down to retrieve screws, I return to my high point. I estimate that I am thirty to thirty-five feet from the top, and as I look up I contemplate the blue bag dangling from my waist. I consider throwing the gear bag up through the hole in the snow bridge—a kind of signal flare that might attract the attention of climbers who are trudging down the glacier from the summit. If they see it and investigate, maybe I'll be found.

It won't be easy though—like throwing an oversized snowball straight up at a streetlamp. It's tempting, because if it works, I won't have to climb all the way out. Staring thirty-five feet above me at the ragged portal leaves me wary: I doubt I can throw this lumpy gear bag straight through it on my first and only shot. If I miss, the bag will disappear down the crevasse with all my meager supplies. Besides, I'm afraid that tossing the bag might be a signal to myself that I have given up on my plan to climb out. And if I've learned one thing so far, it is that I have to act confident, like I am going to make it, even if deep down I'm not sure that this is true.

I decide not to try tossing the gear bag through the hole and instead to count on myself. There is nobody else.

I KNOW FROM all my training and experience that I need to force down water. But even small sips burn; they loosen the blood clots in the back of my throat, making me spit up red-black slime. Seeing the blood reminds me that something could be seriously wrong inside me. This shakes my already tenuous confidence, so I lose interest in drinking.

When I packed my blue gear pouch back on the ledge, hours earlier, the thought of food had turned my stomach, so I didn't bring any with me. Now I badly need those calories but have nothing to eat.

I look down at the ledge, but I can no longer really see the inflatable pad anymore—just the shadowy outline of Mike's feet. I figure it is good that I can't see him, that it is better to focus on the climb. Thinking about him fills me with a sadness that threatens to crush me. The piled snow and padding that separate us make it easier for me to concentrate on what I have to do—*climb*—and leave the bitter sorrow to deal with later.

Hanging, exhausted, my mind drifting, I find myself wondering, *What's Mike's spirit doing now?* In that moment, I have a sense—a comforting feeling—that he is still here with me in the crevasse. Not just floating in a portion of the yawning crack, but filling the entire void.

Perhaps that explains all the times falling ice and snow have sailed past me harmlessly. The upper snow bridge has by now collapsed in several crackling fractures, huge slabs of snow that plunged to the depths of the crevasse. Any one of them could have swept me off my stance or even suffocated me, yet none of them has, and I feel that Mike's spirit is the reason. My partner's still watching out for me while I do my best to get us up this wall.

HAVING LEFT BEHIND several screws, carabiners, and slings as protection in case I fall, now I have to use anything I can to help me claw my way up. With no spare slings left now, at the next screw I clip in a rock-climbing cam, figuring I can use it as a small, open step. I stick my front points into the cam's trigger-wire mechanism and torque my foot sideways. Metal screeches on metal. The fragile cam wires bend grotesquely, but they hold. I stand up, gaining another two feet.

I have one thing going for me that dates all the way back to boyhood: I'd bought the best climbing gear I could. Dad was a blue-collar painter, but he never skimped on safety equipment. He used to say, "Fudge it when ya can to save a buck, but don't be cheap when it comes to gear that people's lives depend on."

So even as a nearly broke college student with big climbing dreams, I scrounged in other areas of my life so I could afford the best mountaineering gear out there, poring over catalogs, comparing specifications, searching out the best deals. Saving money was important, but not as important as having strong equipment.

IT IS A netherworld inside the crevasse. The air near me is below freezing, yet up above—along the snow bridge that looks like a dappled veil, light leaking through in places—the summer solstice sun bakes the snow to the melting point.

Meltwater falls constantly in a frigid drizzle, then freezes after it lands on my jacket and my rope. Each time I move my Prusik along the climbing rope, I fight with that layer of ice, rubbing and scraping at it with gloved hands, trying to clean the rope so the friction knot can bite down. It is clumsy and slow, but I push on, and each foot closer to the surface I sense more light around me. I keep spitting up blood, not knowing the source. It seems like I don't have any major injuries, because I have been climbing for several hours now. But what if something is still wrong inside me? Maybe a broken rib or lacerated lung? The pending sunset has been my self-imposed time limit, but what if I don't have that long?

I look at the wall in front of me and hawk a bloody mix of saliva onto the ice. It drools down for a moment, then freezes in place, distracting me, entertaining me. And it gives me an idea. The bloody spatter will be my tick marks—my equivalent of the small chalk swipes that rock climbers sometimes leave on a wall to chronicle their high points. Those bloody spots of sputum, I decide, will prove to anyone who descends into the crevasse that I tried to get us out, that I tried hard. In some warped way, I seek to turn negatives—like spitting up blood—into positives that will help propel me up, to find tenacity even in the things that scare me.

AFTER A FOURTH, shorter trip down to retrieve my ice screws, I reach a point about sixty feet above the ledge and twenty feet from the top. It is nearing four P.M. and I have been leading—out front, alone, forging the route, placing gear—for about three hours.

My heart aches for Mike; an off-center feeling deep in my gut constantly reminds me that something in the world is very wrong. When I shift my weight from one foot to the other, water squirts out the top of my boot—a blend of meltwater and sweat. Wet nylon clothes cling to my skin and suck heat from my core.

The wall here, already leaning past vertical, juts out several feet to form a small, horizontal ceiling above me. I saw this roof before leaving our ledge and worried then that it would be too big for me to reach past. Now hanging just beneath it, I extend my arm out toward the lip and confirm the worst: I can't stretch the tips of my fingers beyond it. And I am down to just two spare ice screws.

I think about going way back down and pulling out the ice screw near the bottom of my rope. Another one would make life easier. But by now I am so exhausted that if I descend that far, I might not make it back up; I abandon the idea.

I feel tired, so tired. My mind floats to Gloria. Dad. The rest of my loved ones. Thoughts of my family make me wonder about Mike's family. What am I going to tell them?

Thinking intensely about the important people in my life, I feel their energy. I sense the strong presence of Dad, Mike, and some fuzzy blend of my climbing partners hovering nearby. They are silent, watching me closely. Gloria stands a few paces behind them. She, too, holds back from saying anything, but she looks upset. I want to ease her anxiety and tell her not to worry, but I know I can't.

TRYING TO CRANK back up, I lift my ice ax. My arm slowly sinks, my muscles powerless against gravity. Numbness tingles in my left arm and leg. Temporarily unable to advance, I study my position. When I look between my feet, I see my yellow rope trailing down the ice wall, clipped into the three protective ice screws I have left behind every fifteen feet or so. Dangling beneath the overhang with all the vast dark space beneath and around me, I feel like some kind of floating astronaut.

Then I notice something else: Facing one fear after another for hours has tempered me to a resilient calm. Repeatedly grappling with obstacles and adversity has led me to tap wells of fortitude that usually lie hidden and unused. I sense that if I can persist through these moments of fear and doubt, a relieving wave of tenacity will eventually rise to aid me. Just knowing this encourages me to keep hanging on.

When a little strength returns to my arms, I pull myself up until my helmet bumps against the underside of the ice roof. With one foot in a sling, I poke the tips of my other crampon into the ice for stability. I creep that free foot up, then push off hard to lever myself away from the wall in an effort to get a bit more reach. I swing out to the right, like a barn door on its hinges, and stretch out as far as I can, reaching, wincing, and get my right hand up and beyond the edge of the overhang.

With my abdomen muscles quivering with fatigue, I lean back precariously and am able to crank an ice screw about two turns into the wall just above the overhang. Then I run out of energy and let myself drop a few feet in a controlled fall. I sag onto the sling attached to the ice screw just below the roof and rest. After a few minutes, I fight back into the stretched-out position, reach past the lip, and twist the screw a bit deeper into the ice. With about one-third of the screw's length into the frozen wall, I figure it can hold part of my body weight. So with my right arm I hook my hammer over the protruding screw's shaft and pull my upper body high enough so that I can peer past the overhang.

To my great relief, the view up the wall looks less steep than what I've been climbing. Excited that easier ground awaits, I gleefully spit a blood clot a foot higher up the headwall to prove I reached that high. Straightening my right arm out, I lower my head and chest below the roof's lip and intentionally collapse back onto the screw underneath the roof. Guilt jabs me: I saw the wall above, but I hadn't climbed onto it yet, so when I spit my blood mark I cheated. It seems silly, but this somehow sullies the real work and achievement that have gotten me this far. I recognize that no one knows and no one cares about this little progress game except me, but it still feels wrong.

Realizing that I should not have claimed that ground prematurely, I grunt my way back up and out along the roof. I stretch my ice tool farther up the headwall and use the pick to scratch off the red frozen tick mark. Once I have scraped away my own false claim, my conscience is eased, but my arms are tired. I settle back below the overhang, satisfied that I have made amends.

Worn out from that one-minute penance, I rest again, pondering the tough overhang ahead—the crux. Because the crux is the most physically difficult section, it's also usually an ascent's most mentally challenging part. The trick to getting past it is to act confident even though I might be racked with doubt. Hesitating or stalling at the crux wears you out, but acting confident and moving past it boldly will lead to easier ground ahead. Setting protection, then moving on is usually best, so Mike and I have always reminded each other by saying, "Pro and go."

I will be on a much easier section of the wall if I can just get past this crux overhang. I have to keep moving.

I struggle back up, reach out, and continue my slow progress of cranking the ice screw into the wall. My position is awkward, and just balancing in delicate tension while I turn the screw consumes huge amounts of energy. It is like standing on a wobbly chair in a hallway and bending underneath a doorframe to work on the wall in an adjacent room.

After advancing the screw a few rotations I slip, falling onto my rope with a jerk. I need a rest. I want to just hang there—five minutes at the most, no more.

My mind drifts back home, and I start thinking about what it will mean to my family if I get out, what it will mean to Mike's family. And what it will mean to all of them if I don't make it—how no one might ever find out what happened. Thinking of all the grief that this will cause makes me sad and guilty. Sensing these emotions softens me up, and I feel my energy drop.

As my spirits sink, I wonder how much more I can take. My mind loses focus. So tired.

PAIN. MY FOREHEAD stings. Drowsy, I reach up to make the sting go away. I touch the wall and realize that my head is against the ice. I shift in my harness to move away, and when I lift my arm, my jacket feels stiff. Newly formed slivers of ice in the crook of my elbow break away, swirling down into the darkness like little translucent leaves.

How did I get like this? I heft my arm up slowly and look at my watch: four-thirty. How can that be? I drifted off for almost half an hour, sixty feet above the ledge, twenty feet from freedom.

But hanging motionless for so long on the rope has left me

almost catatonic. My mind is dull, my energy is low, and the many pains all seem magnified. Just lifting my arm makes my neck burn.

I'm not sure I can take it anymore. Maybe this is as far as I am going to get. I toy with the idea of not trying to go any higher, but then I remember everyone back home. They wouldn't want me to quit, no matter how much I hurt right now.

I understand that I have to keep going, keep taking the pain for my family. For Gloria. For Dad. For Mom and my three sisters. For Mike's brother, and his mom and dad, so that they will know what happened.

For Mike.

I have to take the risk and misery for everyone in both of our families. And somehow, in my sputtering mind, I guess that might be twenty people, maybe more. I reason that if I take all the pain and effort and divvy it up among all of them, then it won't seem quite so overwhelming. The suffering I have to endure to see any one of them again is individually quite small. Even one foot of anguished progress for each important person will get me up the remaining twenty feet. All I have to do is work a bit harder, endure a little chunk of pain for each of those people, and then just do it over and over again. Repeatedly doing small things, one for each person that matters to Mike and me—that I can do.

I realize that this is not really even about me anymore. I want to live, but I am so far gone now that it's not guaranteed. Even if I can't rally back to action for myself, I must be resilient enough to carry on for the people I love. They have made me all I am and given me all I have. I owe it to them to keep trying. The same is true for Mike and his family: I owe it to them to do the best I can to get us out.

I certainly owe it to Gloria.

Seeing Gloria almost seems too much to hope for. Sharing a long future with her is what I want, but I don't know if I can realistically expect that now. With my body and spirit so battered, I'm not sure I'll actually live very long after this.

Even if I make it out of the crevasse and get to see her for just a minute, that would be something. At least she wouldn't have to live the rest of her life not knowing what happened to me, with me having just been wiped off the face of the Earth. Knowing what happened to us would probably make it easier for Gloria to rebuild her life. So even if I reach the lip of the crevasse, get onto the glacier, and die there—that's a win. Because then she'll know.

This new perspective soothes me. I no longer have to worry about the distant future, or if I'm busted up inside. All I have to do to win is get out of here. And if I get my life back, well, that's a dream almost too big to hope for.

Slowly, I begin moving again. With jerky arms, I stiffly brush the ice crystals from my sleeves. I crane my neck to scout the overhang, then grimace through clenched teeth as pain knifes through my left shoulder. After each rest, it's harder to get going.

If I let myself stop one more time, I may never be able to start up again. But if I just keep moving, I have a chance to make it out alive.

For them.

CHAPTER 15

▲ ▲ ▲

I AM ALMOST through the crux—another couple moves and I'll be past the hardest part. I've seen the headwall beyond the overhang, and once I clip to the screw above the roof's lip, the climbing should get easier. Still a little rattled by my slip into a stupor a few minutes ago, I rush to anchor myself to that upper ice screw, snapping a two-foot-long sling to my chest harness.

Having already made several trips out to the lip, I've got the moves wired. I scoot my left foot high, push my left hip tight under the ceiling, and hook my ax pick through an anchor carabiner clipped to a screw at waist level. Then I stretch to the right and stabilize myself with body tension. My abdominal muscles, torn in the fall and fatigued to their limit, ache and tremble.

To increase the upper screw's strength before I commit to it, I twist it in one more turn with my hammer before my power ebbs. That will have to be good enough.

The leash for the new screw dangles from my chest harness with a carabiner attached and ready to go. I grab that biner, extend my arm toward the nearly buried screw, and open the carabiner's gate. Hooking the biner through the screw's eyehole, I feel a solid tap when the two metallic pieces meet each other, and I see the carabiner settle in. Having finally anchored myself above the dreaded over-hang, I pull my left tool free, sagging happily onto the leash that connects my chest harness to the upper ice screw.

And it's then that disaster strikes.

My body slumps, driving my shoulders up toward my ears, and in an instant, both arms fly above my head, hands flopping uselessly, squeezing my lungs empty with a deep grunt.

My head is too far below the ice roof. Why am I so low? And when I try to breathe, I can't. My lungs are smashed inward. A tight nylon sling pushes hard against my face.

Now I understand: I've blown it.

When I clipped the screw on the headwall with a sling directly from my chest harness, I didn't think it through. Settling all my weight onto that leash yanked the chest harness up and drove it into my armpits, forcing my arms above me and crushing my torso. I hang from my chest harness, suffocating.

I kick my left foot, but my crampon skitters off the ice. Both legs paw the air.

Flailing my trapped arms, my heart pounding, I get my right hand on the two inches of ice screw protruding from the wall. I grab the screw's eye and pull hard, easing some pressure from the cinching chest harness and letting my arms move more freely. Gasping, I suck in a short breath. Then I lose my grip on the screw and slip down an inch. My arms pop back up, and the fight resumes full force.

As the chest harness cuts deep into my armpits, numbness sears my arms. I hear the gurgle and strain of my constricted breathing. The front points of my crampons scrape across the wall, but I find no purchase.

My left hand bumps into the tight leash leading up to the screw. I grasp and pull hard, taking some weight off the harness. With my body an inch higher, I push down with both arms, levering my tri-ceps against the nylon strands of my chest harness. This pumps me up another precious inch and transfers more weight from my chest to my arms. Getting a crampon into the wall lets me push up even higher. Clutching the protruding screw, I do half a pull-up and lift my weight from the chest harness. I pant and recover a bit, but the arm strain builds; I can't hold myself here very long.

With my right hand, I grab the carabiner connecting the leash to my chest harness. If I disconnect, I'll drop below the overhang and lose ground, but if I don't, I'm going to strangle. I fight the biner off my chest harness, unclip, then let go. The anchored rope arcs me back under the overhang, slams me face-first into the ice, and leaves me hanging from my waist harness, stunned but okay. Cowering under the roof, I pant fast, trying to calm myself, pressing a palm against my chest to check for my medal. I chide myself for breaking my pattern and for making such a serious error.

The good news is that the ice screw above the overhang must be solid, and with that piece and leash already in place, clearing the roof should be simple now.

Once I recover, I reach up and clip my climbing rope to the dangling sling first, the way I should have done before. I adjust my Prusik loop tight, then release my grip on the piece below the roof. My torso swings out beneath the upper screw, and my feet slingshot toward the opposite wall. Hanging in free air below the screw, I pendulum back and forth. I close my eyes, worried about the screw pulling out. After the swinging slows, I kick a crampon into the wall for traction, hook a tool on the upper ice screw's shaft, hoist myself up, and connect my sit harness directly to the upper screw. Now secure, I relax my limbs and slump my helmet against the ice wall.

And with that, I'm past the overhang.

THE HIGHER I look, the less steep the headwall seems. It's about eighty-five degrees right here, then eighty, then maybe only seventy degrees about fifteen feet above me, near the top. The climbing should keep getting easier.

With three screws strung out below the overhang, the bottom anchor screw, plus the one I'm hanging from, I have only one ice screw left. I reach up to start pounding it in, but a moment later power drains from my arms and I stop to rest. As I resume twisting the screw into the wall, the wet ice yields easily—a bad sign. The last screw placement was pretty bad, too. I know these will never hold if I fall, and I wonder whether they'll even hold my body weight for long. If one screw pulls and the next can't catch me, I might plummet, ripping out one piece after the next in a zipper fall.

After clipping into the second placement above the overhang, I'm out of screws. The one back below the roof is not doing much good anymore, and I consider dropping down to retrieve it. I'd have more gear, but I worry that I don't possess the arm strength to scale the roof again. If I go down there, I might not be able to get back up. It's too risky to try. I'm exiled to the headwall now.

A new texture on the crevasse wall surprises me. It's coated with hundreds of rough, spherical ice globs ranging in size from plums to grapefruits. Ever-changing frozen environments sculpt water and moist air oddly, but in ten years of winter climbing I've never seen ice blisters like these. I figure the protruding lumps can serve as footholds, so I set a boot atop one, easing the strain on my lower back.

Three and a half straight hours of balancing in jittery aid slings has kinked my back into knots. The new body position provides long-needed relief. After five minutes, I switch feet to give other muscles a break, but as I step onto an orange-sized ice globe, it snaps off the wall. I drop hard onto my sit harness, my foot pawing empty air.

Startled by the mini fall, I curse the ice as adrenaline blasts through me.

I had contemplated aiding up by looping some webbing over the protruding ice globs, just like I've done on rock faces—threading slings around knobby bedrock protuberances we call "chicken heads." But if these ice chicken heads are that weak and untrustworthy, I can't risk hanging from them.

Suddenly, the slide and slump of collapsing snow echoes in the crevasse. Terrified, I throw both arms over my neck and lean into the wall. Holding my breath and listening, I hope I am not in the fall line. Ice chunks splinter in a shattering crash far off to my right. Then I sense a voice nearby: "It's okay. You're safe."

The man's voice came from directly behind me, just a foot away. My brain knows the words were only imagined, but my gut tells me someone is here. I casually glance over my right shoulder, into empty space. I resume facing the milky wall before me, but I sense a strong presence, maybe two. Remembering an old tae kwon do lesson, I stretch my peripheral vision sideways without turning my head, trying to snatch a glimpse. It feels like two people are right behind me, just out of sight.

I casually glance to the right, then whip my head left 180 degrees to see if I can catch them, but all I see is blue light bouncing off the other wall. Of course no one's hovering behind me, and yet I can't shake the strong feeling that two people are there. I feel no fear—I sense that whoever it is, they're on my side, and that they seem to understand better than I what's going on. Closing my eyes, I try to detect their presence.

It's Dad and Mike.

I feel less alone, somehow, even as I struggle to understand it all. With the headwall's angle easing off, I consider free climbing it. It's only about fifteen feet to the top—fifteen feet to freedom, fifteen feet to life. The lure of salvation beckons me.

If I move fast, I think, *I can climb it in a minute.* I latch onto the idea and start calculating how much slack rope to let through my

Prusik loop before I start free climbing. I know I can't be wrong in my calculation: Too much slack, and I greatly increase the chance of disaster if I fall; not enough, and the too short tether might prevent me from escaping from this hole.

I examine the wall again, confirming my fifteen-foot guesstimate to the crevasse lip.

But the snow bridge hole I must climb back through is two feet off to the right. I need a few extra feet of rope to traverse sideways—that makes twenty feet—and then a bit more to make sure that I clear the crevasse lip. This means I need about twenty-five feet of slack. With that much slack, if I slip off the wall I'll drop twenty-five to fifty feet—depending on where I am when I lose my grip—before the rope catches me. That's a huge drop, even onto the best placements, and those last two screws were terrible. If I peel off, I'm looking at a chain-reaction zipper fall. These are horrifying possibilities, but I'm infused with excitement.

I adjust my gloves and ice tool leashes. Still attached to my highest screw for safety, I loosen the Prusik knot and pull through twenty-five feet of slack. I watch the rope loop grow far below my feet, drooping past the overhang. Twice I jig up the slack line, then lower it again, making sure it can't snag and stop me short. The rope's clear. I test-wiggle my fingers and flex my grips on the tools, getting ready to sprint to the top. Reaching to my chest, I feel again for my medal.

I grab the biner that, when released, will thrust me onto the sharp end of a big lead fall above a manky screw. Just one simple unclip and I will force myself to play this terrible hand right now, all in, to free climb up in one great go-for-broke effort. One way or the other, it will be over in the next minute. Perhaps that is what I want the most: for it all to just be over.

I hook my index finger on the biner's gate, ready to open it.

And then I hear a loud voice in my head. It's Dad.

"Stop! Ya can't do it."

Stunned, I pause.

"Ya gotta keep doin' what you were doin'," he says.

"No," I say. "This will be over in a minute. All I've got to do is climb this one section and it's over."

Dad doesn't buy it.

"Ya may not be strong enough. The wall may not be secure enough. And if ya fall, the screw's not gonna hold. You're gonna go all the way down."

"I can't aid climb anymore. I'm out of gear. I'm too tired."

"I know ya want to climb out fast, but the risk is too big. Ya can't do it. The aid climbing's working. Stick with it."

With my forehead slumped against the wall, I squeeze my eyes shut to keep from crying. My internal whining spills over, and in a half cry, half plea I mutter aloud against the ice, "I just can't keep doing this anymore."

My admission of weakness hangs heavy in the damp air. For long, silent seconds my blank mind awaits a response. The answer comes back gentle but solid:

"Ya hafta," Dad says.

Dad has always been right with these kinds of calls. During all my intensely dangerous crawls on electrical tower arms, Dad kept those binoculars glued to his eye sockets and shouted life-protecting instructions to me, his only son. Back then, with my head forced down below the wires and my body struggling not to fall, I couldn't see or analyze all the danger around me, so I had to completely trust his judgment. The same is true now. He wouldn't steer me wrong. Even if I don't like that he's telling me not to free climb yet, I just have to trust him.

There will be no mad dash for the top.

I glumly heft the rope, pulling the twenty-five feet of slack back through the Prusik until it holds me tight against the screw.

THE EMOTIONAL TUSSLE of that false start drains me. As I focus again on the tedious grind of aid climbing, I find myself still in the same bind: I have no ice screws left. I hang from one, the second is planted a few feet below me, and the others are out of reach below the roof, which I dare not cross again. I am now constrained to advancing on just two screws, repeatedly leapfrogging one above the other. This means there can be no more backup screws left behind to catch my fall and there is no margin for error.

My protection placements are so close together now that I don't have to rappel down to retrieve the screw just below me. I simply lean over sideways and reach near my ankles, then twist it out. Bending over so far leaves me light-headed. Then I sit up tall in my harness and twist the screw back in, two or three feet above me. The wall's so soft that half the time I can crank the screw by hand.

Several inches of rotten surface ice, almost like crusty snow, coat the crevasse wall. So I haul up the blue sack dangling from my harness and fish the snow fluke out to try placing it. I hammer the shovel blade horizontally into the wall, hoping I can use it in place of a screw.

As I pound on it, the blade sinks in three inches and starts to bite. But after penetrating another inch, the fluke hits dense ice and stops. With the next hammer blow, the blade skates sideways and shears out. It's no good—the snow-crust layer is too thin to hold the fluke. Disappointed, I jam the fluke back into my gear bag.

I look down. The yellow climbing rope bends under the ice roof, then disappears from view for twenty feet. Halfway back to the snow ledge, it reappears as a dark gray line cutting across an inky wall. With my eyes adjusting to the increased illumination in the upper chamber, I can no longer see Mike's feet—or the pad covering him. Worried that he might not be there, I yank hard on the taut rope below me, feeling it stretch and pull tighter against our mutual bottom anchor. The bottom screw is still there, so Mike must be, too. But for the first time I feel truly separated from my partner.

I'm leaving him behind.

AFTER PULLING ANOTHER screw out from the wall at ankle level, I rest. Then, reaching up, I turn that screw in halfway. There is so little resistance from the soft ice that I use only my hand—no ice tool leverage required. My arms are too tired to reach up far anymore, so I'm just placing this screw two feet higher than the last, right near my face. With my nose six inches away, I watch air-filled, watery slop drool out of this screw's hollow core. The worst placement yet.

I clip the screw and hang uneasily from it. The soft crevasse wall even allows me to kick in footsteps, so burying my boot tips in the wall gives me a good stance. Setting a higher screw into this squishy wall would be false security. Since there're no options left for getting in solid aid gear, I've got to resume free climbing.

I test-kick the wall. My boot penetrates nearly to the ball of my foot. I press my leg down on the foothold and feel the buried front points grab pretty well.

I shift almost all my weight to the kicked step. It holds. Although I am dog tired, the soft snow and moderate wall angle make it possible for me to free climb. I'm less than ten feet from the escape hole, confident that this is the right move—it's different this time. Dad's voice can't talk me out of the risky free climbing now, because there's no other choice.

FIGURING THAT TEN feet of slack should allow me to get my waist to the crevasse lip, I feed that through my Prusik loop, then add five more feet to let me make it onto the glacier's surface. Still leashed to the top screw for safety, I check my gear one final time. All I need now is the strength for five or six moves up and right and I can climb through the porthole to the surface. Taking the last step won't be simple—that open hole doesn't extend all the way back to solid ice, so I'll have to hack away some of the weak snow to reach firm ground.

I reach one tool above my head, nearly touching the underside of the snow ceiling looming over me. When I stretch far to the right, my hammer just reaches the sunshine streaming through the hole. The lingering afternoon sun bathes the steel head in a subtle yellow glow.

I mentally draw that solar power right through the tool and into my muscles, trying to infuse myself with the energy to make it out. The challenge is near my limit, but probably not beyond it— less-than-vertical, soft ice, a warming sun. I'll need to rally more strength, but all I have to do is hold it together and climb well for the next minute, and then I will live.

Pro and go.

I pull in one long breath, then release it slowly.

Climb!

My arms and legs move in a controlled fury: Stick one pick, then the other, kick my right foot into the ice, shake my left foot free from the make-do aid sling, and push myself up in a spray of milky crystals. I feel momentum shift as I leave the comfort of the ice screws and engage the risk of sprinting toward the sun, and life.

With my hips now about eighteen inches past the last screw, I am on my way. Pulling my right tool from the wall easily, I stretch up to place it again, then halt jerkily, as if something has yanked my harness back to the left. I nearly lose my balance.

Confused, my rhythm gone, I snap my head to the left, where I see the sling that's tied to my waist harness still stretched taut back to the last screw. In my excitement to go, I forgot to unclip myself from the anchor. I'm stuck.

I glare at the tight leash as seconds tick past, wasting precious strength. I ponder either cutting the sling so I won't have to climb back to the screw or deliberately dropping onto it and starting this section over. But with such bad protection, I can't fall on purpose.

I must climb back over. As I traverse left to the screw, I burn energy struggling to remove the deep sticks that I'd been so proud of a moment ago. Unable to yank one pick from the wall, I wage a frustrating battle with the tool and self-control. I can't let myself fall fighting this ax, so I wiggle my hand out of the skinny wrist loop, leaving the ice tool stuck to the wall—super risky since unweighted tools sometimes drop out of the ice. If it pops, I'll be marooned with one tool above a shaky screw.

Leaning to the left, I stretch just far enough to unclip the restraining sling from the screw. I'm free. Now I struggle to stay calm and insert my hand back into Mike's too small wrist loop.

I finally pull the ax out of the wall. Afraid to lose momentum, I immediately move back up and right. Grunting with each kick, I smash my front points deep into the soft snow wall and slam each tool down hard enough to embed the entire pick.

My head bumps under the sagging belly of the snow bridge. I'm almost there.

The edge of the open hole beckons just above my right shoulder. I thrust my right arm up the hatchway and wave my hammer frantically, hoping that someone will see me. The great openness so near and the strong light bathing my arm both buoy me.

The sun.

Just below the glacier surface, where the snow bridge meets the crevasse sidewall, I smash my right tool into firm snow. With my left tool I hack away some rotten snow to enlarge the hole above me. The snow bridge is eighteen inches thick and so soft I can push the shaft of my ax up through it easily. Chopping at the roof, I swing my ax rhythmically and the snow breaks away in sticky, irregular clumps. Working from the open edge, I widen the hole, bringing it closer to me.

I keep looking up, my lips sputtering as snow chunks slap my face; I ignore the wet globs sneaking into my jacket. When the snow stops slumping, I see blue sky.

I shove my left ice tool up through the hole and plant it on the glacier's surface. The snow, after cooking in the sunshine for twelve hours now, is soft and wet. The tool plant is decent, but not great.

I kick at the mushy snow but must swing my leg three, four times before I form a foot hold that feels trustworthy. For several minutes I have been furiously driving tools, kicking boots, and smashing snow. My body feels heavy, and I hear myself panting.

After packing down a shaky boot hold, I thrust myself up twelve inches. The snow bridge surrounds my head and upper chest. I am passing right through the weak and traitorous snow layer that collapsed beneath us five hours ago. With my eyes still below the ground surface, I can't see out yet. Instead, my vision drills into the white, lumpy surface two inches from my nose—irregular humps and hollows of corn snow, trillions of crystals loosely bound together by a slippery film of water.

All that's above ground level are my forearms, my ice tools, and the top of my helmet. I straddle two worlds—my legs submerged in the cold, dark crevasse, my arms clinging tenuously to the warmth of light and life.

All the perseverance I can draw from my past pushes me up from below. All the resilience I can gather in this moment keeps me hanging on. All the opportunity I can sense in the future pulls me up from above. Just a few more feet, and I get my life back—Gloria, my parents, my future—even as I sense the black beast clutching at me from below.

THIS IS IT.

Afraid that something will go wrong, I jostle the rope with my foot to confirm that I've got enough slack. I kick one boot and then the other into the snow wall—it's getting softer—then straighten my knees and push myself up. My head pops above the surface. The late-afternoon sunlight ricochets off the brilliant glacier, assaulting my eyes, blinding me. I am going to need those sunglasses I hauled up.

Blinking rapidly, I rotate my head around like a gopher peering from its tunnel, hoping to spy another climber. I see only footprints.

I slam an ax down horizontally on top of the lumpy glacial surface. When I pull on the tool, the pick cuts laterally through the sloppy snow. I set the tool again, but it's no better. I scratch away some garbage snow and swing again. Finally, my pick bites into firmer snow beneath, and I pull myself up a little farther. Setting my other tool also requires a few swings through slush before I finally land a decent stick. I am above the snow bridge now from the waist up.

Pulling my boot from the wall below, I rotate my hip out so I can heave my right knee up and onto the surface. The move shifts weight to my tools set in the oatmeal snow, and a strange sight unfolds in front of me, as if the ground is moving away. Confused, I look at my tools and see the picks inching through the slush.

With my tool placements failing and only one foot in the wall, I gently tip backward—right back toward the crevasse. The last two screws will never hold. With so much rope out, I will fall thirty feet and shock-load that first screw hard, then plummet on down to the next, and the next—maybe all the way to the bottom.

I desperately shove my free leg behind me and touch something solid, momentarily stopping myself. I realize my right boot's making contact with the far side wall of the snow hole I am crawling through. What's keeping me from tipping over backward is the snow bridge itself, just twelve inches over from the weak spot that collapsed beneath me so long ago. With my legs splayed apart, I'm stemmed wide across black space.

I straddle the monster.

I've stopped, but I'm not stable. From my chest to my death-gripped hands, I lie flat on the glacier's wet surface. Pressing my torso against the very top of the icy side wall, I feel the tie-in knot bunch under my left hip. The rope trails back into the darkness snarling just behind me. As I swing and paw, fighting for purchase, my ax carves easily through the wet slop, grabbing nothing.

I feel like my head is going to explode. In this moment I am one with the snow. I'm stalled out, motionless. I lean forward, with my upper body planted prone in mush and my lower half poised upright over the dark void. With all four limbs stretched out, I have no leverage. I know I can't stay like this, but I have no concept of what to do next.

And then I feel it: an uncontrollable shaking in my right leg. It starts in my overstretched hamstring, but in horror I feel it spread to other muscles, until my whole leg is twitching rapidly. Climbers call it Elvis leg, and I have it bad. With all my muscles clenched tight to keep me pinned in place, the other leg starts dancing, too. A climber with Elvis legs is certain to fall in seconds.

And then a calm thought fills my mind.

Go ahead and lunge for it. Your tools will stick. God's going to make 'em stick.

I instinctively push my right leg hard off the weak snow bridge behind me. This shoves my body up and forward, and as I lunge I also swing my right tool down hard. I feel the pick bite into better snow farther back from the rotten crevasse lip.

I drag my body forward through the slop by pulling with all my might on the right tool. It holds. My whole torso rests on the surface now, and most of my weight, too. Not daring to get off the ground, I lie on my stomach and swing the left tool down as hard as I can from my sprawled-out position. The ax head dives through the surface glop, and the pick grabs something solid underneath.

I scoot my body forward another six inches and feel my thighs slide onto solid snow atop the glacier's surface.

Kicking and clawing, I finally slither out of the beast's mouth.

My knees touch the glacier's surface. I'm on top. To let out more slack, I twist back to my left and reach behind to my Prusik loop. I fight the wet knot's grip, but manage to slide it up the rope a bit to make sure I have enough slack to keep moving forward. Both my feet dangle in space over the ravenous black gap. I have almost won my freedom

Embedded in the wet snow, I worm forward another undignified foot. When my boots scrape solid ground, I rise onto my knees and crawl two feet away from the hole. I am desperate to get away from the crevasse lip, terrified that the whole area will crack and crash back into the slot, taking me with it. I consider standing to walk but fear I'm not strong enough, so I crawl on, my head hung low.

A new fear seizes me: that somehow the rope itself will pull me back in. It might snag, or the weight of it—anything, I fear, might happen. I need an anchor. Still on my knees, I sit back on my haunches and jerk the drawstring of my blue ditty bag, pulling it to me. I fumble for the snow fluke and begin pounding it in with my ice hammer. It bites hard, and I get it partway in before weakness forces me to stop, panting. A minute later I drive it home, then clip a biner through the fluke's anchor wire. With stiff hands, I clip my harness leash to the fluke's biner.

Now that I'm directly anchored in, I feel relief bubbling up. I desperately want to get off the rope, but I have to anchor it first so we can get back to Mike.

I have no protection left—no screws, no flukes. The only things left are my tools. With my hammer, I start pounding my ax, handle first, into the glacier. I don't have the strength to lift my hammer with just one arm, so I use both. Although the snow is soft, I manage to drive the ax in only halfway before a new wave of exhaustion washes over me. I bend forward, resting my head and forearms flat on the glacier. After I recover some, I pound the ax the rest of the way in, slot a biner through the ax head hole, tie an anchor knot, and clip the climbing rope to the ax. Mike's anchored in.

Not trusting myself, I double-check my anchor, then Mike's. Finally convinced that we are both correctly anchored in, I untie the rope from my harness. I am a little stunned to see my hand drop the loose end into the snow.

I rise higher on my knees.

"I'm alive," I say, meekly, tentatively.

It feels good to say it.

"I'm alive!" I yell it this time, raising my hands above my head.

I crumple forward and wrap both arms around my chest. My body shakes in broken, choppy sobs. Still kneeling in the snow just a few feet from the crevasse lip, I rock back and forth, desperate in my sorrow and emotional release, talking rapidly out loud to Mike.

"Mike, I'm sorry. Man, I'm so sorry. I'm so sorry you didn't survive...I tried so hard to revive you...I was so afraid to even try to climb...Thanks for encouraging me to try, and for not letting me back away from the fear...Once I started, I stuck with it...You'd be proud how I stayed on the lead. And every time I fell I went back up...I did the climb for me and you both...I tried to do the best I could all the way to the end... I'm sorry you're still down there... I have you anchored... We'll get back and get you out."

FOUR HOURS OF climbing the crevasse wall and my injuries have stiffened my legs. As I start to stand, I list sideways. I shove my left hand into a snow mound to catch myself. Concentrating on balance, I hurl myself up and plant my second foot beneath me, momentarily resting my hands on my knees, then straighten up, swaying.

After a long stare at my watch I finally comprehend that it's after five P.M. It'll be dark in four hours—enough time to walk off the glacier. I'm wet, with no stove, sleeping bag, or food. The rope, my anchored ice ax, and the other climbing gear must stay here so we can get back to Mike, so I have almost no equipment with which to descend. I am in the middle of a treacherous glacier, alone and exhausted. I feel small and weak. I'm out, but I'm not safe.

Crossing a glacier alone is dumb, especially in such a weakened condition. But I just managed to climb alone up that incredible wall; surely I can manage a solo descent of low-angled snow.

Scores of footprints lead down the fall line. After the day's descending climbers moved twenty feet downslope of our snow bridge hole, they all cut right, eastward, perpendicular across our crevasse. Having been beneath the snow bridge for five hours, I know that their trail crosses a bridge section that's thick enough to block the light from penetrating. Their safe and simple passage traversed right over the hungry crevasse just seven paces away from the thin spot I had stepped upon. Seven paces.

I'm on the west side of the crevasse, and to follow the communal descent trail, I will have to get over to the east side via the same snow bridge—and I will be unroped. I know there may be a hundred other slots lurking between me and the glacier's edge about half a mile away, but this one, the monster I just escaped from, feels the scariest. Tempting the killer slot by again crossing the same snow bridge over the same crevasse is just too much. I can't do it.

I stand motionless, gripped by fear and yearning to be off the glacier. I have escaped the crevasse, but I could still die here—wet, frozen, and alone.

Below me, at the edge of the Emmons Glacier, boulders mark where the shifting ice and lurking crevasses stop and solid ground begins. Like a swimmer washed out to sea, I gaze longingly at that distant shore of salvation. It seems so far away.

CHAPTER 16

▲ ▲ ▲

HUGGING THE VOLCANIC rock outcropping far downslope from me sits the rangers' hut at Camp Schurman. I can't quite see its humped roof, but I know it is less than a mile away and 1,200 feet below. I hesitate to yell for help, and for a moment I consider digging a snow cave right on the trail and hunkering down for the night, with a rope tail sticking out of the snow to alert tomorrow's climbers to my presence.

But I'd probably die of hypothermia before they found me.

I have to get help, but when I open my mouth to yell only a croak emerges; my throat's too dry. I drop to my knees and grab a handful of snow—the same wet slop that betrayed me and Mike—and suck on it. After a couple minutes, I feel my voice returning.

I stand, and looking down the mountain, I see movement around the rangers' cabin. I pull out my red balaclava and start waving it over my head.

"Help!" I scream hoarsely, tentatively, then gather all my strength. "Help! Help! Help!"

———

AFTER A COUPLE of minutes, it's obvious that the people at the hut have heard me. Over the next half hour, I watch as they get organized and start moving my way. I decide I'm not going anywhere until they get here—it's too dangerous. I pull my helmet off, plop it in the mushy snow, and sit awkwardly on its dome to stay off the cold, wet ground. Unzipping my chest pocket, I take out my sunglasses and slide them over my eyes. I wrap my arms around myself for warmth, but immediately begin shivering anyway.

Over the next forty minutes, I stand to check on my rescuers' progress, wave my arms, talk some to Mike's spirit, scream, "Help! Help! Help!" and fight to calm myself.

Finally, I hear the metallic clank of climbing gear.

As their rope team of four moves closer, I warn them to be careful—I know they are approaching the snow bridge.

"We're coming," one of them yells. "Just stay there. What happened?"

"We fell in a crevasse," I stammer hoarsely.

"Where's your partner?"

"Still in the crevasse," I yell.

"Does he need help?"

"No, I think it's too late for him," I say.

"Are you hurt?"

"I'm beaten up," I say, "but I think I'm okay."

They move closer to the hidden crevasse.

"You're twenty feet away, be careful . . . You're ten feet away, it's about ten feet across, the snow's rotten. Watch it . . . You're five feet away."

They are almost on me.

"Okay," I hear the leader say, "let's look sharp."

One by one, they cross the snow bridge without a problem. A minute later, they reach me. I am no longer alone.

"What happened?" one of them asks me.

"We fell in the crevasse and we were stuck down there, but I managed to climb out," I say.

"How is your friend?"

"He got hurt real bad," I say. "He stopped breathing and I tried to give him CPR, but he never started breathing again. His lips and gums are blue; I don't think he has breathed for hours now."

I shake uncontrollably, and they help me remove my drenched jacket and wiggle into a dry one they carried with them. They force candy bars on me, and water, and make plans for the leader to descend into the crevasse to check on Mike. Then they set up an anchor system in the snow. Someone asks me if I need to be taken off the mountain right now.

"No," I say. "I can wait."

The lead ranger—in my shaken state, I'm taken aback to hear the others call him "Mike"—prepares to rappel into the depths, and worry overcomes me. Rattling off potential dangers in the crevasse, I spit out everything I can think to tell him. I don't want anyone else to get hurt.

Finally, he backs over the edge and disappears into the hole that opened beneath my feet almost seven hours ago. There is nothing to do but sit and wait for him to return.

The guy tending to me introduces himself as John. He strikes up a gentle, distracting conversation, asking me where I'm from, what I do, that sort of thing. At one point, my tears return.

"My God, my friend's gone," I sob. "He's dead, man. He's down in the hole and he's dead."

"Yeah, man," John says sympathetically, "that's terrible, but we've got you and that's a good thing."

I don't feel very good, but I nod my head in agreement. John puts an arm around my shoulders and gently pats my back.

"It would have been even worse if you were still down there with him," he says.

Finally, the lead ranger emerges from the crevasse.

"There's nothing we can do for your partner tonight," he says. "He's buried under a lot of snow, and it's going to take a big effort to get him out."

Someone asks me if I can walk.

"You'll have to put me in the middle and I'll be pretty shaky," I say, "but I think I can do it."

We spend the next few minutes roping up, then set out with me in the middle position, just in front of a guide named Uwe. Fear seizes me as I approach the indistinct edge of the snow bridge spanning the crevasse, and I suck in a deep breath.

"Watch me," I say to Uwe.

After one big step, I am across. It seems too easy. The snow is soft, my legs are like jelly, but I am walking and stumbling down the mountain. We reach the rangers' hut in about thirty minutes. My spirits sink as I realize Mike and I were just half an hour from Camp Schurman and the safety of solid ground.

In the park service hut I learn that the two rangers are Mike Gauthier and Deb Read and the volunteers are Uwe Schneider and John Norberg. I keep thanking them as they feed me hot soup and tea. I feel like a stranger in a strange world now—all eyes on me. Someone puts me through a light medical exam and pronounces me basically okay—bumped and bruised all over, cuts and scrapes across my face, but seemingly not seriously hurt. It dawns on me how I stink after five days without a shower, but no one says anything.

Read sits down next to me, gently rubs my back, and says, "I'm sorry for the loss of your friend."

"Thank you," I say. "So am I."

I feel like crying but fight it, afraid that if I start I won't stop.

No one wants to ask, but everyone wants to know what happened. In bits and pieces, I relive parts of the climb.

"How much ice climbing have you done?" Gauthier asks.

"Well," I say tentatively, "I've been ice climbing for about ten years, but I'm pretty much an intermediate climber. I can lead seventy-degree stuff when I'm bold, but I've never been able to lead long stretches of vertical ice."

"Well," he remarks, "I believe you, because you say so, but I went down that crevasse and I saw that ice wall. That was an incredible ice lead. That wall was vertical to overhanging. You made a lot of aid placements, your anchors were good, and your rope work was good. I can't believe that you consider yourself an intermediate climber."

"Yeah, I don't understand how I did it either," I say somberly. "I've never done anything like it."

Schneider joins the conversation. "It's simple," he says. "You had the ultimate motivation."

"To survive," I say.

"Yeah," he agrees.

"I feel proud of what I did, but I feel ashamed, too," I say. "My friend's not here and I'm afraid there's something we did wrong, or something I could have done differently."

But one by one, they reassure me. We registered our route; we brought the right gear; we wore our helmets. We were skilled enough to climb the Liberty under icy conditions; we simply ran into bad luck. I appreciate their analysis and support, but already I feel survivor's guilt swelling in me.

My pack and gear are still in the crevasse, part of the ledge holding up Mike. In the upstairs loft I crawl into a dank, Korean War–era sleeping bag the rangers loan me and lie awake as long as I can— frightened of sleep and the nightmares I figure it will bring, frightened that I will scream out in the night. Drenched with sweat, the rank smell of the sleeping bag mixing with my own, I finally drift off.

I SNAP AWAKE. For a few moments, I'm not sure where I am. The blackness and the fuzzy gray light confuse me, and my heart races at the thought that I may still be in the crevasse. But the clank of an aluminum pan downstairs sets me straight. Quickly enough, it all comes back.

I get up, occupying myself with the preparations for leaving. I ask that someone in the park service call Gloria and Mike's family—and a little later, over the radio, I think I hear scratchy confirmation that the notifications have been made. I walk out into the sunshine with some of my soggy outer clothes and lay them out to dry, weighing them down with volcanic rocks. Someone has music playing in the hut, and Don Henley's song "The Boys of Summer" comes on.

The refrain echoes in my head. It's June 22. Summer is here and Mike is gone. I move around the back corner of the cabin, make sure I'm out of the other climbers' view, then let myself cry.

Finally, I gather myself and my gear and get ready to go. I'm vaguely aware of the radio chatter as the rangers plan their effort to retrieve Mike's body, and I know that more rangers with gear are coming in by helicopter.

"We plan to send you out on a chopper, but there's no guarantee," Gauthier says. "You might have to walk out."

I visualize the 5,000-foot descent and dread the thought of hobbling all those miles on my throbbing, battered legs. Not wanting to complain, I just mutter, "I understand."

A little later, a copter lands nearby, and it's time to go. I'm apprehensive—my legs are like noodles, and even the ten-minute walk uphill to the landing zone sounds daunting. I put on a helmet, step stiffly into my harness again, and notice my gashed gear, wet gloves, ripped clothing. It seems as though everything I look at reminds me of the crevasse, reminds me of the gripping terror.

I tie a rope to my harness. Deb Read has the other end, and we trudge to the waiting helicopter. Just before I climb in, she leans in close to my ear to tell me something, but the roar of the idling chopper takes it away. I gesture confusion and point at my ear. She leans in closer and says it again, this time with her hand on my shoulder. I still can't hear it, but when we back a foot away from each other, I see compassion on her face, and I know it was something important, and touching. I force a half smile and nod; then we exchange a quick hug.

The chopper lifts off, and through the bubble I see the immense glaciers of Rainier stretch out below me, slit again and again with crevasses. Flying over the Winthrop and Carbon Glaciers, I spy thousands of slots, some covered with sagging snow bridges, some open. Through the window between my feet, I can see straight down their black throats.

A few minutes later, we land in a green field, surrounded by trees on a warm summer day. After five days of ice, cold, and rock, this new world shocks me. I step out to a throng of waiting rangers.

And thus begins the inquisition, I think.

One of the rangers steps out from the others, shaking my hand. His name is John Madden.

"Just relax," he says. "I'm here to take care of you. If you need anything, just ask. I'm also here to get whatever information we can out of you so we can help other climbers and learn from this incident. There's no pressure, so you take your time, you do what you need to do, and we'll get through it."

"I think I can do it now."

For two hours in a park service office, I spill it all into his tape recorder. My background and Mike's. Our route. The joy on the summit. The disaster on the descent. The climb out.

Finally, he tells me that they want me to get some lunch, get checked out by a doctor, and then retrieve our rental car from the other side of the mountain.

HOLDING THE HEAVY black receiver to my ear, I dial home. It's about noon in Colorado, and Gloria picks up the phone.

"Hi, Glo," I say tentatively.

"Oh, good, I'm glad it's you," she answers, utterly normally. "I was worried when I didn't hear from you last night. How did it go?"

My heart sinks. It's obvious no one has called her.

"The climb up went well and we made the summit yesterday."

"Oh, good," she says.

"But there's bad news."

"What?" she asks. I can hear the apprehension in her voice.

"On the way down, we had an accident. We had a bad accident, Glo."

"Oh, no."

"We fell in a crevasse. We fell about eighty feet into a crevasse on the way down."

"Oh my God, are you all right?"

"I'm beat up, but basically, I'm okay. But not Mike."

"Oh my God, what happened?"

"Mike didn't make it, Gloria."

"What?" she says, her voice barely a whisper.

"He didn't make it," I cry. "I tried to give him CPR and mouth-to-mouth, but I couldn't save him."

"Oh my God, Jim."

Through tears I say, "I made it, Glo. I'm alive. I kept thinking about how I just had to get out for you and Dad."

LATER THAT AFTERNOON, I sit in the sun, talking with Ranger Madden, wondering aloud whether I could have done something differently.

He says, "Sounds like you just had bad luck. There are ten thousand things you could have done differently. Maybe none of them would have made a difference. There *is* something you could have done so that this never would have happened: You could have taken up sailing instead of climbing. But then, of course, you might have gotten run down by a Panamanian freighter somewhere in the Caribbean."

As a law enforcement ranger, Madden has seen a lot of survivors. By way of advice he says, "You might feel the urge to turn in on yourself and not face the world. It's going to be hard, but anybody who survives what you did has to be a fighter. Giving in is definitely not what you're about. I'm sure it's not what Mike was about, either. You have been given a great gift: life. You didn't get that gift handed to you, you earned it. Use it."

Later, Madden drives me around The Mountain to the town of Enumclaw to get checked out.

As I sit in the emergency room, I reek of blood, sweat, urine, and the dank clothes that have been on my body for five days. Dr. Savage checks me over, worrying at first that my wrinkled white feet are frostbitten. After my feet dry, he can tell that I just have mild trench foot from being wet for so long.

An hour later the doctor returns with paperwork and says, "Some of these numbers in your lab work seem impossible for the fit young man I see in front of me. My guess is that you've been running on pure adrenaline for a long time now."

Following X-rays and tests and a lot of pushing and poking, the conclusion is simple: I am terribly beat up, but I suffered no life-threatening injuries, no broken bones, nothing that will require surgery. All that blood I spit up in the crevasse seems to have been from getting smacked in the face, not internal bleeding.

After we leave the hospital, Madden tells me that the crew up on the mountain retrieved Mike's body from the crevasse.

I drop my head backward, close my eyes, and say, "Thank God."

Madden drives to the White River Campground, and we pull in next to the rental car Mike and I left five days ago. I reach into my parka's chest pocket and pull out the car keys I carried up from the crevasse and think: *I guess I get to actually go home.*

In the car, I see Mike's travel clothes, his books. Everything I look at overwhelms me with memories of him.

Then I get behind the wheel and follow Madden on a meandering drive around the east flank of the mountain to the Paradise Inn, on the south side.

I check in, but it's too late for dinner. I buy a bag of Fritos from a vending machine and pick up a bottle of milk and a slice of cherry pie, then wander out onto the deck to eat.

Afterward, I hobble back into the main lobby, feeling eyes on me, and find a pay phone.

It's nine when I call Mom and Dad, midnight in Concord. Dad picks up after one ring. Gloria had told them earlier, so he's been waiting for my call. I picture him sitting at our brown kitchen table. For ninety minutes, I replay the movie in my head, detailing the climb and the disaster for him. At some point, we turn to the future—to what this will mean for me. We talk about my gear; I don't even know where it is. In the crevasse, gone forever? On its way to me?

"Maybe ya should just leave it all behind—be done with it," Dad says.

But I'm not ready. Even now, the day after the worst experience of my life, I'm not ready to declare that I'll leave climbing behind.

"I don't think I should make that decision now," I tell him.

Dad and I are close, but we usually have trouble expressing emotion with each other.

"I love you," I tell him.

"I love you," he says back.

Finally, I hobble into the bar. I order two beers: one for me, one for Mike. I drink them both.

MORNING COMES. MY leg joints are stiff, the muscles very tender. With a single massive blue bruise stretching from my left knee to my groin, my left leg flounders worse than my right one, so I shuffle across my room in an unbalanced, halting gait. My left forefoot remains numb and feels squishy, making the wood floor seem distant beneath me.

Leaning on the bed, the walls, and then the door frame for support, I tread a slow lap around the small room. As the alpine morning light spills in through the lone window, I keep hobbling around the rustic room, trying to loosen up. The walls, floor, ceiling, and furniture are all constructed of the same honey-yellow pine. With each lap, my legs and back relax a little, so I push myself to shuffle once around the whole fifty-foot perimeter without using any support.

I stop at the doorway to the bathroom, and four feet away, just above the old porcelain sink basin, I see myself staring back from the mirror. My eyes look dark and withdrawn, almost menacing. I'm uncomfortable looking at myself.

When I grab the back of a tall wooden desk chair, pain radiates across my left shoulder. I try rotating my head to work the pain out, but I can't turn to the left very far. I worry about it, but it's only been two days since the accident.

The chair scrapes loudly across the pine floor as I slide it out. Using the edge of the desk for support, I sit down awkwardly. With no cushion, the hard wooden chair is uncomfortable. Good. The discomfort will keep me awake, and besides, I don't have the right to be comfortable now, anyway.

I glance out the window. The worn curtains are mostly closed, so I can see only a little piece of the mountain. It's just as well. I could not bear to glimpse the summit right now. Even better, the glacier where it all happened is on the opposite side of the mountain from the Paradise Inn.

From the desk drawer I pull out some stationery. The sheets of paper and the envelope are both decorated in brown ink with a lithograph of Mount Rainier. I study the drawing to see if our ascent or descent routes are in the sketch. I run my swollen finger along the mountain's silhouette and stop at the volcano's apex. This seems to be an image of Rainier's southern side. Slowly, I realize it's the view of the mountain you can see right outside the inn.

Rummaging in the drawer, I find a pen tucked in the back. When I try to hold it, my hand is so puffy that my fingers don't bend right.

I'm afraid to start writing.

I need to talk to Mike so badly right now, but he's gone. Writing to him seems to be the only way. I need to tell him what happened. I've got to tell him how hard I tried to save him, and myself. And I need to apologize—for him dying, and for me living.

Once I leave the mountain today, everything will be different. I will have to face the world. Everyone will want to know what happened, but maybe they'll never understand, because they weren't with us on the glacier. I will have to talk to Mike's family, too. God, how will I possibly be able to do that? What will I say? What can I say?

How am I going to live with this?

I shuffle and align a few blank pieces of stationery. Holding the stack of paper with both hands, I stare at the brown mountain and the words beneath it: Mount Rainier National Park.

I lay the paper flat on the wooden desk. To sit taller in the chair, I straighten my back, ignoring the aches and stiffness. My rigid fingertips crimp around the pen's point. Trying to build momentum, but still unsure, I coax myself onward.

I PRESS PEN onto paper.

June 23, 1992

Dear Mike,

Jesus, man, I'm sorry! I can't believe this happened to you and to us... I swear to God, Mike, I didn't mean to fall into that crevasse and I certainly didn't want to pull you in behind me. God, this sucks...

I stall.
Talk to him.

Everyone tells me that it was all an accident and that it could have been the other way around just as easy. I suppose they're right.

My writing slopes off the page.
Don't stop.

I really enjoyed our climb... God—weren't our bivouacs wild? We were like real alpine hard men—as you said, this climb should make some great stories... I will try and do as the ranger suggested and remember you smiling with an ice ax in your hand on the side of the mountain...

My hand jerks across the paper as I struggle to find the words.
Keep going.

Michael—you would have been proud of my lead—insufficient gear, vertical to overhanging ice, objective hazards (falling snow), time constraints, about ten falls, pro pulling out, never aid climbed before, never self-belayed before . . . and I made it. I always kept going. I took your helmet, pile jacket, and some gear—I was sure you wouldn't mind as I needed it to get out of the hole. I tried to give you what dignity I could. I closed your eyes, put your glasses on, redid your harness, tied you and your gear into the screws so that we could get to you—and while the Therm-a-Rest was initially intended to protect my rope from snarling, it did protect you from snow and ice fall. I was glad of that.

I apologize if my nervousness made you mad or frustrated. Perhaps it was a lack of courage. Perhaps it was foreboding. My crevasse fear did build and build right up to the last few hours and minutes—perhaps I knew.

I assure you that had you gone in first, I too would have dug in for all I was worth and then would have gone right in behind you. I think you know that, though. I truly felt we were friends and partners.

I'm sorry your young and promising life is over, Mike. This stinks—you didn't deserve that. I'm so bummed out and sorry for you, buddy, that I can't describe it—every time I think about the fact that you're dead, I start to cry again.

I'll really miss you popping in from parts unknown for a few days. I'll miss our late nights at Potts and Washingtons. I'll miss our philosophical discussions (and disagreements!). I'll miss rock climbing in the sun with you at Lumpy and Greyrock, and then running down in the storms. I'll miss looking for your blue truck. I'll miss your support for me and your friendship outside our climbing. I'm sorry for all the climbs and things we won't do together. And I'm sorry for all the climbs and things you won't get to do.

I tried to save you, Mike, but I just couldn't do it—nothing worked, *and you weren't getting better—you just got worse. I tried, Mike, but when you were gone I had to save myself. I hope that you understand, and I felt then and now that I had your blessing to take some of your gear and go.*

They say we did things right; that we were unlucky, that these things happen. Well, that may all be true, but it doesn't bring you back and it doesn't make me feel any better. You're still gone, and this still stinks.

I hope that you went painlessly and are now resting in comfort and peace. I shall strive to do what little I can for you and your family. I shall strive to take this second chance I've been given and unfurl my wings and fly with it, not turn inward into a dark ball. I shall strive to live a strong, forward-moving, vivacious life in your honor.

You were my friend and partner, Mike, and I shall never forget you. May your soul be peaceful and spirit calm.

Take care Mike.
Your friend, Jim

I ALIGN THE four scribbled sheets, then fold the stack in thirds. Dragging a wrist across my face, I wipe away the sweat so it doesn't fall on the papers. I slide the letter into the small matching envelope, lick the glue, and carefully close the flap. Before I put it in my pocket, I stare for a long time at this sealed letter, reading the preprinted envelope over and over again: Mount Rainier National Park.

I AM SUPPOSED to meet Madden to sort out the rest of our climbing gear, which has been pulled from the crevasse. I push my breakfast around the plate, staring at a brief newspaper story about our accident.

John takes possession of Mike's things to ship them to Mr. and

Mrs. Price. We finish a few minutes after one P.M. I shake his hand and thank him for his kindness. Leaving the rental car unlocked, I use the bathroom, then return to the car and open the driver's door. Some gear that just came off the mountain has been left on the front seat. It's two carabiners clipped together—one of mine, one of Mike's.

AT THE AIRPORT I call Gloria and then her mother, Marilyn Neesham, and a family friend, Father Peter Mihalic, who obtained the pope-blessed medal I wear. I assure them all that I was wearing the medal and thank them. They tell me they are praying for me and Mike. As we lift off, I try to spot Rainier out the window on the other side of the plane, but I can't see much. It's probably just as well. After what seems like an eternity, we touch down in Denver. As we roll to the gate, I tap the protective medal around my neck.

I am one of the first people off the plane. I see Gloria waiting for me, her expression contorted in sorrow.

"Your face looks bad," she says.

"It kind of hurts," I say, and the tears come.

We hold each other tightly for a time, right at the gate, then finally gather ourselves and trudge out to my pickup. By midnight we are home.

THE NEXT MORNING, I listen to the answering machine's forty messages—there'd been stories in the newspapers.

Finally, I pick up the phone to do something I've been dreading and dial Daryl Price's number. A man answers.

"Hello, Daryl?" I ask.

"No, this is Daryl's dad."

"Mr. Price," I say in a monotone, "this is Jim Davidson."

"Hello, Jim," he says wearily. "How are you?"

"Oh, okay, I guess."

It feels awkward. Every word seems wrong. I ask him if they want to get together.

"Yes, yes," he says. "We've been wanting to hear from you."

We agree to meet later that afternoon.

DARYL'S HOUSE IS only a few blocks from mine. I've never met him—or Mike's parents. I know I owe it to all of them to explain what happened, to answer their questions, to express my sorrow. Gloria and I step out into the sunshine; I need her with me. I have no idea how I'll be received, or exactly what I'll say.

After a ten-minute walk, I find myself standing on Daryl's doorstep, nervous, scared, dreading what lies ahead. Will they blame me for Mike's death? Will they be angry?

The door opens. I see Don Price, a stoic man with a powerful presence.

"I'm Jim Davidson," I say.

After meeting Donna and Daryl, we all sit down in the living room. Gloria sits on my right, holding my hand.

"We just want to know what happened," Donna says in a soft Oklahoma accent. "If you don't talk about it, you'll never be able to live with it."

I start the story from the beginning. Only a few sentences in, my hands—and my voice—tremble badly. Donna gets up and moves over to sit next to me. She reaches over and takes my left hand, holding and patting it while I talk for the next hour or more about the climb, about the fall, about Mike's death. Donna never lets go of my hand, an act of kindness and grace I know will stay with me always.

I consciously shorten the story of my own survival, skipping over big chunks. This isn't about me—it's about Mike. After I finish, Don and Donna both tell me they understand that it was difficult to tell it. I go to the bathroom and splash water on my face.

When I return, the Prices ask me to help them pick out Mike's best slides for his memorial service. They ask about Mike's camera, and I tell them I've already dropped off the film for developing and will be glad to go through the Rainier slides with them and explain everything if they'd like.

"No, I don't think I need to go through the slides," Don Price says. "What you just told me will be indelibly put in my mind. I want the slides and I wanted to hear the stories because they are memories—that's all we have left now."

We talk about the logistics of Mike's memorial service. After good-bye handshakes and hugs, Gloria and I slowly walk home. Gloria says, "While you were gone in the bathroom, Donna said to me, 'The one thing we want Jim to understand is that we never did, and still don't, think Jim was at all responsible for Mike's death.'"

It feels like a heavy burden has been lifted from me. We discuss how incredibly kind the Prices have been to us and Gloria says, "Now I know how Mike got to be so wonderful—he has wonderful parents."

Later that day, Gloria and I drive to the mall so I can buy a new pair of cowboy boots for the service. Mike was a cowboy-boot kind of guy, and it seems to me that wearing a pair to the memorial service would be a fitting tribute. Maybe nobody else will understand it, but I will know.

ON THURSDAY NIGHT—four days since the accident—I steel myself for Mike's memorial service the following morning. Around eight-thirty, the doorbell dings, and I welcome two friends, Rodney Ley and Pat Rastall.

Pat was a coleader on our Aconcagua expedition and a friend of

Mike's; Rodney and I are really just getting to know each other. He had been a good friend of Mike's also, and two weeks ago the three of us climbed in the Lumpy Ridge area of Rocky Mountain National Park, up a route known as Beelzebub—the Devil. Rodney was between me and Mike on the rope. It was the first time I'd ever climbed with Rodney, and the last time I'd climbed with Mike before Rainier.

They sit quietly as I walk through everything that happened, fighting all the time to keep my emotions in check. As experienced climbers, they understand the technical aspects, so we discuss how I escaped with so little gear. They assure me that they will share the details with others in the Fort Collins climbing community so that I don't have to keep retelling the story.

When I shut the door after they leave, it's nearly eleven P.M. I am drained in every way. I head to bed, dreading the dreams that I know will come.

FRIDAY MORNING ARRIVES, and as I prepare for Mike's memorial service, I look in the mirror. The scabs that had stretched across my forehead and down my nose have, for the most part, sloughed off.

I am hurting physically, but I look fine, almost normal. When Mike's dead and I appear to be fine, it makes no sense. How can we be in such different worlds?

On our way to the service, Gloria and I stop to pick up some large prints we'd made for the family: a picture of Mike on Rainier, looking like Joe Mountaineer with a satisfied smile on his face, and a shot of the two of us on the summit. We put them into frames and head to the service.

Before it starts, I ask the Prices if we can meet for a moment. We wander off until we're alone in a secluded part of the chapel.

"Gloria and I wanted to give you something," I say. "We had

these made up for you. Here's one for you, Daryl, and one for you, Mr. and Mrs. Price."

I hand them the framed photographs. I can tell that the pictures of Mike touch them, but it's also obvious how hard it is. Don chokes up for a second.

"I'm sorry," he says. "I'm sorry."

"That's okay," I say, searching for the right words but not finding any.

He and Daryl thank us. Donna hugs me.

"We'll all get through this together," she says.

A little later, I set up the slide projector to scroll pictures of Mike and his many travels. I feel eyes on me; there are more than one hundred people here, and I don't know most of them, yet they all know who I am. With Gloria, I sit near the front at the memorial service, feeling the loss of Mike and the sadness of a hundred strangers right behind me.

DONNA PRICE HAS written a simple note to Mike. It is read at the service.

Mike—

You moved through this world so quickly—like a firefly that glows in the dark for a minute—and then it's gone. We wanted to hold you in our hands—to keep you safe—to share the warmth from your light. We had to set you free—to go your own way.

Love, Mom & Dad.

SEVERAL OF MIKE'S closest friends take some of his cremated ashes high into the Gore Range of Colorado and scatter them in a place where the only sounds are the rush of the wind and the gurgle of streams, where the only sights are the jagged peaks and wide-open sky. Another friend carries the rest of Mike's ashes into the canyonlands of the Four Corners region, spreading them in the red rock country.

CHAPTER 17

▲ ▲ ▲

I HAVE MY life back—my wife and my work and my home. It's all here, and yet I feel empty.

I want so badly not to think about Rainier, not about Mike dead in the gloomy crevasse, not about the terror that gripped me as I fought my way up that wall. But I can't ignore it. On August 29, 1992, nine weeks after the accident, I write in my journal: "I think about Mike all the time now. In the 68 days since the accident, I don't think there was a day I haven't thought of him."

Although I know I can't live like this, expelling the experience from my mind seems wrong, as though I somehow dishonor Mike if I don't acknowledge the regret and sorrow. As though I somehow show disrespect for him and all he gave by simply returning to my old life.

I had heard about survivor's guilt, but didn't understand it. Now I know that the indescribable ache is real. I see a trauma counselor a few times; it helps, but it's not enough.

Even that first night after the accident, as I lay in that dank sleeping bag at Camp Schurman, I told myself I would have to find a place in my heart and mind for this tragedy or I would drive myself crazy. But now I'm home, and the answers don't come so easily.

When someone asks me about Rainier, some days I don't feel strong enough to tell the story; other days I try. During one intense conversation, Gloria reaches over, grabs my forearm, and interjects, "Jim, you're talking in the present tense. It's not happening right now. You're not in the crevasse anymore."

After I struggle through each telling, I feel like I've just boxed ten rounds with Mike Tyson. What happened down there seems too important for me to just let the memories fade with time, but keeping them foremost in my mind for the rest of my life won't work, either. Ultimately, I sit down in a dark bedroom with a tape recorder and spill everything I remember, talking for an hour, then two, then ten and more. After I finish, I know I have the crucial memories saved— they are there, ready if I want to revisit them, safely put away if I don't. The tapes go into a white cardboard box, along with the Rainier maps, my pretrip notes, and a bunch of tattered gear from The Mountain. I store the box next to all my climbing gear.

Every time I walk past that box, I'm reminded. What I don't know is when—or if—I'll open it.

IN THE WEEKS following the accident, my body continually reminds me of what I've been through. A wrong move sends pain through my neck and shoulder blades. Dozens of checker-sized bruises fade from my right leg, but a residual green-blue shadow lingers from the football-sized hematoma on my left thigh.

I eat and drink normally, but shed ten to fifteen pounds the first weeks I'm home. My body and my mind are still amped up, as though adrenaline still pulses through me. One night, after Gloria falls asleep, I vomit blood into the toilet, but tell no one. I figure I was lucky just to get home, so I have no right to complain or expect perfect health.

An almond-sized lump develops in the flesh near my left shoulder blade, and gently pressing it makes my left hand feel tingly and puffy, as if someone's standing on it. My left foot tingles; then the unsettling sensation retreats. One day, pain burns across the front of my left hip, then vanishes. The next day, an ache sears my right hip—a weird, floating pain I can't pin down. Finally, late one Friday night the abdominal burn intensifies, so I visit an emergency room. I have a bulging disk in my neck, intermittently pressing on nerve bundles.

Surgery is an option, but we decide to wait. Given some time, maybe the physical damage will heal. Who knows about the mental stuff.

WHAT IF?

The question claws at me as June 21 plays endlessly in my mind, threatening to consume me. I sit around thinking, or I force myself to stand, walk out the front door, wander the neighborhood under the Colorado sun. I'm home, but not free. I begin working again, but my mind can't escape the crevasse. I've physically survived, but how will I survive the survival?

In an eight-page journal letter titled "To the Mountain Gods" I write:

"How am I to carry this load alone—the self-doubt, the endless questioning? How can I hope to carry it alone? I feel that I am carrying it for myself and for my lost friend. I suspect, from a self-preservation point of view, that carrying it forward and someday leaving it behind for myself will be challenging."

What if?

What if it'd snowed that day? What if we'd lugged our packs to the summit and descended from there instead of retreating to the saddle?

What if?

If it'd snowed that day, we might have called it bad luck because it would have ruined our perfect weather. But it might have been good luck—unknown to us—because it might have helped ice that snow bridge solid, and we might have tromped right across it without a problem, unaware that a crevasse lurked beneath our feet.

If we'd lugged our packs to the summit, we would have been on the main route thirty minutes earlier. That would have been thirty fewer minutes the sun's warming rays would have had to assault the snow bridge that ultimately collapsed beneath my feet.

Gradually I realize that I have to put this aside or I'm going to drive myself crazy.

I decide that pondering the question is healthy but being drowned by it is not, because continually asking, "If?" and "What if?" won't change anything. We made our decisions, and they put us on the Emmons-Winthrop route, in the middle of the Corridor, a little before noon on June 21, 1992. A day earlier or a day later, and the outcome might have been vastly different. Maybe we'd have made it off the mountain without incident, and wolfed down steaks and beers that night. Maybe we'd have stumbled off the edge of the Liberty Wall in the dark. Maybe, maybe.

I find a measure of comfort as I think about the many factors that go into every moment of life.

Decisions. Actions. Good luck. Bad luck. Randomness. Fate. God.

I don't think I'm capable of understanding it all. I figure most things in life, including what happened on Rainier, result from a combination of individual choices as they pan out, with some good and bad luck, some randomness, some fate, and some of God's will thrown in.

I imagine life as if it were a tree, all the branches stretching up toward the sky, splitting, forking, and dividing yet again farther out: As you move out from the trunk, there are many possible pathways. When you make a decision, it leads you down one branch; then the next random event takes you on another new path. Each decision, action, and bit of luck is a fork leading to different outcomes, different branches. Some are sturdy and hold fast, some creak under your weight, some fracture and drop you into unexpected turmoil. .

Mike and I each embraced a life that put us on Rainier, together. On the mountain, Mike and I swapped the lead every hour or so, alternating maybe thirty or forty times over four days. Why was I on the lead then instead of Mike? I don't know. What if we'd done any one of a hundred things differently? I don't know. Why did that snow bridge cave in beneath my feet when a thousand others did not? I don't know. I'll always wonder about those things. But gradually I come to accept that those are the ifs and what-ifs I'll never know the answers to. I'm stuck with that, so I must live with it.

Processing and analyzing the events with my close friends and climbing buddies helps some. Supportive calls and letters bolster me. One day I open a card from Scott Anderson, the geology friend and Aconcagua partner who introduced Mike and me six years earlier. His poignant lines bring me to tears: "Thanks for digging yourself out and sharing your story. You showed tremendous strength. Thanks for doing what you could to bring Mike with you."

I'm lucky, too, that I sense no judgment or animosity from Mike's friends and climbing partners. One is Mark Udall, the executive director of Colorado Outward Bound School. His title made him Mike's boss, but his kindness and climbing expertise made him Mike's friend and mentor. He has climbed all over the world, including the Liberty Ridge, and he had talked with Mike about Rainier before we went there. I met Mark at the memorial service, and right afterward told him, and many of Mike's gathered friends, the Rainier story. Three weeks later, I receive a letter from Mark. In red ink, the envelope bears the Outward Bound motto—"To serve, to strive, and not to yield"—adapted from Tennyson's poem "Ulysses."

"I wanted to write and thank you for sharing the extremely trying circumstances surrounding Mike's death, as well as your own tenacious struggle to survive," Mark wrote, in part. "No doubt you will carry questions around in your mind for quite a while to come. If it is any help, from my perspective, you did all you could and then some. You should be proud. You did what Mike would have wanted and expected you to do. I know Mike's spirit helped you find the strength to climb out of the crevasse."

AFTER MIKE'S MEMORIAL service, a kind relationship takes hold between me and his parents and brother, an extension of my first meeting with Don and Donna and Daryl. Mike's death heaved them and me into a tiny survivors' life raft and set us adrift on a stormy sea of raw emotions. There was every chance our dealings could be strained, maybe even negative, but their character means Mike's parents and brother are cordial, caring, and sympathetic to me even as they forge their own way through their terrible loss.

One day, Don and Donna offer me Mike's most prized possessions: his camera gear. As an underpaid wilderness instructor, Mike devoted a sizable chunk of his modest income to his camera and lenses. When Donna tells me she and Don want me to have it all, she urges me to use it in the way Mike had: to seek and interpret the world's natural beauty.

I unpack the padded box, grasping an Olympus OM-1, its field-battered body outfitted just as I had last seen it on Rainier, with a wide-angle lens and Mike's homemade shoulder strap of half-inch-wide blue webbing. When I flip the camera over, on the bottom I see the engraving: M. D. PRICE. As I clutch his adapters and lenses, I consider that acquiring each expensive item must have cost Mike fifty trail miles and a week of wilderness instruction time. That the Prices have asked me to carry on with his camera gear humbles me into silence.

During one visit that summer, I notice Don wearing an Outward Bound USA pin, its crisp blue-and-silver logo incorporating a symbolic rope and compass. I lean in toward him to admire the nickel-sized pin.

"I remember Mike wearing one like that on Mount Rainier," I tell him.

"Yeah," Don replies, "this is it."

After visiting for an hour, I prepare to leave. Don excuses himself for a moment, then returns and says, "Here, this is for you."

He hands me a smaller Outward Bound pin.

"We found it in Mike's things, and I thought you'd like it."

Stunned into silence for a second, I finally say, "Are you sure?"

"Yes, you should have it," he says.

I begin wearing the pin on special occasions, including a visit to Denver's Outward Bound office, where I chat with Udall and another of Mike's good friends, Andy Maeding. Mark notices the pin on my shirt and asks, "Did you do an OB course?"

"No," I reply, "I always wanted to, but never did."

"You can only get a pin by finishing a course," Andy notes reflexively. "How'd you get it?"

"Oh, sorry. I didn't know. Mike's father gave it to me."

An uncomfortable feeling hangs in the air for a moment.

"I think it's fine that you wear one," Mark says. "You earned it."

FOR MORE THAN a decade, mountains have provided me with recreation, exercise, and joy. They have been a natural temple for my self-improvement, a calming therapy, and a source of spirituality. But the Mount Rainier experience brought loss, pain, and anguish, so as the summer goes on, I'm not certain where mountains now fit into my life.

For years, Gloria and I had heard stories about Nepal from traveling friends. We both wanted to visit the mystical land, and since we planned to start a family eventually, we decided we'd better go soon. In the spring of 1992, before Rainier, Gloria and I had already been considering an autumn trek in Nepal. On Rainier, I told Mike about our Asia plans, and I could tell he was envious.

"Man, I've always wanted to climb in Nepal," he said. "Even if you can't climb on this trip, you should go."

Mike had repeatedly told me tales about two fun-loving and mischievous Sherpa friends from Nepal he worked with at Outward Bound, Dawa and Phurba. Dawa had even come to Mike's memorial service. In the late summer of 1992, I realize I can visit Nepal and see Everest for myself and, in a strange way, on Mike's behalf, too.

I train and test myself gradually on summer hikes, usually with Gloria. Being in the mountains feels good—still fun—even though I don't tackle anything technical. I'm still not sure I'll ever climb seriously again.

With that in mind, Gloria and I hesitate about whether to visit the mountains of Nepal. We decide, finally, to go—mostly for ourselves, partly for Mike, and, hopefully, for some peaceful healing. Afraid that I will spend my life mired in sadness or negativity, I yearn for a way to shed some of the burden, to unshackle myself, and perhaps free Mike's spirit. In my pleading journal letter to the mountain gods, I write:

"For my friend Mike, I have several requests. Allow his spirit to be peaceful, but allow it to roam free. Let him race up and down the slopes with the wind, let him trickle slowly through the canyons, let him spread completely and gracefully across the land with the setting sun. Michael deserved many things in this life he did not get, but he most assuredly deserves these things.

"Of myself, I ask only that you give me pieces of insight that will allow me to try to make something positive of all this. I must pick up the positive and the energy that we both carried, and continue to carry it forward into my life."

On September 21, 1992, precisely one seasonal click after the Rainier accident, Gloria and I set off for Nepal.

KATHMANDU BLENDS THE mystical and the mundane, the profound and the profane. Ascetic holy men wander among slick hucksters hawking trinkets to overwhelmed tourists. Families commit the ashes of their loved ones to the sacred headwaters of the Ganges River, while discarded trash fouls the riverbank.

Gloria and I arrive excited, and enormously relieved to be safe: Two commercial airliners crashed into cloud-shrouded Nepalese mountains in recent months. I'm not in the greatest shape; I'm on heavy antibiotics for an infection in my gut and am supposed to avoid strong sun, drink a lot of water, and brace myself for debilitating diarrhea. It's not the best way to set out on 150 miles of high-altitude hiking and weeks of tent living, but we feel a sense of mission, so we continue.

I want to initiate a Buddhist ceremony in Mike's honor, though I don't want to force anything—especially in a land of delays and the unexpected. I hope for the best but tell myself not to try to control what happens, just to let it all unfold. That's the exact opposite of my natural tendencies. Already this journey is forcing me to grow.

THE NIGHT BEFORE we're to take a small plane to the remote village of Lukla, deep in the mountains, I read Kim Stanley Robinson's *Escape from Kathmandu*, then drift off.

Suddenly, I see Mike, dressed in climbing gear, propped against a wall, lifeless. It appears as though they've just pulled him from the crevasse. Rescuers flank him. I approach apprehensively; Mike is dead, but I sense that he is about to speak.

I snap awake in our dingy Kathmandu bedroom, anxious and sweat-soaked. I calm myself, forcing my breaths at more regular intervals, then eventually doze off.

I see Mike again. He's more lifelike, more animated, as if he's transformed himself to make me more comfortable. He waves me closer, and I instinctively understand that he wants to make it easy for me to say good-bye to him. I can't utter the weighty words.

Mike speaks.

"It's okay, Jim," he says. "'I'm gone now. It's okay to go—go ahead."

I can't speak. He goes on, telling me what to say:

"Say, 'That's it, Mike, I'm sorry but I have to go now.'"

I jerk awake. Gloria's sleeping in the other twin bed. I briefly consider getting up to write about the dreams, but I don't for now. Sometime after a quarter of four, I finally fall asleep again.

Out of sleep's blackness, Mike appears a third time—more vivid and forceful than before. We talk about the first few minutes after we crash-landed on the ledge.

"Were you in much pain?" I ask.

"Only for a minute," he says. "Now there's none. I'm in a good place."

"Were you scared?"

"A little at first," he tells me, "but that faded fast."

"Did you suffer?"

"No, not really," he says. "You went through a lot, Jim, and you did okay. You did the right thing. I'm glad you made it. It was supposed to happen that way."

"Did you stay in the crevasse for a while?" I ask.

"Yes," Mike says. "I tried to help and watch over you. You have to let it go and move on with your life. Enjoy everything. I am okay now, and you should be, too."

I awaken suddenly, tense and exhausted. Mike's visits feel so real, they seem like more than dreams. Later that day, when I chronicle the experience in my journal, I conclude that Mike is trying to ease my mind, trying to encourage me to reclaim my life. That he's trying to give me some peace by getting me to say good-bye to him. My partner Mike is urgently working to help save the part of me that is still stuck on the ledge.

WE HIKE ALONG the verdant banks of the Dudh Kosi (Milk River), up through the Khumbu Valley toward Mount Everest. Every day we pass ice-covered peaks that soar two miles above our heads. Looking through Mike's OM-1 viewfinder, I snap frame after frame, trying to capture the Himalayan giants he'd hoped to scale. I feel that I'm looking through the lens for him.

As I study these majestic peaks, my eyes scan possible ascent routes—even as I remain officially noncommittal about whether I will return to climbing.

By the time we reach the holy monastery of Tengboche five days later, we speak a little Nepali and our guide, Prem Lakpa Sherpa, understands that we wish to have a ceremony, a *puja,* for Mike's spirit. At twenty-five, Prem Lakpa is young, but as a savvy guide from a strong Buddhist family, he requests an audience with the second-highest lama at the monastery, Lama Nawang Zampu.

Gloria, Prem Lakpa, and I cross an open courtyard and walk along a stone-lined passageway, ducking under the heavy drape that serves as a door and taking a seat in the darkened room where the lama has lived for decades. Flickering yak-butter candles throw dancing yellow light across ancient Buddhist *thangka* paintings. The middle-aged lama has walnut skin, short-cropped black hair, and calm eyes. In Nepali, Prem Lakpa explains how we want this *puja* for Mike. The lama nods and tells Prem Lakpa to bring us back the next day.

After picking at our breakfast the next morning, we return to the lama's chamber, where it's even darker than it was yesterday. From the next room we hear the lama pounding a drum and chanting rhythmically. Eventually, he finishes, then joins us. He smiles and unwinds a newly made string of eleven prayer flags—an auspicious number, he tells us. Impressed, Prem Lakpa explains that the lama hand-printed Tibetan prayers on these flags last night, then stitched them to a connecting string. He is pleased that we seek to hold a *puja* for our departed friend. I touch my index finger to the Outward Bound pin on my jacket.

The lama picks up an ancient metal incense burner and walks back and forth waving it under the stretched-out flags, which are of five different colors, chanting.

"He is blessing them," Prem Lakpa tells us.

When I close my eyes the sounds and smells permeate my memory and I feel carried off by the chanting. I sense an otherworldliness I have not felt before.

As the lama hands me the prayer flags and silk blessing scarves, called *katas*, I respond as I have seen Nepalese greet other monks: With a deep bow, my palms clasped together before my chest, I say, "*Namaste*"—I greet and honor the divine within you.

This has all gone much further and better than I had dared hope. But the experience is not over. Lama Zampu speaks to Prem Lakpa, who excitedly translates: We can now meet the highest lama at the monastery, the *rinpoche*, who is revered as the reincarnation of a previous great lama. When we arrive at a deeper part of the monastery, we remove our shoes and sit on long benches padded with yak-wool blankets until the *rinpoche* glides in and we stand. He is a slight man, about sixty years old, with a shaved head and orange robes. After the *rinpoche* sits, Prem Lakpa follows, and finally Gloria and I do, too, careful to mimic our guide's moves. Prem Lakpa approaches the *rinpoche* with our prayer flags. The revered *rinpoche* takes some blessed rice, blows on it, then sprinkles it across the flags to bless them. He then blows on all the rice in the small paper sack and hands the bag and flags to Prem Lakpa. In the distance, through ancient stone walls, I hear the low, bass murmur of other chanting monks.

After we quietly sip coffee together, it is time to go. Prem Lakpa stands, bows toward the *rinpoche,* and backs out of the room, staying bent forward in reverence. Gloria and I do the same, traverse unlit hallways, then step into the pounding sunlight. We mill about in small circles, stunned by the experience and our good fortune. The three of us take turns touching the blessed flags, rice, and scarves we now have for Mike's *puja.* Because the *rinpoche* rarely meets with foreign visitors, Prem Lakpa says, "Very lucky for you. Very lucky for me."

TWO DAYS LATER, we carry our prayer flags, rice, and *katas* toward a summit. We are at 18,000 feet and the air is half as thick as at sea level, so we plod up the trail. My pulse races way past 120 beats a minute, and I fight off a familiar altitude lethargy I haven't felt since Aconcagua years ago. With each step, Gloria shatters her previous altitude record of 14,000 feet.

I have picked the rocky summit of Kala Patthar—"Black Rock" in Hindi—as the place for Mike's *puja.* Resting at the foot of Mount Everest, Kala Patthar overlooks the Khumbu Glacier and the south side Everest base camp, and is surrounded by a dozen peaks more than 20,000 feet tall.

We had left our campsite in Lobuche village before dawn and had seen the rising sun tint the Khumbu Valley the same burnt orange as the *rinpoche*'s robes. It's midmorning now, and the sky is deep blue. At the 18,514-foot summit, there are already some piled rock pillars that we could hang our prayer flags from, but Prem Lakpa says it will be better if we make our own. We gather flat rocks, and Prem Lakpa stacks them into raised rectangular piles. With the three of us wearing our *katas,* Gloria snaps photos while Prem Lakpa and I unscroll the prayer flags' string and secure it to our two rock towers. Each wind-driven flap of a flag sends a prayer up to the gods. Following Sherpa and Buddhist traditions, we set out small pieces of food as an offering to the gods.

I had hoped to feel joy, but I don't. This blessing ceremony will be my good-bye to Mike. I have been clutching him close to my heart for months now, and today, on this windswept Himalayan summit, I must set him free—for my sake and his. With Everest towering above us, snowy mountains stretching to the horizon, and blessed offerings from Tengboche's high lamas, it is the best good-bye ceremony I could have envisioned. I want to speak, but I cannot.

Prem Lakpa leads us through the *puja,* standing with his arms raised beneath the flapping flags, chanting in Nepali.

(Later, he will translate his words: "Mike, dead friend of Jim, this *puja* is for you and your spirit. It is a good *puja* as we have very special prayer flags made and blessed by the lamas, as well as the *katas.* You were a good man, and this *puja* is for you.")

As he chants, Prem Lakpa tosses rice toward the four cardinal directions. I seize the idea to cast blessed rice at each landmark around us. I turn slowly in a clockwise circle and, mimicking Prem Lakpa's style, flick pinches of rice at the peaks of Everest, Nuptse, and Lhotse, toward the Khumbu Glacier, the Lo La pass, and Tibet, at the summits of Pokalde, Taboche, and, finally, to the west, Cho Oyu.

Gloria hands me the camera and takes some blessed rice, tossing it into the air as the wind gently flutters the flags. Tears pour from my eyes, and I can't see through the viewfinder. Prem Lakpa encourages us to save some blessed rice, to "bring it home and put on your altar." I resist; I have no altar at home, and this *puja* is for Mike, not me, so I intend to expend all the blessings and goodness here. I am determined not to take anything physical away from this ceremonial place. This is good-bye.

A pained look creases Prem Lakpa's face, and he hugs me, saying, "I am so sorry, sir."

Gloria joins us, and we three huddle together, saying nothing, letting the tears seep down our cheeks.

"GLO," I ASK, "can I have a few minutes alone here?"

Gloria and Prem Lakpa descend a hundred yards down Kala Patthar and tuck in behind a black boulder, just out of sight.

I breathe out long and slow, and then begin speaking impromptu and aloud.

"We're here to do a *puja* for you, Mike. Couldn't pick a better place, eh? I have to leave you up here, Mike. You have to be where you are, and I have to live my life. I'm going to miss you, Mike—you were a good man, a good partner, and a great friend. We had a lot of fun, didn't we?"

I reach to the right chest pocket of my purple parka, the same one I wore on Rainier, tug open the zipper, and fish out a carabiner I have carried halfway around the world. Mike's carabiner. The one I cut from his harness.

Though I have tinkered with it over the months, the locking gate is still seized shut. It takes a lot of force to permanently jam a locking carabiner, so it serves as stark physical proof of how hard I fell and how hard Mike fought to stop me. Our combined energies from the moment of the crevasse fall are bound up in this stuck biner.

"Look," I continue, "I brought your biner. I was alone when I took it from you, and I'm alone when I'm giving it back to you. It's your biner, Mike. I was only holding on to it for you, and now I'm giving it back."

I thrust it skyward to show him, teary-eyed but smiling, then extend the locking biner up toward the same alpine landmarks at which I tossed rice. I present his biner toward Everest's summit last of all.

Then I look around for the deepest bedrock crack I can locate near the summit. I crouch over the fissure and let go of the biner. It slithers down out of sight, clattering against the black rock as it settles in deep. I do not want anyone to find it. I scrape my hands across the hardscrabble ground, scooping up sand and rock dust. I carefully pour it into the crack, burying Mike's carabiner, and with it a tiny part of the raw pain from the crevasse.

In my mind, I speak to Mike again, telling him that we do not need to talk directly anymore, at least not too often, that we both need to do well with where we are now. A sense of peace—almost happiness—settles on me.

I descend a few paces down the ridge, then turn back toward the summit, trying to imagine where Mike might be now. I can picture him sitting on the top, looking west at the mountains, facing away from me. I sense him smiling, but he doesn't turn toward me.

"*Namaste,*" I mutter aloud, grinning. I feel Mike answering me—"*Namaste,* Jim"—in a rising, happy tone.

I turn away from the summit and begin my journey home.

CHAPTER 18

▲ ▲ ▲

THE GRAY GRANITE is warm under my fingertips, each handhold rough and secure. We are six pitches up the Twin Owls formation at Lumpy Ridge on a perfect first day of summer. Each time the rope moves, a biner above me clanks against bedrock. Wiggling the wired nut gently, I get it to pop loose; then I push it up and out of the crack, reversing the pattern Rodney used to place it half an hour ago. Rodney, my partner and friend, is just a little bit above me now. He had been Mike's close friend, too—the three of us had climbed together just before Rainier—and he was there as I struggled to deal with all that had happened in that crevasse.

With 450 feet of rock behind us and just ten feet to go, I pause to soak in the joy of climbing and the satisfaction that the route is nearly complete.

Coming back to Lumpy with Rodney today has been the right thing to do.

It is June 21, the anniversary of Mike's death.

During the first few years after the accident, the twenty-first day of June was torturous. On each one, I hiked alone, checking my watch often as I thought about exactly where Mike and I were on

Rainier at precisely what time. Even though I tried to make the summits of those memorial hikes happy, they never were.

But now seven years have passed, and I'm marking June 21 by climbing with a good buddy. Rodney and I are reclimbing a route I had been on twice before with Mike. Today feels like an upbeat honoring of Mike and the rewarding pastimes he cherished, ones we still embrace. Being here has spurred me to tell old stories about Mike, about our previous successful ascent of this climb, and about how we had fun the other time even though we got rained off. As Mike's old friend, Rodney is happy to listen to the tales and tosses in a few doozies of his own, like the story of the night he and Mike passed a bottle of whiskey back and forth while Mike recited some of his original cowboy poetry.

Rodney and I have swapped the lead back and forth today—three pitches for him, three for me. We're moving well. I look up and see his rock shoe–clad feet dangling off the final belay ledge just ahead.

"Hey, I'm almost there. You got a cold beer ready for me?" I joke.

"Not quite," he replies. "You gotta carry my pack to the truck first. Then maybe I'll give you one."

It feels good to be up here again. The mountains, the movement, the impromptu teasing with my climbing friend. There will be some somber moments tonight, perhaps when I check in with the Prices to see how they are doing. But even so, I sense the balance tipping toward a more joyful heart. Instinct tells me that it's going to be better now.

FOR FIVE YEARS after the Rainier accident, the mountains were just a small part of my world. Life had taken a new direction: Gloria and I became parents with the arrival of our daughter, Jessica, and then, two years later, our son, Nick.

Working as an environmental consultant and helping raise our young family meant that I had to put climbing off to the side. I still ventured into the mountains during those years, doing some hiking, backcountry skiing, even a little rock climbing, but no serious alpine climbs. Still, I would look at old climbing slides and feel the mountains' tug. The sight of an elegant snow ridge would raise familiar emotions: excitement and anxiety, joy and fear.

During those years, I couldn't decide whether to embrace mountaineering again. Climbing had brought me the worst experience of my life in that crevasse. And at the same time, it had compelled me to be my best on the most difficult day I have ever endured.

Just as I'd postponed my decision on whether to resume climbing, I hadn't established a definitive place in my life for my memories of Rainier, and Mike. The slides, tapes, maps, ice screws, and tattered gear from that fateful trip still sat in a cardboard box, waiting.

Then one day, five years after the disaster, Rodney asked me a question that forced me to finally decide whether I was still a climber: "Are you interested in helping me lead an expedition to Nepal?"

After much soul searching, Gloria and I considered what it could mean. We both recognized that climbing was my chosen pathway to growth and self-refinement—my calling, based on passion, not logic. One night, after tucking the kids into bed, we returned to the discussion.

"Glo," I said, "I know it'll be tough on you, and a little risky, but I really want to go. You know how big this is."

"Yeah, I know," she said. "I'm not thrilled about it, but I understand."

She paused, then asked, "What if something happens, though?"

"I can't promise one hundred percent that nothing'll happen," I said softly.

"I know. That's the problem."

In the end, I was swayed by the huge opportunity it represented, not just for that one trip but for an unknowable spectrum of possibilities, and for the chance to reclaim a core part of who I am. And so I soon found myself coleader of an expedition to Nepal.

Thus it was that six years after Rainier, I once again hiked up the Khumbu Valley. The roaring waters of the Dudh Kosi and the pungent smell of rhododendrons seemed the same, yet I had changed. Last time I had been scared and scarred as we trekked toward the *puja.* Now I was composed and confident, using my experience to help teach, guide, and protect ten young climbers. I still carried the pain of losing Mike, but from it I had extracted the motivation to live a bigger life, to wrap my arms around adventure, to challenge myself by returning to Nepal as an expedition leader instead of remaining fearfully shackled to my desk, plodding through my middle years. Nearly losing my life gave me the courage to strive for a richer existence and the determination to pursue it with vigor.

People sometimes say of the recently deceased, "He died doing what he loved." I heard that a few times about Mike. I thought it far better, and much more important, that Mike *lived* doing what he loved.

Ultimately, I heeded the lesson, determined to live doing what I love. That meant climbing mountains. Yes, I had to strike a balance between my passion and my responsibility to care for my family, but shutting out that ardor in fear of the possible risks seems a dishonor to the gifts of health and life I still possess. Returning to Nepal seemed especially appropriate: I honored Mike there on the first trip with a *puja,* and on the second one I honored him, and me, by passionately embracing this life-affirming pursuit.

In Tibetan Buddhism, the never-ending cycle of birth, life, and death is symbolized by the endless knot. Rodney and I saw the symbol frequently as we trekked and climbed across Nepal for a month. The endless knot has many interpretations, and one that speaks powerfully to me is the interweaving of the spiritual path with the flow of time and movement. I feel that Mike and I are connected threads in some endless knot.

I THINK MIKE would be pleased that helping people grow through invigorating mountain experiences is part of my life's purpose now. I teach some climbing classes for Rodney at CSU's outdoor program and lead an expedition every other year; these pursuits have added new dimensions to my climbing and my life. Passing on my hard-won knowledge feels right. For these groups I sometimes present slide shows to share climbing stories and provide some insight into what all these adventures have taught me. My most intense experience, Rainier, might be a compelling tale to relate, but I am not confident that I will be able to tell it, and not sure if I should.

Nevertheless, I feel the urge to share what happened on Rainier, who Mike was, and how I survived. As the years go by, I also feel a growing obligation to pass on what I learned through those struggles in the hope that it might help someone else face and overcome their own harsh challenges. While I was in the crevasse, Joe Simpson's survival tale convinced me there was a remote chance to escape, and that belief helped spur me to action. Perhaps I have an obligation to share my story, so that others who hear me might one day tell themselves: "If he did that, I can do this."

In a cosmic way, I wonder if sharing the lessons from surviving Rainier is part of the reason that I am still alive. Having already spoken at hundreds of science conferences, I wonder if I can tell the Rainier story publicly in a way that might offer strength or inspiration. I ask myself: Should I share this? Can I do this? Is it right? If I pursue it, can I properly honor Mike?

I see Mike's parents a few times each year, and it feels like we are old family friends now. I feel an obligation to check with them before I speak or write about that terrible time in the crevasse. Over lunch one day, I nervously ask for their thoughts about me possibly sharing what happened to Mike and me.

"If you're asking for our blessing, you have it," Don says.

One night in 2003, a frenetic kind of energy overtakes me, and soon I am in front of a computer screen, searching for an appropriate place to share the Rainier story. Staring at a webpage, I find the Rainier Mountain Festival—a gathering that celebrates the mountain, bringing in climbers who relate their stories and show pictures and answer questions. I feel certain that I must go there and tell this story.

That September, I'm in Ashford, Washington, on the southwestern flank of The Mountain, standing in a stuffy garage-sized tent in the shadow of the very peak that took Mike's life and changed mine forever. I steel myself to speak publicly for the first time about what happened in the crevasse.

I have no idea whether I can do it. A good friend, Scott Yetman, stands by, ready to escort me off the stage if I falter, if my emotions choke the words from my throat.

It takes all the courage I can muster to stand on that volcanic soil and tell the tale. I fight my way through it and see the audience stare back wide-eyed. After I finish, I am wrung out emotionally. I stand outside the tent door and shake hands with some of those who listened. One middle-aged woman approaches me with her two adolescent girls. After prompting the kids to thank me, she says, "I'm so glad my daughters were here to hear this."

"Really? I worried about you wishing that they not hear this intense experience."

"No, I wanted them to hear it. Now if they're in an accident or a difficult situation, they'll know how much people can do, that we can do incredible things if we try our hardest." She grips my hand with both of hers and says, "Thank you for sharing with us."

Her comments stun me. They run over and over through my mind. That evening, while eating grilled salmon with Scott at the festival cookout, I look toward Rainier's summit, hidden behind the conifer forest.

Maybe this is what I'm supposed to do.

IN TIME, I recognize that the most important things I learned were not about scaling overhanging ice walls but about what allowed me to climb out of that crevasse. Life is full of scary crevasses. Illness, accidents, and financial disasters can appear without warning. Seemingly secure institutions like banks, businesses, and marriages collapse, just like snow bridges weakened by the sun. At some time, everyone will fall into one of life's crevasses; mine just happened to be a crack in the ice. Crawling out of these crevasses, overcoming life's challenges, is something each of us must face. Finding resilience for surviving and thriving through adversity is part of everyone's climb.

ULTIMATELY, I PUT aside environmental consulting to concentrate on my work as a full-time speaker. The progression developed naturally—the more I spoke, the more I was able to distill what facing the terrible situation in the crevasse had revealed to me. Although the dark terror and horrific circumstances had made me want to hide and quit, I'd had to constrain these natural reactions enough to think and work my way out of the crisis. I'd had to accept the harsh realities and face them—the sooner, the better.

Now I am able to tell others that facing and analyzing their problems gives them a chance to determine which factors they control. In my case, I had no control over the steepness of the ice wall or the depth of the crevasse. Fixating on things you cannot control is pointless, disheartening, and debilitating. Instead, it's critical to identify the factors within your control and then act on them with vigor. I could control how I used the rope and where I placed my precious gear, so that is what I focused on. By tenaciously applying themselves to the things that can be acted upon, people can overcome incredibly difficult challenges.

Finding the courage to act under duress is among the toughest things most of us will ever face. I believe people can reach into their past to find the incredible strength needed to take action. By remembering loved ones in your life and honoring their faith in you, you can tap the deep well of strength that you innately carry, and this will give you courage. I found strength and courage in the lessons my father taught me, and through my bond to Gloria. Just touching the medallion I wear whenever I climb reminds me of that.

In a crisis, the bravery to act can also be crystallized right in the present moment through our commitment to those who face the challenge with us. In my weakest moments, I manifested the willpower to act by honoring the deep-rooted mutual commitment Mike and I shared.

But strength from the past and courage from the present moment are only part of the equation. The promise of a better future—in my case, the promise of life—is a powerful motivator. Like the crux of a climb, the hardest and scariest moments of life's harsh challenges are often fleeting, and are soon followed by less difficult times. Knowing that the future will inevitably become easier than the momentary crux can serve as an anchor with which you can draw yourself forward.

Sharing these messages becomes a powerful outlet for all I took from Rainier. It is how I honor Mike, how I extract something positive from the negative. It is how I wrestled with my demons, and pinned them to the ground.

———

SOMETIMES AFTER A presentation, I hear variations on the same questions. Did Rainier change me? How did surviving affect me? While a traumatic event can induce dramatic changes, I made no major alterations to my life or lifestyle. I lived in the same town, stayed married to the same woman, and hung out with the same friends. For a while, I thought maybe I should have been dramatically changed by the tragedy on Mount Rainier. In the end, I concluded that I would not be one of those people who buy a Harley and ride off in search of something. I believe this lack of dramatic life shift was not some inability to learn or change on my part but was, instead, affirmation that I had been largely living life on target for myself even before the accident.

Resources in the world are not distributed evenly, including the precious gift of time. The point is made when my mom dies shortly before Jessica is born. The lesson is further driven home when Dad dies suddenly of heart failure while I am climbing Denali. Over the years, Dad and I had become even closer, and I looked to him as a dear friend and wise adviser. His death hits me hard and makes me realize that at forty-one years old, I have only so much time left.

Surviving Rainier, and experiencing the sad loss of Mike and my loved ones, drives home the fact that I had better make sure I am living my life well. So I begin to vacation a little more and work a little less. I spend less money on things and more on experiences. I free myself from relationships with unpleasant or untrustworthy people. Each of these refinements has some costs, but they are just minor surcharges to live a life that I can look back on fondly when my journey concludes.

Mountain climbing is risky and rewarding, painful and powerful. Climbing provides an intense crucible that reveals much about human frailties and capacities. The distilled learnings from my mountain travels are invaluable to me.

THERE ARE THINGS I carry in my head and my heart. The memories of Mike. The lessons I took away from Rainier. The knowledge that I found a way to be at my best in the worst situation.

There are other things, ones I can hold in my hands, that are also precious to me.

Mike's blue pile Patagonia pullover, the one he wore on Rainier, the one I climb in each June 21. One of his snap-button western shirts. His Olympus OM-1. And the one that always brings a smile to me: a T-shirt that exemplifies Mike's wit, his sense of humor. On the front of the gray shirt are three ships out at sea, with two American Indians standing on a cliff, watching. Angling below the sketch are these words:

In 1492, Native Americans
discovered Columbus
lost at sea!

And then there are the two carabiners, both dull aluminum and lightly scratched. As I hold them now, they are much alike, except one has a small band of red tape wrapped around it. That one belonged to me, the other to Mike. Retrieved by rangers from somewhere deep in the crevasse, the carabiners were clipped together on the mountain, then later dropped onto the front seat of our rental car just before I left the mountain alone after the accident. They are two links in the chain that connects us.

I have never separated them—there is no "mine" or "yours" on the mountain, only "ours." Sometimes, I think about having them welded so that they can never be taken apart, so that this last physical tie to Mike can never be broken.

On one of the carabiners is my tattered *kata* from Tengboche—

the silk scarf blessed by the *rinpoche* before Mike's *puja*. I tied it on after Gloria and I returned from Nepal a few months after the accident and I've never removed it.

And I have never removed the folded piece of notebook paper stapled around the other carabiner. In black ink on one side is a note from one of the rangers who sent our linked biners down from the mountain on June 23, 1992.

> *These belong to Mr. Price or his partner.*
> *They need to be sent to John Madden, Longmire.*

I stare long and hard at the other side of the paper. There, in blue ballpoint ink, is a note signed by Madden, the ranger who investigated the crevasse fall. That note contains a few simple words:

> *Jim, These were just delivered.*
> *You did all you could.*
> *Life is a gift!*

CHAPTER 19

▲ ▲ ▲

OVER TWENTY-SEVEN years of climbing, I have loaded my pack a thousand times, but never as carefully as now. This morning I have double-checked my gear against printed lists, mental lists, even against my instincts. There can be no oversights as I'm preparing for the biggest summit push of my life: into the Death Zone, all the way to 8,201 meters.

Within the hour, my teammates and I will begin rallying for our final four-day push to the top of Cho Oyu, at 26,906 feet, the sixth highest peak in the world.

TWO DAYS PASS. It's September 23, 2009, and I am at Camp 3. It took me more than three heart-pounding hours today to make the 1,200-foot snow climb up from Camp 2. With every brutal step, I set a new personal altitude record, and here at 24,600 feet, just sitting in the tent leaves me fighting for air. Soon we will go on bottled oxygen for the first time, then try to catch two or three hours of sleep before our planned departure to the summit at eleven to-night.

Before I lie down, I need to confirm that my down suit's left chest pocket holds the critical items I carry on all serious climbs.

Photos of Glo and the kids. My amulet box holding a Tibetan coin from the Tengboche lama, Mike's Outward Bound pin, and my Denali Pro pin earned by helping with a high-altitude rescue in Alaska.

I warm my icy hand against my bare neck until sensation returns to the fingertips. Then I reach deep into my down suit, under all the layers, groping for my necklace, tracing along the familiar thin chain to the medal Gloria gave me twenty-six years ago.

It's seven P.M. I need to sleep, but can't. Trying to relax and to point myself toward success, I bring to mind reassuring thoughts expressed by friends and family members, and the supportive words of climbing buddies at my going-away party. I mentally match each section of the summit push ahead with experience I have gained on other high peaks around the world.

I can do this.

I look at the black inked messages of love that I asked Glo, Jess, and Nick to write on the left forearm of my red down suit. And I reach out mentally to those who will protect me. I ask Dad for the determination to keep going. I ask Mom to help me get back down to my family. And I ask Mike to watch over me.

AROUND MIDNIGHT, I reach the famous crumbling rock section above 25,000 feet called the Yellow Band. With Kay-Two, a Tibetan guide, nearby, and with some fixed lines to clip into, I cannot fall far. But I can falter. I place my crampon points carefully on tiny limestone ledges, and press down hard.

Do it like ya mean it.

Moving my head fast sends my oxygen-starved brain swimming,

so I learn to make slow, smooth motions. I try gliding through this alien environment as we push farther up into the darkness. On steep sections, I inhale so hard from the oxygen mask that I sound like Darth Vader on steroids.

The stars have never seemed as bright as they do here at 25,500 feet. I keep checking my watch and altimeter. We are moving fast. When I detect orange light flashing intermittently in the valley far below us, I worry that I'm seeing things, that perhaps my brain is too oxygen-deprived. But then I realize I'm looking down on the flattened tops of massive thunderclouds illuminated from within as lightning sets them ablaze.

I should eat and drink, but it's so cold that insulated water bottles freeze and food sets up rock hard. The altitude and the hours roll by. When my altimeter reads 26,000 feet, a distant voice in my mind shouts encouragement.

Stick with it.

Just as Dad taught me as a kid, I keep checking the stars to confirm our direction. We've spent several hours going southeast, directly at the Orion constellation. At first Orion was partially hidden behind Cho Oyu's summit, but as he has risen higher, so have we. Now his full, friendly outline sparkles in front of us. Then, as we swing east toward the big drop into Nepal, Orion takes a protective flanking position to my right.

At 26,500 feet the terrain eases. We are on the final march across the summit plateau—an agonizing 400 yards. Mount Everest sits twenty miles dead ahead, and I can see a black spot where its bulk blots out stars. A biting wind picks up around three-thirty A.M., and stopping, for even a minute, feels impossible.

The slope flattens more. My mountain sense tells me we're almost there. The altimeter reads 26,900. In my headlight beam, about fifty feet ahead, I see a small snow bump crowned with a sacred *kata* and bits of frozen food offered up during an informal *puja*.

The top of Cho Oyu.

The northeast wind pushes hard on my left side. It's gusting to about thirty miles per hour, masking the sound of my boots or ax hitting the crusty snow. All I hear is my ragged breaths and the wind-driven hood of my down suit flapping wildly against my left cheek. Though each torturous step makes my legs feel heavy, excitement churns them forward.

I'm gonna make it!

With ten feet to go, I think about everyone back home. I wish they could know what's happening right this instant. With my heart and mind, I broadcast out to them: "I'm okay. We're going to summit!"

I take a final stride and lift my massive high-altitude boot onto the highest snow mound. Next to the food offerings, I rest my gloved hand on the snow and touch the summit.

My thirty-year dream comes true.

The first two members of our team who summited have just started down, so Kay-Two and I have the top to ourselves for a few precious minutes. We hug and slap each other's backs through inches of pile and down. Surrounded by darkness, with little to see, I look at the blue-white stars instead: spectacular.

Remembering my summit tradition, I ask Kay-Two to snap a picture of me holding photos of Gloria, Jess, and Nick. Tears of joy and relief slip from my eyes. The other eight members of our team are on their way up here, but we can't wait long. At four-seventeen A.M., numb hands and toes force our retreat, and we start down.

AFTER REACHING CAMP 3, I refuel and rest briefly, then begin the descent toward Camp 2, at 23,600 feet. Now out of the Death Zone, each person on our team finds his or her own pace, with two people descending ahead of me, and our leader, the Sherpas, and most of my teammates coming down an hour or more behind. Climbing alone down the modest snow slopes below Camp 3, where there are no fixed lines, I plunge my ax in hard, then take two careful steps downhill. I repeat the process over and over.

No mistakes.

My slow pace allows me to absorb the experience.

During forty-seven years of living and twenty-seven years of climbing, I have had successes and failures, opportunities and obstacles. Though it hasn't always been easy, I have endeavored to keep moving forward.

I took breaks from climbing, but I always returned. The mountains, I know, are as much a part of me as my skin. The things I find there make me stronger and more resilient. They infuse me with the determination to rally back after I get knocked down and the willpower to engage both the challenges I choose and the adversities thrust before me.

The perseverance instilled in me by my family, my partners, and my experiences allows me to press on far longer than I might think possible. Even this climb of Cho Oyu has been a microcosm of that repeating cycle of resilience: engage, persevere, rally.

NOW THE DESCENT is happening faster than I'd like. Knowing that I may never again be in such a rare place, on such a fine day, right after a special summit like Cho Oyu, I want to linger.

At 24,000 feet, I find a flat snow ledge, so I stop and sit. The midmorning sun tracks across the Himalayan sky. With no one in sight, I am alone with my joy and my thoughts. I scan the seemingly small 20,000- to 23,000-foot peaks below me, and see the brown plains of Tibet stretch to the northern horizon.

My oxygen mask feels tight on my face. I realize it's because I'm smiling so hard. I loosen the straps and let the black mask dangle below my chin. Delighted, I spontaneously speak aloud:

"Dad, Mom—I did it! I finally made the top of an eight-thousand-meter peak, just like I always wanted to.

"Mike! I touched the top, man. I touched the top for both of us. Thanks for watching out for me up there.

"Thank you all for helping me become what I am. I got to be here, to climb this awesome mountain, and now I get to go home. To Glo, and Jess and Nick."

I'll probably never be here again, so I soak in the view for a few more minutes and then stand slowly, reluctant to leave.

Four hundred feet below me, I glimpse some climbers trudging uphill. I cannot be alone in this place, this moment, much longer. Soon the magic will slip away.

It is time to move on. Somewhere there's another mountain, waiting. The climb continues.

ACKNOWLEDGMENTS

This book would not have been possible without the trust, kindness, and support of numerous people.

To Don and Donna Price and Daryl Price, we offer profound gratitude for allowing this story to be told, for sharing stories about Mike, and for granting us permission to quote liberally from his journals and other writings. We will never adequately be able to thank the Prices for their grace. We hope that in some way this book is a tribute to Mike, and to a life well lived.

In addition, we can't say enough about others who were close to Mike and who opened their hearts and their memories to us: Bob Jamieson, Deb Follo Caughron, Joanne Donohue, U.S. senator Mark Udall, and Dr. James Work.

We are eternally grateful to Jim Trotter, Jim Sheeler, Andrew J. Field, Mike Littwin, Rodney Ley, John Calderazzo, and Kerrie Flanagan, all of whom offered thoughts and direction that shaped and improved our manuscript immensely. Additionally, Kerrie and the Northern Colorado Writers deserve our gratitude for bringing the two of us together at the group's 2007 conference—and for supporting this project in more ways than we can count.

Portions of this story were originally published on the pages of the *Rocky Mountain News*. We thank John Temple, the *Rocky's* longtime editor and publisher, and the E. W. Scripps Company for the permission to use those words.

None of this would have been possible without the best agent in the world. Dan Conaway at Writers House believed in this project—and in us—before we knew we could do it. Knock wood! Thank you also to Stephen Barr at Writers House, whose support and thoughtful insights improved our manuscript, and to Simon Lipskar, who arranged our first literary blind date with Dan.

Luke Dempsey and Mark Tavani and the entire team at Ballantine Books—especially Dennis Ambrose, Bonnie Thompson, Ryan Doherty, and Jessica Waters—have been a joy to work with. We knew five minutes into our first meeting that we wanted to work with Ballantine, and over the ensuing months that faith was rewarded again and again.

JIM DAVIDSON

To Mike Price: Your talents, friendship, and mentorship made our many adventures grand fun. That day on Rainier, you used those gifts to save me. Thank you, Mike. You will be with me always. I am very thankful for the kindness of the Price family, Don, Donna, and Daryl. You all have been gracious, friendly, and supportive from the moment I met you.

My parents, Joe and Jean Davidson, gave me a solid upbringing and a zest for life. Thank you, Mom and Dad. I am especially grateful, Dad, for all those years working by your side, where you taught me the skills, will, and resilience that would one day save my life. To my sisters, Pat, Linda, and Joanne, thanks for sharing our journey through life.

My friend and climbing partner Rodney Ley: I have much to thank you for. You helped me reconnect with climbing, the climbing community, and myself. During one hundred expedition days and ten times that many days at low altitude, you have been a leader, a wingman, and my co-conspirator in fun.

Over the years I have been fortunate to climb with solid partners. During my formative climbs, I appreciated the companionship of Joe Berlin, Tom Engleson, Jim Seines, Mark Piantedosi, Chris Flood, Patrick Heaney, Scott Anderson, Daryl Miller, Pat Rastall, and many more. I have also been fortunate to share a rope with Shawn Zeigler, Terry Parker, Marlene Swift, Scott Yetman, Megan Burch, John Calderazzo, and Alan Arnette. Through climbing classes and expeditions, I have been invigorated by many student climbers too numerous to list here; I wish you all safe travels to the mountains and beyond. Special thanks to Mike Gauthier, Deb Read, Uwe Schneider, John Norberg, and John Madden for helping to get me off The Mountain. Thank you to the family and friends who welcomed me home.

I appreciate the many writers who have encouraged and taught me, including those at the Lighthouse Writers Workshop and the Northern Colorado Writers. Many colleagues at the National Speakers Association have assisted me, most notably my mentor and friend LeAnn Thieman, who saw potential in me and helped bring it forth. A special thanks to Joe Simpson for writing *Touching the Void*, as it inspired me to believe climbing out of a crevasse was possible.

For my coauthor, Kevin Vaughan, I am quite thankful. Like swinging leads on a tough climb, partnering with you on this book adventure has been exhilarating. As a journalist and coauthor, you are indeed solid. Along with Kevin, the *Rocky Mountain News* kindly let me work with savvy, sensitive professionals like John Temple, Jim Trotter, Chris Schneider, and Wes Pope.

I am most thankful for my wife, Gloria, and our children, Jessica and Nick. Gloria has been a loving and supportive partner through all the twists, turns, and loops of life. Gloria, through your words, actions, and deeds, you are a shining role model for me and our kids. Jessica and Nick, thanks for showing me fun, for giving me hope, and for making me proud.

KEVIN VAUGHAN

To Jim Davidson, who I met at a time when I was searching for my next interesting story, I offer eternal thanks for his trust in first allowing me to tell his amazing tale of tragedy and, ultimately, triumph on the pages of the *Rocky Mountain News*. I treasure the partnership and the friendship that grew from that and culminated in this book.

I was lucky at the *Rocky* to work for John Temple, an editor who fostered an environment where a writer could dream big. I can't say enough about the adventure that was my eleven and a half years at that paper, and how sad I was the day its owners shut it down. I also offer thanks to *Rocky* editors Deb Goeken, Carol Hanner, Eric Brown, Cliff Foster, Steve Myers, Tonia Twichell, and especially Jim Trotter, whose contributions to the newspaper series "The Crevasse" and to this book were invaluable and whose friendship is even more meaningful.

Over the course of my writing career, I have been shaped by many gifted and talented editors and storytellers, whose influence I feel in every sentence I write. That began nearly three decades ago with Greg Pearson, a professor at Metropolitan State College who made me believe in myself in a way I never had before, and continued with Bob Spencer, Bill Spencer, Bob Davis, Rich Abrahamson, Chris Cobler, Tony Balandran, Mike Littwin, Todd Hartman, Sara Burnett, David Montero, Jim Sheeler, Lynn Bartels, Chris Barge, M. E. Sprengelmeyer, Charlie Brennan, Michael O'Keeffe, Jeff Kass, Hector Gutierrez, Tina Griego, David Olinger, Jennifer Brown, and the late James B. Meadow. Thank you all.

At *The Denver Post*, Editor Greg Moore threw me a lifeline at a time when I thought my journalism career might end. I don't know what I would have done without it. His support, and that of news director Kevin Dale, helped make this book possible.

Chris Webster helped me stay sane through it all.

I offer a lifetime of gratitude to my late father, Pete Vaughan, and my mother, Linda Vaughan, for the gentle way they allowed me to figure out my life without the pressure of having to be what they wanted me to be. And to my sister, Rebecca Vaughan, and her husband, Peter Illig, I say "thank you" for teaching me something new every time we talk.

Finally, to Colleen, Forrest, Morgan, and Sawyer, I offer my heart. A writer is supposed to always find the right words, but there aren't any big enough to explain what each of them means to me. Their love, support, and patience—and their tolerance of the missed meals and middle-of-the-night phone calls as I pursued the story of the day—sustains me. Their hugs are my medicine, their smiles my sunsets. They make my life complete.

SOURCES

The authors strove at all times to re-create events as accurately as possible. In addition to Jim Davidson's deeply seared memories, the authors relied on other materials that confirmed key details:

- A series of tape recordings dictated by Jim in August 1992 in which he recounted everything he could remember of the tragedy on Mount Rainier that had occurred six weeks earlier. These twelve hours of tapes formed the basis for much of the on-mountain dialogue involving the climbing partners.
- Jim's letter to Mike Price, written on June 23, 1992, before Jim departed Mount Rainier.
- A tape recording of investigating ranger John Madden's interview with Jim the day after the accident.
- Original National Park Service accident reports.
- Jim's notes, maps, photos, and files about the 1983 Mount Rainier attempt and the 1992 Liberty Ridge climb.
- Jim's writings about the accident, which he began in the fall of 1992.
- Newspaper stories about the accident from *The Denver Post,* the *Rocky Mountain News,* and the *Fort Collins Coloradoan.*
- Approximately thirty hours of interviews with Jim conducted by Kevin Vaughan during research for the 2008 *Rocky Mountain News* series "The Crevasse."

- Jim's eighteen personal journals since 1981, covering many climbs, expeditions, trips, and other experiences.
- Jim's extensive photography collection, including the pictures he and Mike took on Rainier.
- Personal correspondence between Jim and a dozen friends from 1983 to 2010, especially just after the 1992 accident.
- Gloria Davidson's personal journals—in particular, her recollections about Jim's call from Rainier and about the day they met the Price family.
- Jim's medical records from his emergency room visit the day after the accident.
- Mike's master's thesis, "Tracking the Spirit."
- Mike's complete journals from his 1981 adventure in the Yukon, his 1991 trip to Antarctica, and numerous other writings of his, access to which was granted by Don and Donna Price and Dr. James Work, a retired professor at Colorado State University and the adviser on Mike's thesis.
- A tape recording of a phone message left for Jim and Gloria by Mike in the year before the accident.
- A memory book from Mike's memorial service made available to the authors by Daryl Price.
- Interviews with the following people: Don and Donna Price, Daryl Price, Rodney Ley, Bob Jamieson, Mike Gauthier, Joanne Donohue, Deb Caughron, and Dr. James Work.

ABOUT THE AUTHORS

JIM DAVIDSON is an accomplished climber and inspirational speaker who shares lessons distilled from a lifetime of mountain adventures. Since 1982, he has climbed across the United States and been on high-altitude expeditions to Alaska, Argentina, Bolivia, Ecuador, Mexico, Nepal, and Tibet. Formerly an environmental geologist with his own consulting firm, Jim is now a professional speaker with Speaking of Adventure (www.speakingofadventure.com). Jim lives in Colorado with his two adventurous kids and his very tolerant wife.

KEVIN VAUGHAN is a staff writer at *The Denver Post*. A graduate of Metropolitan State College, he has written extensively on the sports supplement industry, the tragedy at Columbine High School, and the criminal justice system. He has been honored numerous times for his journalism. He lives in Colorado with his wife and their three children.

ABOUT THE TYPE

This book was set in Sabon, a typeface designed by the well-known German typographer Jan Tschichold (1902–1974). Sabon's design is based upon the original letterforms of Claude Garamond and was created specifically to be used for three sources: foundry type for hand composition, Linotype, and Monotype. Tschichold named his typeface for the famous Frankfurt typefounder Jacques Sabon, who died in 1580.